INSTRUCTOR'S MANUAL AND TRANSPARENCY MASTERS TO ACCOMPANY

CASE STUDIES IN BUSINESS ETHICS

SECOND EDITION

MARIANNE M. JENNINGS
Professor of Legal and Ethical Studies in Business
Arizona State University, College of Business

WEST PUBLISHING COMPANY
Minneapolis/St. Paul   New York   Los Angeles   San Francisco

WEST'S COMMITMENT TO THE ENVIRONMENT

In 1906, West Publishing Company began recycling materials left over from the production of books. This began a tradition of efficient and responsible use of resources. Today, up to 95% of our legal books and 70% of our college texts and school texts are printed on recycled, acid-free stock. West also recycles nearly 22 million pounds of scrap paper annually—the equivalent of 181,717 trees. Since the 1960s, West has devised ways to capture and recycle waste inks, solvents, oils, and vapors created in the printing process. We also recycle plastics of all kinds, wood, glass, corrugated cardboard, and batteries, and have eliminated the use of Styrofoam book packaging. We at West are proud of the longevity and the scope of our commitment to the environment.

Production, Prepress, Printing and Binding by West Publishing Company.

 TEXT IS PRINTED ON 10% POST CONSUMER RECYCLED PAPER PRINTED WITH SOY INK™

CONTENTS

Using the Manual

This instructor's manual consists of four parts. In the first portion you will find key discussion points, observations and additional information for each of the cases in the book. The second part contains Advanced Instructional Materials (AIM) that offers some background on business ethics: what is it? what different views exist? what is the terminology? what questions do we ask when faced with an ethical dilemma in business? These materials can be used for your own background information or presented to the students in lecture or reading format.

The third portion of the manual contains transparency masters for the cases. These transparencies offer illustrations and diagrams of the often complex interactions of the characters in the cases. The students will thus be able to visualize this interaction as opposed to mentally keeping track and who did what and when.

The final segment of this instructor's manual, and new to this edition, is a test bank. Many instructors asked for help in developing exams for their courses. This test bank offers a variety of question formats and topics along with answers.

Each case is covered in the manual. The title of the case appears at the top of the page. If there is a transparency associated with the case, its number is noted directly beneath the case title. There is then a section called "Answers and Key Discussion Items." The questions from the book are answered along with embellishments and additional questions to ask the students as a follow-up. In those cases where the legal and ethical issues cross, there is a heading, "Legal Issues" in which the law as applied to that particular case is discussed.

The materials were developed with both students and instructors in mind. The instructor is given additional resources as well as notions for the stimulation of discussion. Students enjoy the benefit of instruction that leads to the heart of the difficult dilemmas presented in the text.

Good luck as you proceed with instruction in an area that is critical to your students in their business and personal lives. I hope the materials are helpful to you. If you have questions or suggestions, please feel free to call at (602)965-9488 or write to me at Box 873706, Arizona State University, Tempe, AZ 85287.

Marianne M. Jennings
Professor of Legal and Ethical
    Studies in Business
College of Business
Arizona State University
IADMMJ @ ASUVM.INRE.ASU.EDU

An Overview of Business Ethics

If you are using the book as a supplement to your discussion of ethics, the introductory materials need not be covered. If you are using the book as a portion of a course that contains an ethics component, you may wish to begin with a discussion that summarizes the introduction in the text. There are transparency masters as noted in this summary to enhance your lecture or discussion as this background material is presented. You may wish to draw on the Advanced Instructional Materials (AIM) that appear in the second part of this manual to provide you with more depth for your discussion and/or lecture. Transparency masters for those materials are also included with the transparencies in the final portion of this manual.

Outline of Introductory Materials

I.   An Ethical Climate in a Business is Critical

    A.   Poor ethical choices can lead to devastating losses and often business failures
        e.g.:   Orange County, Barings Bank, Union Carbide, Beech-Nut, E.F. Hutton, BCCI, Salomon Brothers, Johns-Manville and others covered in the text

    B.   Good ethical choices can have positive effect on earnings
        e.g.:   Ethical firms are able to pay dividends consistently
                Ethical firms offer investors a better return

II. Why Business Ethics?

    A.   Connection between profitability and ethics/values
        Note: Collins and Porras - BUILT TO LAST
        Note: Ethics Resource Center Study on value of shares in ethical firms
        Note: CEOs belief that ethical standards strengthen your competitive edge

III. What is business ethics?

    A.   The application of moral standards to business dilemmas

    B.   Types of dilemmas (<u>Use transparency 1 to show categories</u>)
        Text is organized according to these categories of dilemmas

IV. Recognizing Ethical Dilemmas

    A.   Recognizing ethical dilemmas - Observe the language of

justification used when people face an ethical dilemma (<u>Use transparency 2</u>)

    B.   Categories of unethical behavior (<u>Use transparency 3</u>)

V.   Resolving Ethical Dilemmas

    A.   Blanchard/Peale model (<u>Use transparency 4</u>)

        1. Is it legal?
        2. Is it balanced?
        3. How does it make me feel?

    B.   Front Page of the Newspaper Test (<u>Use transparency 5</u>)

    C.   Laura Nash model (<u>Use transparency 6</u>)

        1. Have you defined the problem accurately?
        2. How would you define the problem if you stood on the other side of the fence?
        3. How did this situation occur in the first place?
        4. To whom and to what do you give your loyalty as a person and as a member of the corporation?
        5. What is your intention in making this decision?
        6. How does this intention compare with the likely results?
        7. Whom could your decision or action injure?
        8. Can you discuss your decision with the affected parties?
        9. Are you confident that your position will be as valid over a long period of time as it seems now?
      10. Could you discuss your decision with your CEO, board, friends, boss, family?
      11. What is the symbolic potential of your action if understood? if misunderstood?
      12. Under what circumstances would you make exceptions to your position?

    D.   Perspective: Use that of a reporter or a wage earner

VI. Resolution of ethical dilemmas requires practice in applying the various models.

Make assignments of cases according to your class coverage or use the indexes in the text to assign cases by company, business discipline or topic.

1.1 Commodities, Conflicts, and Clintons

<u>Use Transparency 7</u>.

It will help students visualize the parties' roles and interrelationships.

<u>Answers and Key Discussion Items</u>

1. Mrs. Clinton was then the wife of a top law enforcement official in the state of Arkansas. Mr. Blair was legal counsel for the state's largest company, a firm that was heavily regulated at both the state and federal levels. Mr. Blair's advice on commodities trades introduced a quid pro quo element into the Blair/Clinton relationship. Tyson's and Blair's interests in regulation were from a business perspective. Mrs. Clinton was the spouse of the state's top regulator who was also a candidate for governor. The front page of the newspaper test tells us there was a conflict here.

2. Whether Mr. and Mrs. Clinton would or would not have been influenced by the helpful advice is not the issue. Their interests are at odds as regulator and regulated. The most skeptical could argue that the advice was a way of making significant campaign contributions outside the legal limitations. There is also the appearance of impropriety.

3. The appointment of the Tyson executives subsequent to Mr. Clinton's election as governor creates the appearance of quid pro quo. Tyson's regulatory treatment post-Blair advice is some evidence that the advice was given in exchange for favorable regulatory treatment.

4. Yes, Mr. Clinton did have a conflict of interest. Direct influence is often not used because of prohibitions -- statutory prohibitions because of public official standing. Hence, family members are sought out for influence. Influence once removed remains influence and Mr. Clinton had a conflict through his wife's conduct.

5. Mr. Espy's actions as Secretary of Agriculture provide some indication of the introduction of a quid pro quo. Further, Tyson was perceived and treated as a friend of the Clinton governorship and presidency.

6. Yes, Mr. Espy had a conflict. He was accepting items of value from a firm he was responsible for enforcing the law against and regulating. As a former member of Congress, Mr. Espy did not realize the distinction between lobbying activities when one is a

legislator as opposed to influence activities when one is the enforcer/regulator. Lobbying is an activity protected by the First Amendment. Influencing regulators and enforcers is obstruction of justice.

7.   Under the American Bar Association's Model Rules of Professional Responsibility, Mrs. Clinton would have a conflict because of her husband's position in government. However, partners of Mrs. Clinton in the Rose law firm could represent Tyson without a violation of the ABA rules. Again, the lack of a violation of the rules is not necessarily the test for ethical conduct. This representation does not survive the newspaper test: it looks bad to have the governor's wife's law firm awarded the legal business of the state's largest company, a heavily regulated one at that.

8.   None of the decisions made in this case from Blair's advice to hiring the Rose firm to Espy's actions to the hiring of Tyson executives can survive the front-page-of-the-newspaper test. Transparency 7 demonstrates how interconnected and interdependent the parties were and the likelihood of expectation of favorable treatment was high.

9.   What is your intention in providing trading advice to Mrs. Clinton? What is your intention in taking trading advice from Mr. Blair? Are you as confident about your decision over the long term? Could you disclose your decision publicly? All of these questions could be applied to Mrs. Clinton's decision to accept the trading advice, the Rose law firm account, the Tyson executives being hired and the Mike Espy situation. As we examine these decisions now, they have created image and other problems for all those involved. The Laura Nash questions would have helped at the time.

10.   In conflicts of interest, the issue is not whether one has been influenced. The issue is whether a situation has been created in which influence is possible. The introduction of quid pro quo into the relationship is the ethical breach.

Legal Issues

Indirect campaign contributions may be a problem here. The commodities trades and the sufficiency of cash coverage for the trade may present some legal issues. Laws against bribing public officials may apply as the Espy investigation continues.

1.2   The Realty with the Disguised Ownership

<u>Use Transparency 8</u>.

Helps students visualize the interaction among the many parties in the case.

<u>Answers and Key Discussion Items</u>

1.   Tonopah engaged in deceit, dishonesty, profit at others' expense and fraud.

2.   Algonquin perceived Tonopah to be its agent. Arguably, the parties had an agency relationship. Even with ownership Tonopah continued to serve in a function of providing a service to Algonquin for a price.

3.   Tim was in a difficult position. Like so many of us when we discover unethical or illegal conduct by others, he was reluctant to get involved and bring it to the attention of Algonquin. He had the additional difficulty of carrying the appearance of sour grapes if he did speak up and make accusations. Also, Tim needed to be concerned about slander and libel. Anything he would say to someone else must be 100% factually accurate and verifiable because of his liability for saying something so damaging about a business to another business. Anonymity was not really an option for him because only those to whom Charkoff and Owens spoke would know of the kickback. Hence, his identity could not be protected. Have the students put themselves in Tim's position. Ask them to describe how Tim will be treated and perceived if he does disclose the kickbacks. Won't Tim's assertions be difficult for him to prove? Since Tim didn't do anything wrong, should he be involved in any of the problems? Wasn't Tim the only one who was harmed by all the conduct?

4.   As with many ethical dilemmas, self-destruction is not necessary for Tim to do the "right" thing. Tim should suggest to Bob Ward that he and Algonquin investigate the full transaction. Tim need not be the accuser or the investigator. Tim should simply let Ward know that he understood the terms of the agreement to be different and offer the suggestion that the finances be audited.

5.   Be sure to have students bring out the fact that when bidding processes and businesses are conducted in this manner, everyone suffers because the process is not objective. The higher costs are passed along and issues of quality and qualifications are no longer relevant. Although Tim seems to be ancillary, he is the key to fair bidding practices in the future.

6.   Yes. Both sides engaged in commercial bribery. Both the payor and

1.2 The Realty with the Disguised Ownership (cont'd)

the recipient can be charged with commercial bribery. Let the students know that many attorneys general are using older statutes on commercial bribery that have been dormant for many years to prosecute this type of behavior. The new focus on commercial bribery has come about because of the concerns that everyone suffers when there is commercial bribery. We all pay higher prices and we have no guarantees of quality, good faith, trust. In short, when the capitalistic system breaks down, there is harm to more than just the party who lost the bid. There is societal harm. You could use the Italian government as an example. After the clean-up of corruption in the government in 1994, the costs for building their freeways there were DOWN by 50% because bribes and other kickbacks were no longer involved.

Legal Issues

Tonopah was an agent for Algonquin and violated the fiduciary obligations agents owe their principals. Agents are to act in the best interests of their principals and disclose any interest they may have in transactions involving the principals. Tonopah and Charkoff and Owens all made secret profits from the deals with Meals-to-Go and Algonquin would have a legal action for breach of those duties. Additionally, Charkoff and Owens and their firms may have violated state criminal statutes with their fees if they are construed to be non-contract related.

1.3 The City Council Employee

Answers and Key Discussion Items

1. No matter how much Bimini needed graphic art work and no matter how good a graphic artist Jake Gilbert is, the newspaper accounts of this relationship if Houston hires Gilbert would be unfavorable. The relationship would be depicted as a suggestive pay-off in which Gilbert's position on billboards is supported by a business dependent upon the continuation of billboard advertising for survival.

2. The headline might read:

   Unemployed Council Candidate Now Employed By the City's Largest Billboard Beneficiary

   The Best Kind of Campaign Contribution: A Job

   Council Candidate Working for Billboard Proponent

3. No. There is no difference. Whether working directly for Bimini or working in a position Bimini obtained for Gilbert, the result is the same: the introduction of quid pro quo into their relationship. Gilbert can no longer vote his constituency or conscience, he must consider Bimini's personal help as an expectation of favorable treatment.

4. Gilbert should not be submitting a bid. The potential for public embarrassment and conflict is too high. His being hired simply cannot be adequately explained or justified. The conflict is so great here that the nature of the bid is irrelevant. He should not be bidding, period. If he does bid, Bimini should not hire him. The potential for damage to them is great as well.

5. Gilbert cannot avoid facing the billboard issue if he is running for office. There is no way to take the job and do a credible job of running for and holding office. He simply cannot take the job.

6. Yes. Gilbert has a conflict of interest whether he is a direct employee or under contract.

Other Observations

The long-term impact of a decision to hire Gilbert would be damaging to Gilbert's, Bimini's and Houston's reputations. Independence is perceived, not explained. Both will cost themselves the issue that concerns them the most.

The students will identify with Dewey because he is an employee who has seen the implications of a decision to hire Gilbert either as an employee or a contractor. Dewey is but a manager who possesses little authority and little job security. Challenge the students to think of ways Dewey might approach the problem:

    a.   Preparation; examples of other elections in which similar relationships have destroyed candidates and cost businesses;

    b.   Appearance of impropriety; the newspaper test

    c.   Laura Nash; will I feel as good about this over the long-run?

Legal Issues

In many states, the contracts (either for the work or for employment) might be classified as indirect campaign contributions that might have to be disclosed at a minimum and, quite possibly, could be considered contributions in excess of many of the states' maximums established by campaign finance reform laws.

1.4 The Firm Workout and the Fonda PhD

Answers and Key Discussion Items

1. Yes.   Dr. Kosich's affiliation should have been disclosed. Further, the argument could be made that Kosich should have elected not to participate in the evaluation because of his conflict.   If Kosich did not opt out, *Shape* should have standards for the use of experts on its "independent" evaluations of exercise tapes and any other products rated by the magazine. *Shape*'s credibility suffers when these types of conflicts and controversies arise. Competitors in a crowded and intensely competitive field have taken each other on in a battle of words.

2. The direct comparison form of advertising can be a helpful source of information to consumers. They were slightly misleading in that the true identity was withheld and that was not disclosed up front.

3. Dr. Kosich is a well-known expert in the field and is used as a consultant by many firms.   His credentials are outstanding. However, Dr. Kosich, as a paid consultant to the Fonda tape production, lost his standing as simply an outside expert. Whether the bias did or did not enter into his evaluation of the tapes, the perception is that the ratings are tainted by someone who benefits, at least indirectly, from the success of a particular tape.

   Dr. Kosich should have refused to participate in the evaluation. At a minimum, if he was to participate, his affiliation should have been disclosed. Dr. Kosich has a conflict of interest. Conflicts of interest are often difficult to spot. Many do not recognize them until the conflict is later established, as in this case, in a very public and embarrassing way.

4. Direct response is good information for the consumer.   If the economic standard of perfect information is to be achieved in the marketplace, consumers must know from others how effective a product is and what they can expect. Comparisons must be done fairly and accurately to contribute effectively to the marketplace knowledge.

5. The FIRM is enjoying ongoing success and continues to grow in the market.   Their   success   is   instructive   in   terms   of   honest advertising. The conflict of interest and the extra help in the evaluation still did not ensure success for the tapes that benefitted.   Despite the unfair advantage, the quality product emerged in the market and has survived. The case offers an illustration of ethics and survival and the lack of ethics and the consequences.

Other Observations

1.4 The Firm Workout and the Fonda PhD (cont'd)

Shape magazine should screen its evaluators for such conflicts.

Legal Issues

Direct confrontation advertising is currently permitted and, indeed, encouraged by the Federal Trade Commission (FTC). However, competitors must be cautious in their direct confrontation advertising to be certain that the claims made are accurate. Under infringement laws, statements made about competitors' products that are inaccurate can serve as the basis for a suit by the competitor.

1.5 The Chain of Command and Purchasing

Use Transparency 9.

Answers and Key Discussion Items

1. Deidre is in a tense spot with which students can identify. They know the correct decision to be made but may be feeling some pressure from a superior to make a different decision.

    Deidre should make her recommendation as she has evaluated it and give her justifications. It is a business decision based on concerns about the viability and reliability of a new business. Deidre can also explain that Chelsea's is price-competitive and that she would be willing to consider Chelsea's once more references and a track record are available.

2. Hoffman should not reverse Deidre because it undermines her authority and confidence as the person responsible for purchasing. Also, Hoffman needs to consider the appearance of board presence and pressure being used to force the company to enter into contracts it would otherwise not choose. Troubles in the company at any time will bring a laundry list of these types of transactions that will prove damaging to Hoffman, Triple Plus and Chelsea's. Hoffman is in a position to explain to Wasson that his daughter's firm looks very good to them and that once she establishes a record with some smaller accounts, purchasing would be willing to have her work with them.

3. No bid information should be given to Chelsea's as a favor to Sam Wasson. See below.

4. Many corporations' ethics policies require directors to disclose conflicts of interest; i.e., situations in which they or a family member benefit through a contractual relationship with the corporation. Wasson may have that obligation here.

5. Hoffman's intervention would send a signal to employees about the way the company does business and how contracts are awarded. It may seem like a one-time intervention, but Hoffman would actually be establishing the tone for the company. Employees would learn that who you know is the standard for behavior and not what's best for the company. Hoffman's intervention would do damage to the ethical atmosphere of the firm.

Legal Issues

Both Sam Wasson and Frank Hoffman are fiduciaries of Triple Plus. The transactions they enter into must be in the best interest of the

1.5 The Chain of Command and Purchasing (cont'd)

corporation. Since the purchasing manager's decision has been made, neither should use their authority or influence to change that decision. Further, the disclosure of bid information in advance would be a violation of those fiduciary duties.

1.6 Conflicts of Interest in Referrals

Answers and Key Discussion Items

1. Tina is in a difficult situation as she tries to manage the outside activities of physicians, a generally independent and private group. However, Tina needs to think of the various stakeholders affected by her work and decisions. She also needs to think of the long term. Today's high medical care costs, cutbacks in insurance coverage and increasing government regulation demand a responsible approach to cost-containment and conflicts of interest. Tina should institute a mandatory disclosure policy. Tina should take a proactive position, citing current regulation, the Blue Cross study and the Department of Health and Human Services' policies. Tina should implement the policy after discussions with physicians and explanations of her concerns.

2. As a patient, I would want to know who owns the facilities. There might be the need for a second opinion. There might be the need to investigate costs at other facilities. I should be told if the person ordering tests is going to make money from those tests.

3. Whether or not the physicians would be self-serving is not the issue. The appearance of all of the physician-owned facilities is that there is a conflict of interest. The physician owners do not make money if patients are not referred to their facilities or services. A newspaper story about the incestuous relationships between physicians and their companies would not be favorable for them or Tina.

4. Possible headlines:

    Physicians Earn From Prescribing Tests at Their Labs
    Prescriptions for Profit: Your Doctor Might Own the Lab
    Doctor-Owned Labs Earn Lavish Profits in a Captive Market

Legal Issues

Many states already mandate disclosure when a physician makes a referral to a self-owned lab. The AMA position is behind the times in terms of legislative coverage of disclosure.

1.7 Donations and Vendors

<u>Answers and Key Discussion Items</u>

1. Conflict of interest; ethical tone for the hotel; commercial
    bribery

2. No, it won't matter what the bid is. There will be a perception of
    a problem. Also, the parties need to think about the impact on
    employees of their interrelationships. Perception of quid pro quo:
    you give me business, and I'll donate to your wife's cause. All 3
    should be concerned about the long-term impact on their
    reputations.

    Although the mention is subtle and the endowment is noble, the
    CEO's wife is being set up for a path of pressure from Sherman. In
    this initial setting the interaction of the endowment and the
    bidding seems remote. However, Sherman's will forever have the
    ability to hold the endowment threat over the heads of the CEO and
    his associate dean wife.

    The hotel CEO could find himself in a position of having to defend
    his conduct to board members and shareholders once the connection
    is made public (probably in an unflattering newspaper story).
    Sherman's bid may indeed be the lowest, but it will not eliminate
    the newspaper coverage of the relationship between the parties.

3. Yes, unless appropriate steps are taken (see answer to #4).

4. An easy way around the problem is to have the associate dean bring
    someone else in (from the university development office or another
    college) to handle the potential contribution from Sherman. She
    need not even discuss the reason. She could explain that
    endowments for the scholarship fund are handled by another official
    or, if she felt more comfortable explaining, that because of the
    bidding someone else was being brought in to work on this pledge of
    funds.

5. Yes, as noted in answer #2, the relationship looks cozy, and the
    University should be concerned about its reputation and
    obligations.

<u>Legal Issues</u>

The hotel CEO simply needs to exercise his fiduciary duty with respect
to the corporation and not have the issue regarding his wife's job
affect the bidding process or decisions in which Sherman will be a
party. The questions about fiduciary responsibility can be eliminated
through detachment of his wife from the endowment negotiations.

1.8　The Quality Kickback

Answers and Key Discussion Items

1. A key Laura Nash questions arises here: What are your intentions in making this decision? Why is Caremark using other physicians? Is it truly for quality control or is it an indirect means of giving a kickback? One could argue that regardless of its intentions, the probable result of this program is the perception that the payments are indeed kickbacks. The press coverage is not favorable regardless of the motivation.

    We are all harmed by programs such as this. Costs are increased overall and it is possible that physicians' independent judgments are affected by the payments received from Caremark for their evaluations.

2. It is possible to make an argument that the home care should be monitored by a physician -- beyond just the usual patient check-ups. However, it should be actual supervision and review of the care, not just payment for a sign-off.

3. If there is no work involved and no actual monitoring, the arrangement could create the perception that physicians are well paid for doing nothing with the hope that they will refer their own patients to this particular home care service.

4. No, compliance with positive law is NOT the standard for ethical behavior. Many activities are legal on the surface or by explanation but are really nothing more than violations of the spirit of the law, as here. Monitoring is permitted, but it must be meaningful.

Legal Issues

Some medical malpractice defense lawyers would argue that Caremark's policy and procedure is a good one for establishing the quality of home care so that for any lawsuits filed for malpractice there is evidence of independent monitoring. Hopefully, the monitoring allows early intervention in the event of poor decisions, lack of action or incompetency on the part of the actual or primary physician.

The fine line on Caremark's actions between "safe harbor" and "kickback" is its intention in using the physician monitoring program.

Note:　On June 16, 1995, Caremark agreed to plead guilty and pay $159 million in civil damages and criminal fines. C.A. "Lance" Piccolo, Caremark's CEO, stated, "I just feel genuinely bad that it happened, and I'm glad it's over."

1.9 The Loan Officer and the Debtors

Answers and Key Discussion Items

1. Shelby, a character most students will identify with, is faced with the classic problem of a new culture and old employees who "have always done it this way." Shelby may find herself in the difficult position of having to turn to someone other than her immediate supervisor for "ethical relief." It may be "just the way business is done", but it should be changed. Shelby is absolutely correct. Shelby will need to express her concerns directly to Ben. She should do so with good preparation. She should use the bank's own code of ethics as well as examples from other banks to demonstrate her position. She should pursue other avenues in the bank if she is unable to convince Ben of the need to avoid the appearance of impropriety. Alternatives would include a hotline, the ombudsperson, audit department, legal counsel and Ben's supervisor. She should look to the persons who are committed to changing the bank's ethical culture and enlist their support.

2. The conflict with the potential borrower paying for the collateral evaluation trip is that the pressure to make the loan increases. The payment necessitates more direct contact and the passage of funds from the potential customer to the bank regardless of the loan decision.

3. The payment for the collateral evaluation trip opens all kinds of doors: will the travel arrangements be "excessive?" how much can the potential borrower expend in making the arrangements? how fancy will the facilities for the loan officers be? Many banks include policies in their codes of ethics that specifically preclude loan officers from allowing potential borrowers to pay for their collateral evaluation trips.

4. The solicitation of donations from bank loan officers is a less direct and more subtle type of pressure that says to the debtor, "either I contribute to this or I am going to lose my line of credit." It is a means of applying pressure to customers who want to maintain good relationships with their loan officers. Many banks, again, have specific provisions in their codes of ethics that prohibit loan officers and others responsible for loan approval from soliciting contributions (in-kind or otherwise) from loan customers to avoid the appearance of pressure.

5. The voluntary contribution of a firm would be accepted but bank employees would not solicit such donations from customers.

6. Again, Shelby needs to present her concerns in a well-reasoned manner. Research on other banks' policies would help as she presents her concerns.

1.10   Incidental Beneficiaries of the Philanthropist's Estate

Use Transparencies 10 and 11.

Answers and Key Discussion Items

1. This is a classic case of a series of conflicts that arose as fiduciaries, given responsibility for the management of funds and properties, managed those funds and properties as if they were their own funds and were to be used for the benefit of themselves and others around them.

2. The Nathan sale should never have occurred unless at least the appraisal figure was paid and there was full disclosure to an independent panel of the foundation or an independent panel of the university.

3. Madison Graves had a conflict of interest. The award of the listings for the properties should have been done on a competitive basis. If Madison won the bid, as selected by an independent panel, then his commissions and results would have been more palatable.

4. The sales of the properties themselves were deservedly reported with questions. An appraiser should not also be the purchaser of the property unless there were other independent appraisals conducted when the appraiser indicated a desire to purchase the property.

5. The managers of this fund behaved as if the property was their own, in the wrong sense. They ignored propriety and the obligation to maximize the return on the contributed property. Managing funds as if they were your own in the trustee sense means managing them so that you take appropriate precautions and do all that you can to maximize profits.

6. A good foundation member would have set up a system of checks and balances and demanded more independence in the transactions. Also, the responsibility of effective management was required and the lapse of the lease option is evidence of a problem in adequate management.

7. Yes. Forms, processes, and approvals for members dealing with the foundation would be helpful. These processes anticipate public disclosure and provide above-board means for approval.

Legal Issues

1.10 Incidental Beneficiaries of the Philanthropist's Estate (cont'd)

There are duties imposed upon managers of trust properties and funds. This case shows self-dealing and breach of the duty to manage the funds and property prudently. The disclosure of interests in the various firms, employees and appraisers dealing with the foundation would be necessary. Documents would be required disclosing all of the assets and their disposition. The university, as a beneficiary, would have the right to claim losses for any mismanagement.

1.11　　　**The Secretary of Agriculture, Chicken Processors, and Football Sky-Box Seats**

<u>Use Transparency 12.</u>

<u>Answers and Key Discussion Items</u>

1.　No, the value is not the issue. Taking these items, regardless of amount, introduced quid pro quos into Mr. Espy's relationships with the companies he was supposed to be regulating. As a cabinet member and member of the executive branch, Mr. Espy has enforcement responsibilities that preclude the acceptance of any form of gift, regardless of value.

2.　No, Mr. Espy's reimbursement does not eliminate the questionable values introduced in the relationship by his having taken items in the first place. Mr. Espy cannot accept items and then reimburse. Mr. Espy simply cannot accept them in the first place.

3.　Front page of the newspaper test - looks like sale of influence Blanchard/Peale: Is it legal?

　　No; this type of conduct in the executive branch, particularly by a heavily regulated company could be called bribery. Is it balanced? No, introduces an unfair advantage to those with access to the secretary. How does it make me feel? Although initially Mr. Espy was not troubled by it all, the aftermath demonstrates that the gifts should have been troubling; creating conflicts of interest.

4.　Yes, Mr. Espy allowed the introduction of quid pro quo into his relationships; his acceptance of benefits created a sense of obligation.

5.　Mr. Blackley's dual paycheck was a problem; possibly illegal; government employee's outside compensation is regulated. Mr. Blackley's orders on inspections give the appearance of impropriety.

　　Tyson's furnishing of lodging and flights to a member of the executive (i.e., law enforcement) branch of government was a conflict.

　　The Tyson scholarship to Mr. Espy's girlfriend was just shy of an out-and-out cash payment; a definite conflict.

　　Sun Diamond's conduct was suspicious -- who paid for it? Appearance of a conflict.

　　Dallas Football Game -- gift of tickets and transportation are conflicts.

Answers and Key Discussion Items

1.   Sheila is in a position no one enjoys and very few know how to handle. She is the killjoy. However, Sheila needs to keep in mind some of the questions from the Nash test: could I discuss this trip with the CEO, with the Board, with my family? will I feel as good about this decision over the long run? If she is unable to convince the others and the supervisor of her concerns about propriety, she needs to use whatever avenue the company has available. She might try someone outside her immediate supervisor's supervisor such as the legal department or the audit department.

2.   Foregoing the trip is enough for Sheila personally but when the incident is later discovered, her ability to take a position and advocate it will be questioned. Many people view Sheila as being in a no-win situation. In fact, Sheila's principles afford her an opportunity to demonstrate leadership skills. She might consider offering examples of other similar incidents from other industries and firms and the results to demonstrate the repercussions for the members of her group.

3.   No, the CEO sends a stronger message if Sheila is retained. It would help employees to understand that choosing the correct action ensures protection. If she is fired when she had nowhere to turn, all employees will be reluctant to stay.

4.   No, firing the agents is not too harsh. The ethical tone of the department is pervasively poor. Cleaning it out is a good idea because these purchasing agents simply could not see the ethical issue. Whether there are bids pending is not the issue. The perks Rydman is offering will cloud the judgment of the purchasing department in future bidding processes. This type of conduct will not survive the front page of the newspaper test. The trip would simply be reported as the purchasing department accepting trips from a supplier and the appropriate conclusions would be drawn by the public. LA East is in a particularly sensitive position because it is a regulated public utility. Life for these types of firms is one in a fishbowl. Public scrutiny is intense and merciless.

Legal Issues

No statutory violations have occurred. However, the purchasing department is compromising its independence and its duty as an agent for the company to secure those contracts that are most beneficial to the principal (the utility).

1.13   **Pharmaceutical Honorariums to Researchers: Graying of the Line between Industry and Academic Research**

<u>Use Transparency 13</u>.

<u>Answers and Key Discussion Items</u>

1.   There are several ethical dilemmas present. First, there is the integrity of research and researchers sponsored by the company. The donation of royalties to the University where the studies on Retin-A were conducted raises questions about the results because of the interest the University has in the success of the product. The payment of honorariums to researchers and physicians to sponsor symposia on the product again raises issues about the independence of the views of participants.

A second ethical dilemma is Ortho's winking use of a product for a purpose not yet approved by the FDA. The irony is that the media would continue to tout the product for Ortho and it probably did not need to risk strained relationships with its regulator.

A third ethical issue concerns the universities and their policies with respect to royalties from companies and honoraria paid to faculty members.   Issues of research integrity and academic autonomy arise.   University administrators must evaluate these relationships and develop positions and policies for accepting donations and for professors participating in company-sponsored symposia in which they receive honoraria.

2.   Kligman's results should be verified independently.   Another university has done so. It apparently will only help the position and eliminates the questions raised by Kligman's work and conflict of interest.

3.   All universities should have generic policies in place for patents and royalties in which they hold an interest and for which members of their faculty have done research. Possibilities for handling the possible poor reflection on research integrity include:

a.   Supervision of research by consultants or outsiders;
b.   No direct financial benefit to researchers; and
c.   Public disclosure of interests and interrelationships.

4.   The harm in having individuals use the drug for an other-than-approved-purpose is that the test results have not been subjected to third-party scrutiny. It is possible that people would be misled about its capabilities.   It is also possible that appropriate warnings may not be present for this secondary use. This is a no-harm, no-foul argument.   If no one is hurt, the

conflicts and the lack of approval are moot issues. But, would we
want everyone operating this way? even on drugs where the
potential harms are more significant?

5.   Level of satisfaction now should not control whether disclosure is
      made. The universities and pharmaceuticals should be forthcoming
      about disclosures to avoid future issues of allegations of
      impropriety, particularly if something goes wrong with the drug.

6.   Research cannot be released without prior review; research may be
      withheld; negative research findings may be minimized; any research
      findings will be questioned because of close connections and
      financial ties.

7.   Corporate finding goes to students, not physically to researchers.
      Research council for review of work.
      Independent researchers affiliated with university researchers.
      Research supervision.
      An interest in the sales of a drug for which you are doing the
      research creates an almost unfixable conflict of interest.

Legal Issues

A company can advocate a product only for its approved use. The product
can't be marketed as an anti-aging creme. Indirectly, Ortho is doing so
by enjoying the benefits of media reports on research findings that were
incidental to the creme's primary use as an anti-acne creme. Ortho can
make no claims in ads regarding this use but the sponsored symposia and
the studies in the media permit its disclosure of an alternative use.

1.14   The Sale of Sand to the Saudis

Answers and Key Discussion Items

1.   If you can't trust Ms. Morris now, how can you trust her as an
      employee? Ms. Morris is bringing proprietary information to you.
      Her information looks like a solution in the short-run.   In the
      long-run you will be forced to cope with her tendencies. She could
      do the same to you.   You will also be working with someone who
      knows that you hired her because of improper information. You are
      both on the line at all times.

2.   Silt, Sand and Such is harmed by your decision to hire Ms. Morris.
      You and your firm will be harmed over the long-run. Is this the
      type of information you would want disclosed on the front page of
      a newspaper?

3.   Could you trust her? Would Silt, Sand and Such sue you for Morris
      breaking a covenant not to compete? Would you come to rely on
      "easy" fixes for meeting goals?

4.   Ms. Morris might be under a covenant not to compete and you could
      be held liable.   If it is proprietary information, it might be
      theft. Many students will respond that this type of thing is done
      all the time: employees leave and take information with them.
      However, "it's always been done," and "if we don't do it someone
      else will," are not justifications for actions, they are signals of
      ethical problems.   This information is not just operational or
      technological. It is information unique to one firm and developed
      solely by that firm.

5.   No, there would be no trust in your relationship with Morris. She
      betrayed her former employer. She could betray you.

Legal Issues

It is possible that your firm could be sued for interference with
contractual relations. You really don't know how much negotiation has
gone on and what groundwork has been laid for the contract. The use of
Ms. Morris's information could throw your company into a costly legal
battle.

1.15   The Employee and the Reporter

Answers and Key Discussion Items

1.   The students should try to place themselves in Jim's position. He
      has a good working relationship with a reporter who has helped
      Jim's company over the years. Jim wants to maintain that
      relationship. Jim also holds some resentment toward his own firm
      because of the cutbacks. However, Jim needs to apply some of the
      Nash questions: to whom do you give your loyalty? whom will your
      decision affect?

      Jim's loyalty should be to his company absent illegal and harmful
      conduct. Here employees are going to be harmed by the cutbacks but
      it will not help the employees to learn of their fates in the
      newspaper. Whether Jim agrees with the CEO and the management
      consultants on the plans is not the issue. Those decisions have
      been made at the appropriate levels. Those responsible should be
      given the opportunity to communicate with affected employees and
      offer them the dignity of fair treatment. Jim's conduct only harms
      the employees. It will not change the outcome.

2.   Jim should give the plan to Larsen immediately after the employees
      have been notified. He can still preserve his relationship.

3.   Yes, Larsen probably would have discovered it, but that does not
      justify disloyal behavior on Jim's part. Chances are Jim will not
      come forward with a confession. However, Jim could do so and
      explain his, perhaps misguided, desire to maintain a good
      relationship with Larsen and hopefully help the company in the
      long-run. Coming forward will be easier for Jim than having the
      company discover by its own investigation who was responsible.

4.   Have students examine the consequences of Jim coming forward. They
      may want to consider that his supervisor and CEO will find out
      anyway and stepping forward may help. They should consider
      economic impact; i.e., loss of their jobs.

1.16 The Rigged Election

Answers and Key Discussion Items

1. Mr. Gunty was trying to get an edge on the job market. Contact with speakers through the president's position might give him an opportunity not available to others.

2. Chances are many students did not care about the club officer positions. But many are hurt by Gunty's actions. The process is undermined, the credibility of the organization and institution are hurt. If those tactics are allowed to continue, they eliminate equal opportunities for all students to hold office.

3. Anonymity offers some security. Often it is used when there is insufficient evidence available and an investigation is warranted.

4. Many students make the point that this is "just school" and that the standards are different. Standards of personal honesty are always the same. Further, have the students examine the consequences to Mr. Gunty. He is known to his classmates and readers of the <u>Wall Street Journal</u> as someone who cheated on something as insignificant as "just school." Could you count on Mr. Gunty in an honesty sense in any setting? Mr. Gunty's long-term damage to his reputation is significant.

    Further, Mr. Gunty may have encountered life's worst punishment: having to write an extra paper!!!

1.17   Puffing in the Resume

Answers and Key Discussion Items

1. The point should be made that there is nothing wrong with presenting yourself in the best light possible. The line for unethical resumes is crossed when the information is not accurate. For example, you could put "Denny's Restaurant Manager," or you could list your activities, "Coordinated scheduling, handled purchasing, performed payroll, customer satisfaction, etc." and then list Denny's as the place of employment. Saying you performed those management duties when, in fact, you were a fry cook would be unethical. It is wrong to place false information in a resume. You may not have the chance to correct it.

2. Rather than misstate the degree, you should take care of the debts or fines. Either way you handle this one, you are going to have to disclose unethical behavior. You have not defined the problem accurately. Why go through the job process having to explain why you don't have a degree? Get the degree.

3. A thirteen-month lapse is not so unusual these days. Concealment from a prospective employer will only damage your relationship even if you do get the job. And, as the Honeywell case illustrated, deceit is something an employer can use against you at any point in the employment relationship.

4. There is a difference between marketing yourself effectively and lying. You should never claim to have a skill, degree or prior employment experience that you do not have. The lack of candor will ensure that you don't keep the job you do get. It all works out the same. The idea in an employment search is to match skills, experience and personality with the right job. The lack of candor only postpones the ability to find that position.

5. Puffing is acceptable so long as there are no false impressions. Misrepresentation may get you a job, but it may also get you fired. It is a high risk activity and a truly short-term solution.

Legal Issues

If you are bidding on a contract and fail to disclose information about yourself or misstate or overstate your qualifications, there could be statutory penalties as well as an action for fraud or misrepresentation. Your misrepresentations on your resume can be used against you later on as a justification for firing you.

1.18   The Glowing Recommendation

Answers and Key Discussion Items

1.   Jake's dilemma is an interesting cross between ethical commitments, legal issues, and the liability of a firm for employee recommendations. Jake has agreed to be a reference, so he must answer the prospective employer's questions. Jake does have some good things to say about Bob--he is conscientious and a hard worker. The absence of information on his skills should alert an observant employer of gaps that should be checked with others.

2.   Another dilemma will arise if the new employer calls Jake and asks for the information intentionally left out. It is at that point that you need to talk with Bob. This talk should have been conducted long before Bob went job hunting. It should have been conducted as part of Jake's responsibilities as a manager. Jake has the obligation to use his employer's resources wisely and allowing Bob's work efforts and habits to continue over the years was not an effective use of anyone's time or resources. Jake's loyalty to his friendship took priority over his loyalty to his employer.

3.   Yes, Jake, like many of us, has failed to confront an uncomfortable situation head on. He needs to address the problem, which is more than the reference request.

4.   Many glowing recommendations are given to be rid of employees. It is neither balanced nor ethical to do so. These recommendations harm both the employee and the new employer.

5.   Not when employment/supervisory issues are involved. We often tell "white lies" to avoid offending a friend. We should not tell white lies about employees and their work.

Legal Issues

The area of recommendations from employers is fraught with legal pitfalls. As a result, many employers follow a policy of simply stating whether an employee would or would not be rehired. However, these policies do not preclude the personal types of references and recommendations Jake agreed to provide here. Jake should understand his liability for statements that are inaccurate (liability to Bob). There has been liability imposed for glowing recommendations for employees who later turn out to be disasters as well as slander/libel liability for poor references.

1.19   The Good Business Reference

Answers and Key Discussion Items

1.   You need to define your role. You are a reference with respect to
      the lines of credit. You are not a reference for the quality of
      their printing.   You could preface any remarks you make by
      explaining that the printing company is simply a credit customer
      and you would be a business reference only. Unless you are also
      using the printer for your materials, you are giving second-hand
      information.

2.   If you do use the customer as a printer, you should be candid about
      your experience and assessment as well as your belief in the
      printer's potential. There is a compromise here. The disclosure
      of accurate information may help the potential customer in working
      out deadlines and establishing proofing procedures.

3.   No, because you cannot offer any opinion beyond just that of a
      creditor.

4.   Yes, it would possibly be defamation to speak beyond your direct
      information as a creditor.

Legal Issues

Use caution to be sure your information is accurate.   Inaccurate
statements would be slander or libel (depending upon their form) and if
a contract is not awarded as a result, there may be bases for a suit for
intentional interference with contractual relations.

1.20   The Unofficial Government Contract and the Account Sale

<u>Answers and Key Discussion Items</u>

1.   This is a classic conflict of interest. The situation has arisen because you did not remove yourself from the negotiations and sale process from the outset. Your loyalty is to your employer and the information should be disclosed. The fact that the information is unofficial is irrelevant. You have already made the first mistake in handling the sale.

2.   At this point, you should disclose everything and let the employer decide about the contract and your fate.

3.   Yes, to avoid these problems and conflicts, someone else should have handled the sale from the outset.

<u>Legal Issues</u>

In some states, this type of self-dealing would be criminal.

1.21 Radar Detectors and the Law

Answers and Key Discussion Items

1. Radar detectors are indeed a means of facilitating violations of the law. The fact that "everyone speeds," "everyone has them," or "the speed limits aren't right or are unfair," does not change the illegal nature of the activity.

2. Suppose that someone is injured or killed because of your speeding, would you be morally responsible? Therefore, it is immoral to violate the laws. The laws were established for a purpose and we can question that purpose and work to change the laws but self-determination of inefficacy does not permit violations. The laws are positive law enacted in a utilitarian sense: the most good for the most people. There is a certain element of morality even in the speeding laws.

3. Radar detectors facilitate violations of the law. Radar detectors have no purpose beyond evasion of the law. Ask the students if they would be comfortable running a very profitable business that manufactures radar detectors and other similar devices.

4. Many students feel this way: speeding may be against the law, but it's arbitrary.

Legal Issues

As any student knows, speeding brings fines. The activity is illegal. Discussions will attempt to justify it, but until the laws change, it is unethical.

Special note

This topic will be a particularly sensitive one because "everyone does it."

1.22   The Ethics of Looking Busy

Answers and Key Discussion Items

1.   Jane's focus should be:

Am I giving an honest day's work for my pay?
Am I being honest with my employer?
Am I taking something that doesn't belong to me (my employer's time)?
Is it fair?
Is it balanced?
How would Jane feel if someone she was paying to work for her behaved in this fashion?

2.   Employees who need flexibility should request it and not engage in Jane's behavior (which is dishonest). Flex-time is an option more and more employers make available.

3.   Jane does not have enough work that she feels comfortable leaving for long stretches. Jane may not progress as quickly in the organization without the necessary, "How can I help?" attitude as opposed to her current, "How much can I get away with?" attitude.

4.   No one should ever say or do anything that is dishonest at the behest of a supervisor or co-employee. A proper response is "Jane, or Ms. Nugent, I'm a good worker who will do anything that I am asked, but please don't ask me to say or do anything that is less than honest." When Jane's conduct is discovered (and it always is), Jane's secretary may go too.

5.   Firm management should revisit the basis for evaluation: quality time vs. quantity time. As employers consider the impact on employee family life, stress, health, etc., long hours may not be the only key to success and should not be a basis for evaluation. Further, employees are finding ways to deceive the system. Hours spent (or perceived hours spent) are obviously not indicative of work as we see from Jane's antics.

2.1   Ann Hopkins, Price Waterhouse and the Partnership

Use Transparency 14 to show the choices in language made in the evaluation of Ann Hopkins.

Answers and Key Discussion Items

1.   The partnership evaluation system appears to be widely-dispersed, uncertain in criteria, and not policed for violations of equal employment laws. In fairness to Price Waterhouse though, there was a time when such decisions (those for partnerships) were considered immune to EEOC attack (they were not classified as employment decisions).

2.   One of the intriguing aspects of the case is why none of the partners, particularly any of the other women, ever spoke up and objected to the language and bases for Hopkins's evaluation. The process of group think results from peer pressure being applied to such an extent that those forms of conduct and types of statements that would otherwise be wrong and offensive are ignored.

3.   The subjectivity was troublesome only because it allowed sexism to enter into the decision-making process. There is nothing wrong with not awarding a partnership to someone who is obnoxious, alienates the staff and is offensive in manner. These types of professional decisions on life-long commitments to employment necessarily include personal elements. However, in this case, and in many other employment cases, those issues were not the focus of the evaluation. The focus of the evaluation was Ms. Hopkins's appearance and her role as a woman in the workplace. In developing a procedure for evaluating potential partners, the firm should consider criteria such as revenue generated, relationships with staff, work compatibility with other partners, client satisfaction and others that are relevant, gender-neutral and serve to incorporate the concerns about the partnership decision.

4.   The concept of "mixed motives" was covered in the U.S. Supreme Court decision. There may have been legitimate concerns about Ms. Hopkins' partnership "fit", but they were manifested in gender-descriptive terms.

5.   The firm would have to have a diverse workforce. Top executives would have to support diversity by their hires and promotions. Basing decisions on experience and qualifications would become the firm's set of standards.

Legal Issues

The partners had concerns about Ms. Hopkins' fit into the partnership and those concerns are legitimate. The violation of the Civil Rights laws (and specifically Title VII) came as those concerns were translated into gender-descriptive terms.

2.2 Handwriting Analysis and Employment

Use Transparency 15 to show types of handwriting and the conclusions drawn by the experts on that writing.

Answers and Key Discussion Items

1. Handwriting is so easily altered that questions about its accuracy exist. Also, it seems to be an imprecise science when compared with drug-screening tests. However, many managers see it as a way to discern personality traits and those traits that make, for example, a good salesperson.

2. Handwriting analysis appears to be no different than a personality test. Questions exist about those types of evaluations as well. There appear to be contradictions in the experts' analysis of the same handwriting. Also, applicants have the ability to change handwriting samples just as they have the ability to control answers on a personality test.

3. As the transparency shows, there is great disparity among experts on treatment of handwriting. The question that arises is how much value such analysis brings to the employment decision. Managers are perhaps better served relying on interviews, questions and work samples.

4. Privacy issues may exist but handwriting is not an invasion of the person. Handwriting is part of working and not a taking of something that would not otherwise be seen. If the analysis are accurate, then a great deal of information is available to an employer that would otherwise not be available. Presently, handwriting seems to be a little bit of wizardry that enjoys some success.

5. Legally, many firms have run into discrimination problems because tests not really related to employment skills serve to screen out certain races. Depending on the analysts, it is possible women could be screened out of certain jobs. A valid accusation of discrimination via disparate impact could be made especially given the discrepancies in handwriting analysis.

2.3 Health and Genetic Screening

<u>Answers and Key Discussion Items</u>

1. The use of the results of genetic screening is perhaps the real
    concern in any employee testing of this sort. If the results are
    being used, as in Israel, to avoid unnecessary risk and exposure in
    the workplace based on genetic composition, it is helpful. If, on
    the other hand, the screening results are used to deny employment,
    deny health insurance coverage or refuse to hire on the grounds
    that the employee's children would require additional medical care
    because of genetic diseases, there would be an invasion of privacy.

2. The clash is between the ability of all of us to overcome inherent
    defects and the use of pre-screening to prevent giving us the
    opportunity to do so. The use for all employees seems overly broad
    and carries the potential of exclusion of employees not on the
    basis of qualifications, but inherent composition. If carried to
    its extreme, some people would be essentially not hireable because
    of their genetic composition.

3. DuPont's program appears to have been implemented to prevent
    illness, not as a tool of discrimination or arbitrarily. Concern
    of making employees ill is at the heart of it.

4. The screening on the basis of sickle-cell anemia could result in a
    disparate impact on particular races. Although screening might be
    intended to ensure safety and put high risk employees in other
    jobs, the effect may be to preclude certain groups from higher-
    paying jobs.

5. Yes, DuPont's goal appears to be protection of employees;
    minimizing illness. Unfortunately, statutory protections clash and
    DuPont may lose.

6. The ADA provides that employment cannot be denied or terminated
    strictly on the basis of illness if the employee is able (with
    reasonable accommodation) to do his or her job. DuPont thus could
    not simply exclude sickle cell anemia victims so long as they can
    do the job.

<u>Legal Issues</u>

The U.S. Supreme Court has already ruled that an employer may not use a
woman's fertility or possible fetal exposure (and the resulting dangers
or permanent damage) to exclude women from certain jobs that are higher-
paying, but also higher in risk. The use of a genetic screening device
that impacts a particular race would probably meet the same fate in a
judicial challenge.

2.4   The Smoking Prohibition

Answers and Key Discussion Items

1. Many companies take a different approach and attempt to have employees make the voluntary choice to eliminate unhealthy activities through educational programs, incentives and additional health insurance coverage costs for those who do smoke.

2. The interests of the employee's privacy are at risk as they clash with the interests of the employer in keeping employees healthy and keeping the cost of health insurance down. A utilitarian approach says that in doing the most good for the most people, eliminating smokers reduces health coverage and ensures that more people will have coverage.

3. There is an interest in health costs, passive smoke and safety of other employees. However, the issue of rights is also present. The ban on off-the-job smoking is a violation of individual freedom. As pointed out by one legislator in the case: if you permit off-the-job control, where do you draw the line?

4. It is not discrimination to refuse to hire smokers. Title VII includes no category for protection for voluntary conduct that translates into exposure for other employees as well as additional health insurance costs for the employer and other employees.

5. The exclusions for hazardous activities are quite common. Again, the employer is trying to provide the best possible coverage at the lowest possible price and exclusion of these employees achieves that goal. Again, refusal to hire on these bases is also not discrimination. The employer does make an investment in an employee in training, benefits, etc. and implements policies such as this to ensure that there is a return on these employee investments.

    Many insurance policies that cover key individuals include clauses that prohibit these activities during the period of coverage. For example, film stars would carry large policies on them because of the costs involved if they are unable to complete a movie. These activities are prohibited during the course of the movie shoot to minimize risk.

2.5   DUI and Deliveries

Answers and Key Discussion Items

1. The employer is balancing the privacy rights of the employee with the rights of society. Safety on the roads is imperative as so many others' rights are affected when irresponsible drivers are driving.

    The students should recognize that in this case, the DUI screening is simply good business. Safety of the drivers affords the company a good reputation. If drivers are, in fact, under the influence, their errors are likely to injure others and cost the company a great deal in litigation and public relations in the event of the discovery of the employee's drug or alcohol abuse.

2. Random means a larger net. Announced means temporarily clean employees. Notice is more dignified, but not as effective as determent.

3. There are various approaches to testing. Some employers require all employees to be tested. Other employers only require employees who are involved in positions that affect public safety to be tested. Other employers require officers and those employees in safety positions to be tested. The officers are tested to show compliance and good faith.

4. Testing employees who are involved in an accident may not be a choice. Law enforcement agencies may do that for you. It would be best to test all the drivers, require it periodically and then perform random tests. Employees and potential employees should all be told clearly the policies and procedures on drug testing.

5. Drug-testing is similar to the invasion of privacy that occurs when we go through the screening devices at the airport. It is an invasion of privacy, but one we are willing to accept because of our overriding concern for safety.

6. Testing only suspicious drivers minimizes the invasion of privacy, but minimizes the deterrent effect of a testing program. You may not have a large enough net to catch offenders.

7. Many people differ on the action that should be taken in the event of a positive result on a drug screening. Many employers take the posture that it is a violation of company rules and there is immediate termination. These policies tend to dominate in employment situations where public safety is at issue (drivers). Other employers take the position of a warning and mandatory drug rehabilitation and education programs. Accuracy is ensured through follow-up testing or the ability of the employee to use an independent lab.

2.5   DUI and Deliveries (cont'd)

8.   Counseling, retesting, rehab programs, reassignment, stress reduction

9.   Two labs; employee's choice of labs; latest technology

10.   You should inform drivers of testing as a precondition of employment and your ongoing test. Being candid up front is fair and ethical.

2.6   Corporate Anthropology: Is the Boss Spying?

Answers and Key Discussion Items

1.   Many argue that spying is the only way the employer can monitor effective performance. Many maintain that electronic surveillance is just a more sophisticated means of having the supervisor walk around and observe employees at work. On the other hand, the electronic surveillance is relentless -- employees are never given the opportunity for a "let-up."

2.   Many argue that they are the same with one exception: an employee can see a supervisor walking around and respond. They can't "see" electronic monitoring. They don't know when they're being watched.

3.   The right to privacy while doing one's job has not been recognized. Employers have the right to observe, correct and monitor. The advance disclosure of the monitoring seems more fair to most employees. However, in an ethical sense, shouldn't an employee always be performing his/her job effectively? Isn't the employee accepting wages in exchange for doing what is asked by the employer? In other words, should it make any difference in the way an employee acts whether or not he/she is being observed?

4.   Employees are told of the monitoring and can thus assume they are always being observed. There are no surprises. Employees know their conduct is watched.

5.   The desk is slightly different. Some elements of private life are within the desk and the invasion here is not directly related to job performance. Observing an employee work at a desk is different from actually going through the desk when the employee is not there.

6.   The nature of the employee's work can make surveillance more or less necessary. Telephone work must be monitored in a specific way and those monitors give employers information about how long the calls take, whether more operators are needed and whether the operators are following company guidelines on information, courtesy, etc.

Point out that hotels and other service industries have used customer satisfaction surveys as a means of monitoring employees for years. If anything, those surveys are less objective since customers can recount encounters with employees in their own words without adding a different perspective. In-house observation at least collects the full information.

2.7 The HIV-Positive Physician and the Hospital's Liability

Answers and Key Discussion Items

1. The hospital will never avoid lawsuits. The disclosure was made voluntarily so that the hospital did not add additional counts of negligence for the failure to notify the patients so that they could take appropriate precautions and, if necessary, undergo early intervention treatment.

2. The case is a very delicate balancing of the interests of the physician who is HIV positive, his privacy and right to work and the interests of the patients who expect not to be exposed to some disease beyond that which brought them to the hospital for treatment. The hospital has an obligation of providing safe medical care. The HIV-positive physician presented a health risk to the hospital patients. The court strikes a balance by revealing the exposure to the patients without revealing the identity of the physician. All the needs are met without undue invasion of the physician's privacy.

3. The patients' health are at risk by contact and they should know of the physician's illness. Privacy interests are outweighed by risk of exposure.

4. The remoteness of the chance of contracting the disease from a physician was acknowledged by the court. However, the court also acknowledged that, rightly or wrongly, the public is wary and frightened of the AIDS virus and views it as existing at epidemic proportions. The court agrees with the public perception to the extent that the disease should not be taken lightly.

5. Dr. Doe's medical career is necessarily curtailed because of the risk to patients. Dr. Doe should have consented to disclosure because of the potential harm to the patients.

6. The perception of the hospital is affected by the disclosure. The physician's career is affected by the disclosure. However, if you were a patient, would you want to know that your physician was HIV positive? Will the presence of the disease preclude individuals from certain types of professions and employment? Will they be permitted in those professions but have difficulty succeeding?

Legal Issues

The students should be made aware of the Americans with Disabilities Act which prohibits discrimination in the workplace on the basis of physical disabilities that do not interfere with the ability to perform the job. The statute is still new and litigation related to AIDS and the protection under the Act will be forthcoming. Also at issue will be statutes like the Pennsylvania one which involve court orders for disclosure and whether the federal law preempts such disclosure standards.

2.8   The Affair Between the Gatekeeper and the Operations VP

<u>Answers and Key Discussion Items</u>

1. The affair concerns the company because the officers interact in areas subject to internal controls. Also, the affair affects the reputation of the company. Also, issues of morality arise. At the officer level of a company, these types of relationships can turn into cases of sexual harassment and often result in the neglect of duties.

2. Most employees in Verdi's shoes would let the situation go and not tell anyone except in a gossip sense. If Verdi knows either Deborah or Raymond, he should talk with them individually and express his concern and the concerns of others in the officer group. Verdi should help them to understand that their behavior will eventually cost them their positions. His failure to act could be very harmful to both of their careers. He may be helping by confronting them with the matter directly.

3. Myers is not trying to impose his moral standards. There is a general moral standard regarding marital fidelity and Myers is simply trying to run a company that does not include an officer group that ignores this moral standard.

4. Many companies, at one time, had policies prohibiting fraternization among employees. If the employees did fraternize, one had to leave or be transferred to a different facility. These policies ran into difficulties with Title VII of the Civil Rights Act because of their unfair impact on women.

    An appropriate company policy would be one that prohibits personal relationships among employees that could result in the compromise of work habits, internal controls or the company's reputation. One of the difficulties in a case such as this one is developing an appropriate policy that does not violate Title VII. It must be gender-neutral and address personal relationships generally.

5. Verdi should disclose the information -- company controls may be at issue. The company and many individuals will be hurt.

<u>Legal Issues</u>

Some state and local laws prohibit discrimination on the basis of sexual orientation. A court ruling involving a Wal-Mart policy on prohibition of employees marrying was found violative of Title VII.

2.9   E-Mail, Voice Mail, Fax -- Is There Corporate Privacy?

Answers and Key Discussion Items

1.   Just as with monitoring, employees need to know that their uses of these forms of technology are monitored. Courts have been clear in stating that employers own these technologies and employee rights to privacy in them in the workplace do not exist.

2.   Full disclosure upon hiring of access and monitoring; ongoing reminders of monitoring.

3.   Yes, some employers have an e-mail/voice mail disclosure/monitoring form given to all employees.

4.   It would be unfair of employees to use work equipment and facilities for private use -- employees don't have rights for private use of employer facilities.

5.   Never put anything in e-mail, voice mail or fax you are not willing to have disclosed to anyone in the company.

6.   Yes, tapping into electronic devices is quite easy. Espionage using these technologies is quite common. For a salesman to tap into another company's technology is dishonest and unethical. It falls into the category of taking things that don't belong to you.

7.   These forms of communication open the door for false messages such as contract offers, acceptances, bids, etc. Guaranteeing authenticity requires passwords, changes in passwords, etc.

Answers and Key Discussion Items

1. Braun's conduct was clearly sexual harassment. Many men in Braun's situation justify the conduct as follows: 1) it's private; 2) she "asked for it"; and 3) it was just a pass. However, the worst part of the case was the inaction of management with respect to the complaints lodged by Ford and the continuing conduct of Braun. Responses to conduct such as Braun's must be quick and harsh. Termination may be necessary.

2. Braun and his managers had different perceptions about what constitutes sexual harassment. As in many headline cases today, the conduct is not perceived to be sufficient to warrant investigation, reprimand or even a sympathetic ear.

3. Because the tolerance of sexual harassment has been high in the past, modifications of attitudes requires reinforcement and reminders. Someone else speaking on behalf of Ms. Ford could have helped her resolve the case sooner than it was resolved. There is a tendency is a group situation in which no one is speaking up to allow unethical and illegal conduct to continue. An additional voice could have made the difference for Ms. Ford and the resulting damages she experienced.

Legal Issues

Sexual harassment and a sexually hostile environment are prohibited under Title VII of the Civil Rights Act. Additionally, some states, such as Arizona, permit sexually harassed employees to recover from employers and managers individually on a tort theory for the failure to take necessary steps to eliminate the harassment experienced.

2.11   The Attorney and the Law Clerk

Answers and Key Discussion Items

1.   Mr. Heinze's conduct went on for so long because he was in a position of authority, no one complained for a number of years and many of the women he encountered were concerned about his influence on their career progression. Everyone who knew of Mr. Heinze's conduct bears some responsibility for the outcome of this case. Again, the issues were probably perceived as a joke and few women were willing to come forward thinking that "this must be the way everyone runs an office."

2.   The Council may not have known of Mr. Heinze's conduct but it did employ him and is responsible for the tortious acts of its agents and Mr. Heinze was certainly an agent. As such, the council is financially responsible.

3.   Whether the state should be responsible in a legal sense was not the issue for the judge. The issue for the judge was that the state should assume responsibility for such agents and that the only way to attract the attention of the state and ensure that another Mr. Heinze could not happen and that these types of independent employees were given greater supervision, was to assess a large verdict against the state. If the state knew of Mr. Heinze's pattern and had prior complaints, there would be legal justification for the award. The judge's verdict and assessment was a strong signal to the state to become more actively involved in the supervision of its employees who operate in a somewhat independent fashion.

Note for the students that the taxpayers will eventually end up footing the bill on Mr. Heinze. The students generally have good notions about the fairness of this decision. Have them discuss the state's (and ultimately the taxpayers') liability.

2.12 Stroh's Swedish Bikini Team

<u>Answers and Key Discussion Items</u>

1. The ads get attention and sell beer but also offend a large segment of the market: many women. The image of women in the ad is demeaning. The ad may not sell beer -- that should be the first question as the marketing manager evaluates the campaign.

2. The court would balance the censorship issue with the need to regulate advertising and a peculiar need to regulate sales of and ads for alcohol.

3. It is a difficult connection to draw between the ads and an atmosphere of harassment in the workplace for the five women. The ads are external but do send a message about the culture of the decision making-level in Stroh's. That message may be perceived by workers and carried out at various levels in the company as justification for poor treatment of women, sexist remarks and the displays of photos and pictures.

    The tenuous ad connection could be eliminated as the focus of the complaints, and the women can have their workplace objections discussed. The fact that the connection is tenuous does not mean that the culture at Stroh's does not lend itself to the worker perception that women are to be perceived and treated as in the ad.

4. These ads and many others similar to them may draw in some sales. However, the ads can also bring the wrath of customers who are offended. Women need not be abandoned in making advertisements for beer; their role model should remain something other than a scantily-clad blonde. Stroh's should also be concerned about the tone the ads set for the company.

2.13 Tops Guns and Sexual Harassment

Answers and Key Discussion Items

1. At an event which was at least indirectly sponsored by the Navy, the gauntlet was not just party fun. It was harassment because the women were not voluntary participants and the convention was one related to their employment. Sexual harassment is covered both at the workplace and at events sponsored by the employer. While the conduct occurred at a party, it was an employment-related party. The initial response when women complained was "boys will be boys" or "she should have known" or "that's what you get when you go to parties with heavy drinking", etc.

2. The situation was one with which the men were familiar. They had been to Tailhook conventions and understood the nature of activities on the closed floor. For the women involved, it was a new experience and prior knowledge of behavior patterns did not exist. These arguments were made by top Navy officials, i.e., what do you expect from aviators who have been partying for 3 days?

3 and 4. Both the senior officers and the hotel management acquiesced in the sense that no action was taken to limit the drinking or control the conduct on the floor. The senior officers, many of whom are now gone from the Navy, tolerated the conduct as "that's the way it has always been done."

5. In a peer-pressure situation, no one was willing to speak up or take action. The hotel was interested in retaining the convention ("if we don't do it, someone else will").

6. The conduct in the gauntlet was horrendous, but the conduct of Spigener was worse. He showed a lack of respect for Ms. Coughlin and his actions constituted sexual harassment. The Navy has instituted a sexual harassment hotline.

7. The Navy's Tailhook incident has been one that has highlighted the change in the composition of the military and the lack of change in the conduct and attitude of the men who have dominated the military for so long. The reaction to the women's complaints created more difficulty than the party conduct. No one seemed to care about the complaints which sent a signal that the conduct was acceptable.

8. Again, the lack of action caused public outrage and demonstrated the problem.

    Note: The Navy is considering a ban on Playboy magazines for all enlisted personnel and officers. Ask the students to discuss this ban.

2.14   Hooters: More Than a Waitress?

Answers and Key Discussion Items

1.   It is obvious from Hooters' ads, the attire of the waitresses, the
      name and the T-shirts that the restaurant chain has a focus on
      sexual entendre. The whole restaurant theme seems to say to women,
      "Avoid this place if harassment is a problem." The issue is not
      whether knowledge is critical. Knowledge is obvious. The issue is
      whether Hooters and its theme should be regulated in some way.

2.   Despite the theme, Hooters managers should ensure that harassment
      of workers does not occur.

3.   Managers can set the restaurant tone by intervening when workers
      are uncomfortable with customer behavior and by a asking those who
      can't control themselves to leave.

4.   Students will debate the issue whole-heartedly. A former student
      shared a dilemma: he needed hours for continuing education for his
      license renewal. The seminar that would give him the hours he
      needed in time for renewal was being held at a Hooters restaurant.
      He felt uncomfortable going but needed his continuing education
      hours. What would you do?

2.15   On-the-Job Fetal Injuries

Answers and Key Discussion Items

1. The policy was designed to protect women of child-bearing capability and their fetuses. The policy of Johnson Controls had the best intentions and was based on sound legal advice: avoid liability for fetal exposure in certain jobs. The difficulty was that no choice was given and the high-exposure jobs were the ones paying the most money.

2. Freedom of choice is a good alternative with the exception of possible problems for the fetus who is left with exposure but no choice. This lack of choice on the part of the baby may still spell future liability for Johnson Controls.

3. The issue here is one of balancing the mother's rights for equal employment with the child's rights of freedom from injury, damage, etc. The difficulty lies in dictating the conduct of the mother for the benefit of an individual who cannot speak, but may be injured. The legal decision focused on the rights of the mother.

4. As the director of human resources, faced with the implementation of the U.S. Supreme Court decision, I would quickly develop a disclosure statement and waiver. All workers would be given both. Exposure to lead can be dangerous for men as well. With universal coverage, the waivers and signatures are an employment requirement and not a requirement for women only (or women of child-bearing years).

5. Whether the U.S. Supreme Court made the correct decision in subordinating the rights of unborn children remains to be seen. In the opinion there is a footnote regarding the possibility of state litigation with respect to insurance coverage of such birth defects. State law might permit recovery against the company even though the U.S. Supreme Court was mandating that women be permitted to hold those jobs that might result in the liability issues.

Legal Issues

Many employers are affected by the *Johnson Controls* case. Hospitals with technicians and other personnel in x-ray and nuclear medicine, nuclear plant workers, and VDT workers would be affected. Any exclusionary policies must be eliminated.

2.16   Wards Cove: Salmon Cannery Jobs

Use Transparency 16 to show differences in types of jobs available during the canning season.

Answers and Key Discussion Items

1.   The court found there was no intent to discriminate. Students should consider some of the practices listed on the transparency such as the separate eating and sleeping quarters. A program that provides training to move cannery workers into noncannery jobs would eliminate the perception the community and workers have about discrimination.

2.   An affirmative action program could be used for training and moving workers from unskilled to skilled positions. Such a program would even be legal under the Supreme Court's most recent ruling on affirmative action because this employer has a past history of disparate treatment.

3.   Statistical matches are difficult types of cases to make. The workforce of a particular employee may not mirror the general population but this lack of direct match should not be a presumption of discrimination.

4.   Under new Supreme Court decisions, statistical matches are not required. Any statistical base used must be of qualified applicants, not the workforce or community population generally.

Legal Issues

The *Wards Cove* case and others decided in the same court term were thought to make it more difficult for plaintiffs to prove discrimination under Title VII. Congress passed amendments to Title VII in 1991 that largely eliminated the extra burden of proof imposed by cases such as *Wards Cove*. However, as noted in #4, new Supreme Court decisions have further clarified definitions of discrimination and imposed new requirements for affirmative action programs.

2.17   Denny's: Discriminatory Service With a Smile

Answers and Key Discussion Items

1.   When the news of these incidents became public, the senior management was surprised. Clear signals about racial discrimination were not making their way down to the restaurants and restaurant managers.

2.   Apart from the financial costs, Denny's had a public relations nightmare. Further, it is impossible to know how much business was lost as a result of this public disclosure.

3.   Denny's needs an educational campaign and a reward system for employees on diversity issues. The organization needs a theme of tolerance, openness and above all, compliance with the law.

2.18   Richard Woolley: The Long-Term Engineer

Answers and Key Discussion Items

1.   There is a balancing of the interests of the employer in having the flexibility to reduce the employment force and costs with the reliance of employees and their expectation of some assurance of employment with advance notice of termination.

2.   The balance is achieved by some small measure of due process.   The employer should have procedures to be followed for termination and the employee should be entitled to expect that those procedures will be followed.   Materials such as employee handbooks and company policies and procedures form the bases for this due process.   Apart from the legal and ethical requirements, these procedures are sound management principles that permit the individuals to grow and make changes as they receive formal feedback.   Morale improves when employees feel there are protections built into the process for them and that they will be given the opportunity to change before they are terminated without explanation.

3.   The changes in employee protections do cut down employer flexibility.   But the loss of flexibility is a response to perceived employer unfairness in dealing the employees.

4.   Hoffman-LaRoche's concerns about lawsuits would be justified if it did not implement processes and procedures for warnings and terminations.   The courts are simply requiring due process.   So long as there is a process, law suits are minimized and employers will prevail.

Legal Issues

Employment at will has been subject to significant judicial modifications.   In many states, employees cannot be fired where it would violate public policy (whistle-blower protection) or where an implied contract exists between the employer and employee by virtue of handbooks or policies and procedures.

2.19   Catherine Wagenseller: The Fired Killjoy

<u>Use Transparency 17 for a chronology of events</u>.

Answers and Key Discussion Items

1. The conduct outside the hospital was brought into the hospital. The case study points out the dangers that companies face when employees socialize either officially or unofficially. Their standards of behavior, moral standards, etc. may differ and the employee who does not join in becomes a fifth wheel. The outsider attitude is often carried into the workplace and made a part of personnel decisions (as here). Personal standards, morals and beliefs should not be the subject of personnel actions. Those attitudes and beliefs are uniquely individual and should not be subject to conformity in order to retain a job or enjoy fair treatment on the job.

2. The river activity harmed Wagenseller because she was not comfortable with it and she was a captive audience. Once she was on the raft trip, there was little that she could do to remove herself from conduct that she found offensive. A good utilitarian question here is: what if everybody behaved this way? how would society appear?

3. Wagenseller should have first talked with Smith to express her concerns. Perhaps they could have communicated better and avoided the eventual showdown. Then Wagenseller could have spoken to others for protection.

4. The termination did not fit the sequence of Wagenseller's employment development. A good supervisor would have asked more questions and delved more deeply into the rapid turnaround in attitudes about her work.

5. The termination sent the signal that supervisors had ultimate control over standards of propriety and employees who complained, did not participate or distanced themselves would suffer the consequences.

6. A mix of employees is critical, especially in team work such as emergency care. However, the differences in standards do not necessarily equate with the inability to work together. She was able to work with the team before "Moon River" and presumably she could continue if the exposure episode had not been brought into the workplace.

Legal Issues

See Case 2.18 for discussion of employment at will protections.

2.20   Beech-Nut and the No-Apple-Juice Apple Juice

Use Transparency 18 for a chronology of events.

Answers and Key Discussion Items

1.   While no one was harmed by the apple juice, it was fraud to tell
     consumers it was apple juice and charge apple juice prices. Also,
     there was the possibility that a baby might have had an allergic
     reaction to the chemicals in the product. Parents need to have
     content information before giving the juice to the babies. Selling
     no-apple-juice apple juice was unfair to the buyers, the users and
     the competitors of Beech-Nut.

2.   This was a company that had no avenues for employees to report
     problems they suspected and did not have the appropriate culture
     for responding to problems and questions that were pursued
     diligently by employees. LiCari made sure he had his facts
     straight and he did follow the lines of authority, the proper plan
     for a whistle-blower. The problems LiCari encountered were that
     nobody at any level wanted to listen to him. Even LiCari's
     circumstantial evidence should have been taken seriously and
     followed up on.

3.   Circumstantial evidence is not conclusive evidence. Often whistle-
     blowers look foolish when they do not have full information. Here,
     the evidence was, however, quite strong.

4.   Beech-Nut was facing tremendous competition and the need to keep
     prices down. The ease of the substitution and its low cost made
     the continuing dependence on a chemical concoction necessary.

5.   LiCari is an honest and conscientious man who did everything he
     could and explored every avenue to try to help the company correct
     its problems. LiCari wrote anonymously to the FDA because of his
     conscience, but did not want to be involved in the process of
     investigating or have his name revealed to Beech-Nut. Discuss with
     the students the ethics of anonymous tips. Accuracy can be
     difficult to verify and follow-up is impossible. Should the person
     be willing to accept the consequences that follow from coming
     forward? Compare LiCari to Anita Hill and her allegations against
     Clarence Thomas. Should she have come forward while still employed
     by Judge Thomas?

6.   LiCari's identity was revealed eventually but he wanted to remain
     anonymous to avoid the public scrutiny, stress, and hassle.

7.   Hoyvald and Lavery are still subject to state charges that are
     pending. But, it is important for the students to realize that

criminal conviction or not, these two men are now unemployable and will spend most of the money they earned on attorneys' fees in defending their cases. The criminal charges may be the least of their problems. There are no positive aspects to their running Beech-Nut during this time. Their careers are finished, personal disgrace (guilty or not) follows and shareholders, employers and customers will continue to resent their conduct.

Legal Issues

The FDA requires full disclosure of all product contents on the label. It is a felony violation of federal law to mislead or mislabel intentionally. Also, the sale of apple juice with no apple juice constituted fraud.

2.21   NASA and the Space Shuttle Booster Rockets

Answers and Key Discussion Items

1. Manuel Velasquez draws the line on moral responsibility for deaths
    that result from products with those who made the ultimate decision
    to go forward with a product; not with those who helped in its
    development, fact verification for it and documentation of harms
    from variations in use. Those who made the ultimate decision to
    allow the launch in the colder temperatures despite advice to the
    contrary, would be morally responsible.

2. Ask the students if they would have been comfortable placing a call
    to NASA when the decision, made against their advice, was made.
    Ask them if such action outside their supervisory lines is
    justified because of the issues of human life.

3. Locke's comment is a classic illustration of an attempt to quantify
    one of the basic rights that cannot and should not be quantified.
    A human life is viewed as priceless and any reference to relative
    cost is not only offensive to most people but costly to the company
    in terms of public relations.

4. Absolutely.   The information about the risk beyond original
    specifications and risk levels should have been covered and
    considered. Perhaps this information should have been controlling.

5. Such support for a position is gained through the persuasion of
    others about the moral/ethical correctness of your position. Mr.
    Boisjoly could have convinced others of the risk, the loss of life,
    the risk to the company, the program and how worried he was. He
    could convince fellow engineers of his concerns and then as a group
    they could convince management and NASA.

6. Everyone had bought into the risk according to the specifications.
    The astronauts did not realize they were being launched under
    conditions not included in the specs. They had not assumed the
    degree of risk the cold temperatures brought. The decision should
    have been made by NASA with full information and not with any type
    of assurance that there might be performance when, in fact, no one
    knew whether they would work.

    Note: Discuss with the students the lives of McDonald and
              Boisjoly after the booster rocket failure. Are all those
              who point out wrongs punished? Does it seem like ethical
              choices lead to self-destruction? Are their setbacks
              temporary?

7. Yes. Engineers had safety concerns. Managers had concerns about
    contracts, earnings, public relations, etc.

Dow Corning and the Silicone Implants: Questions of Safety and Disclosure

<u>Use Transparency 19 to show the history and ownership of the silicone implant manufacturers</u>.

<u>Use Transparency 20 to show the chronology of events for Dow Corning</u>.

<u>Answers and Key Discussion Items</u>

1.   Manuel Velasquez holds the test for moral responsibility to be: who had the ultimate decision-making authority for the product? The engineers, designers, and production employees who follow orders would not be morally responsible under the Velasquez test. However, Velasquez ignores the feelings of those who worked on the product. Whether they would or would not be held responsible on an accountability test will not change the fundamental personal feelings they will have about having worked on a product that injures many, often leaving permanent damage. The information on the 1975 study should have been disclosed -- people can then make a decision based on full disclosure.

2.   For employees like Talcott, and LiCari in the Beech-Nut case, the failure of the company to take action and their anticipation of harm to others means that their resignations are necessary to alleviate the moral responsibility they will feel.

3.   Ask the students to put themselves in Talcott's shoes and whether they would have done more or less. Remind them about the issues of their livelihood, peer pressure and company pressure so that they appreciate how difficult circumstances were.

4.   Freedom to choose is a moral right. But choosing should be based on full information and accurate disclosure. In this case, there are differing views about the implants. Some women would very much like to have the choice because of their need for reconstructive surgery. They weigh the dangers with the self-esteem problems and want the option of the implants. Such an option is viable but there must be full information so that the choice is made with an accurate weighing of the risks.

5.   The FDA not only has a moral responsibility, it is charged by Congress with the enforcement of the law. Those products that cause harm (as documented for the FDA), must be recalled. The FDA waited for too long a time in handling the problem and should have required warnings or a halt of future sales.

6.   Dr. Rudy was attempting to get full information to physicians. But the problem was that the information needed to go directly to users

2.22   Dow Corning and the Silicone Implants: Questions of Safety and Disclosure (cont'd)

so that full disclosure and freedom of choice were assured.

Note: Ask the students if choice is most important in this case. Also ask them why companies are hesitant to respond to issues raised by employees with respect to safety. Explain to them issues of profitability and the pressures to increase sales.

Dow Corning declared bankruptcy in June 1995. The settlements remain in jeopardy as the Chapter 11 proceeding continues.

2.23   The English Teacher and the Football Players

Answers and Key Discussion Issues

1.   The grade should not be changed. Ms. Robbins should not succumb to pressure. Ms. Robbins should seek help outside her department and perhaps outside the university such as through the NCAA or the athletic conference offices.

2.   The department chair should support Ms. Robbins and uphold the longstanding academic policy of faculty autonomy. Ms. Robbins has been fair and given the students extra opportunities.

3.   Yes, the integrity of the grading system is impaired. All those students who earned their grades have been treated unfairly. Further, the football players will carry the same credentials as those students who have done the work and passed and the credibility of the institution is diminished when it is discovered that they, in fact, cannot do the work.

4.   Ms. Robbins was more than fair to the students. If anything, she was unfair to the other students in giving the athletes additional opportunities.

Legal Issues

The NCAA would be interested in investigating the grade incident for possible rules violations and penalties. Ms. Robbins may have been terminated in violation of public policy and would enjoy recovery under one of the exceptions to the employment at will doctrine. Indeed, a case from the University of Georgia brought an instructor there a verdict in excess of $1,000,000.

2.24   Orders of Shoot to Kill

Answers and Key Discussion Items

1.   Using the Velasquez test, those who gave the orders to shoot to
      kill would be morally responsible and not the guards who carried
      out the orders. However, this definition of moral responsibility
      does not mitigate the feelings of a violation of rights that the
      border guards might have.

2.   There are times when laws that are passed or procedures that are
      implemented violate basic principles of rights and justice. In
      these cases, positive law is in itself unethical. In these
      circumstances, the violation of those procedures or laws is
      justifiable. Positive law compliance is not always ethical
      behavior. Such compliance may not be enough or it may be a
      violation of natural law.

3.   The decision to shoot and miss was a compromise -- not direct civil
      disobedience but a means of avoiding a violation of the rights of
      others.

4.   The trial and conviction are done with the hope that others placed
      in similar situations in the future will follow their consciences
      as opposed to the dictates of those in power. Justice requires
      compensation. Whether a conviction satisfies that requirement is
      subject to debate.

5.   Knowing the demands of the job should have been a deterrent to
      those committed to principles of justice. It is important to have
      the students realize that any job may involve an order from an
      employer to commit a wrong act; one that violates the law or one,
      as here, that violates the rights of others. Speaking up in the
      form of refusing to take a job or discontinuing the employment may
      be required. In the immediate sense, they lose their source of
      income. Over the long term, however, they avoid the fate of these
      guards.

2.25   The Changing Time Cards

<u>Answers and Key Discussion Items</u>

1. The harm fell upon the taxpayers who eventually foot the bill but also upon other contractors who share in an indictment of dishonesty. The harm fell upon shareholders as GE works to regain its reputation.

2. Mr. Gravitt did a difficult but ethical thing in reporting the time card violations. He followed the correct steps in trying to remedy the problem and gathered his information carefully. He was in a culture that did not provide the opportunity for self-correction.

3. Mr. Gravitt did violate the privacy of another and company procedures in the methods he used for the collection of his data. Ask the students if the ends Gravitt was able to accomplish justified the means he used. Is it permissible to violate one rule in an attempt to remedy other violations?

4. Tepe's moral responsibility test follows that of Velasquez; those making the orders are responsible, not the soldiers who carry them out. However, this test fails to take into account the consciences of the soldiers and their recognition that something wrong is being done. Mr. Tepe's attitude is a means of ignoring wrongdoing.

5. That type of executive philosophy teaches employees that no questions can be asked and that you do what you're told regardless of what you think. Breaking the law becomes easy in such an amoral atmosphere.

6. Incentive programs which base compensation on revenue only are programs that invite employees to cheat, be dishonest and "do whatever it takes" to meet goals.

7. GE would need:

    (a) a more open atmosphere
    (b) different compensation system
    (c) different management philosophy and attitude
    (d) hot line
    (e) statement of values
    (f) ombudsperson office

<u>Legal Issues</u>

Under the new Federal Corporate Sentencing Guidelines, corporations can mitigate criminal penalties by demonstrating the presence of a code of ethics and training for employees in the area of ethical decisions. The companies can also mitigate criminal penalties by showing they had a hotline for employees to call and report wrongdoing.   Further, the companies can reduce penalties by voluntary compliance.   If they come forward with violations that are self-discovered, judges can take their self-reporting into account in sentencing.   These guidelines make it necessary for people such as Mr. Gravitt to be able to come forward and receive a response.

Also, Mr. Gravitt is the beneficiary of a federal law that permits reporting employees to recover portions of the amount they report is involved in wrongdoing.   Legal incentives now exist at the federal level for ethical compliance.

2.26   Child Labor and Burgers

Answers and Key Discussion Items

1.   The books should be left in the restaurant. There are penalties associated with concealment of records, so it is more than an ethical choice.

2.   The harm is to the teenagers who may not be able to properly determine the need for constraints in work hours. Employers took advantage of young laborers and the laws were passed for their protection. Other employers who honor the law are harmed in a competitive sense because they are unable to use teenage labor as much.

3.   Ken faces questions of loyalty to his employer, possible loss of his source of income and the problems of violations. Ken should let the Labor Department do its investigation and be willing to accept whatever penalties may result. At this point he is uncertain about violations, so he should let them have full access to determine whether this in fact is the case. Ken faces personal penalties for concealment if he hides the books at home.

4.   Ken's values/standards:

      a.   Loyalty to employer
      b.   Earning a living
      c.   Dishonesty/honesty
      d.   Obeying the law

2.27   The Extension of Benefits to Partners of Homosexual Employees

<u>Answers and Key Discussion Items</u>

1 and 2.   Lotus and other companies plunge themselves into a public and company debate when policies regarding "significant others" are adopted that specifically reference the "significant others." As the comments by employees demonstrate, people have profoundly different feelings about the morality of homosexuality. Other employees are concerned about the difficulties of having to disclose their personal relationships.

3.   Employees feel the way they feel. There is great emotion on both sides of the issue in Lotus, in other companies, among the public.

4.   To adequately cope with the complex issues of "family" in today's society, Lotus and other companies should regroup to provide dependent coverage. Dependent coverage could include, for example, anyone who resides in your household who is not covered under another insurer's or work policy (exceptions could be made for full-time student-children who reside, temporarily, elsewhere). Not only does this definition resolve the problem, it would permit employees who have the responsibility of parental care to provide coverage for those parents. This type of definition is neutral and not as likely to stir the emotions expressed by employees in this case study. The coverage is provided in a generic as opposed to specific declaration.

2.28   Seattle's Comparable Worth

Use Transparencies 21 and 22 to illustrate comparable worth concepts.

Answers and Key Discussion Items

1. Comparable worth represents a confrontation between the economics of wages and the fairness of wages. Wages adjust to what the market will or can bear. Comparable worth is a wage system based on factors other than what the market is willing to pay. Rightly or wrongly, the market adopts salaries according to principles of supply and demand. Raising wages or reducing wages at rates different than the market will result in the outflow of workers described in the case.

2. The argument against comparable worth is one made based on what happened in Seattle: defections from comparable worth systems to market systems. Quality workers are lost because market forces continue.

3. Economists argue that women should move into different fields as opposed to undertaking major realignments in salaries that may cost the employer making the adjustments its work force. On the other hand, the American Association of University Women has taken the position that women should be able to choose their careers and professions based on their abilities and likes and not have to perform in a lower-paying job simply because it is female-dominated.

4. A generic discrimination suit based on field salary disparity is not a possibility under existing law. Current anti-discrimination laws afford protection only in cases of different pay for the __same__ work, not comparable work.

5. Have the students discuss their feelings about working in a city like Seattle where wages are suddenly adjusted as they were here. Would they favor it? Would they leave their positions? Ask them to evaluate whether comparable worth systems are too complex.

6. The issue remains a sensitive one and has created problems and a talent drain. It should be revisited.

Legal Issues

As yet, the absence of comparable worth systems has not been a basis for a Title VII discrimination suit. The Equal Pay Act only requires equal pay for equal work. Women and men doing the same jobs must be paid the same wages. The act does not require a comparison of similar jobs and an adjustment.

2.29   Unequal Earnings

Answers and Key Discussion Items

1.   The students need to discuss market issues (supply and demand) and the impact on wages. The disparity appears to be market-driven. Either the market could be adjusted or women could change the professions they have traditionally chosen. The American Association of University Women has taken the position that the market values of jobs that are traditionally female are at a lower rate and this bias will not self-correct. Further, their position as stated in the case, is that women should not be forced into careers and professions they do not enjoy. The wages should be adjusted to make careers that have been traditionally female more attractive.

2.   The gap is closing as progress is made against discrimination and as women progress. Comparable worth is often offered as an alternative to close the gap. The difficulty is that employees then leave and go to employers that have not adopted a comparable worth system.

3.   Other explanations include women electing different career paths, electing part-time work, electing flex-time. Some elections mean less pay, but it is a voluntary choice. Also, leave taken for children sets back the earning scale for women for at least a short time.

4.   Legally there are only the constraints of the Equal Pay Act. Equal pay for equal work is all that is required. Similar jobs need not have equal pay (similar in skill levels or responsibility as in comparable worth systems).

Legal Issues

Only the Equal Pay Act is indirectly involved. Equal pay for equal work is its standard and there have not been successful cases under the Act using a comparable worth standard.

3.1   BCCI and the Role of Internal Auditors

<u>Use Transparency 23 to show the complexity of BCCI and its various subsidiaries around the world</u>.

<u>Answers and Key Discussion Items</u>

1.   Yes, if management is engaged in fraud, it is possible. It is not, however, impossible to spot the issues and problems with piercing questions based on experience.

2.   At a national meeting of internal auditors a speaker asked the question, "How does a BCCI happen with competent, international auditors auditing its books?" Her speech went on to explain that a BCCI happens because many people recognize what is happening but don't know how or fail to bring it to the attention of those who can take appropriate action. As a board member she reflected on how very possible it would be for members of the boards of BCCI subsidiaries not to realize the extent and nature of BCCI's activities if management had hidden information from the auditors or if the auditors were missing signals and failing to alert the board.

      In some instances auditors are misled by management and it is the position of AICPA and FASB that it is not the responsibility of auditors to detect management fraud unless the auditor specifically agrees to do so. Thus it would be possible for an auditor to issue a clean opinion in a BCCI case because the wrongdoing would be hidden from the auditors. There has been some pressure on auditors from the investment public, investment regulators and as a result of large settlements and verdicts against auditors in cases like BCCI to undertake detection of fraud. The clean opinion reflects the auditor's work and review of appropriate samples. No fraud or other misdeeds might be detected.

3.   Various red flags are touted by plaintiffs' lawyers in cases against auditors as means of detecting fraud. One such flag would be a young senior management and a CEO and/or chairman who is a full generation older (as in the Charles Keating/Lincoln Savings and Loan case). Other red flags would include complex paper trails that are difficult to follow. Another red flag would be the denial of access to books and records of subsidiaries. Cash flow issues, rapid sequences of capital offerings and one-time gain recognitions to boost earnings would signal possible difficulties.

4.   A member of the audit committee has very little choice because of SEC regulations. The information would have to be disclosed and action taken to eliminate the activities. In the event there is a refusal for action to be taken, the audit committee directors would be forced to resign.

5.   Fraud can be detected generally by signals as noted above and by non-quantitative factors such as experience in human nature and personalities, an ability to detect evasiveness and the personal strength to note flattery as a means of avoiding detection.

6.   As subsequent indictments of both Clifford and Altman suggest, it seems unlikely that they could have held the positions they held and defended BCCI as much as they did in so many intricate financial dealings and not know of the nature of BCCI. They were serving as officers and directors of a subsidiary and defending the parent company in litigation. Further, they were the beneficiaries of loans that enabled them to make substantial profits in stock deals.   Clifford and Altman had no incentives to report any problems in the BCCI operations or subsidiaries, although technically such reporting would have been their responsibility as board members.

7.   A great deal of focus and discussion has been held regarding the need to avoid another BCCI. Its incorporation in Luxembourg and its large number of multinational subsidiaries made it difficult for any one nation's regulators to detect exactly how the finances of BCCI were being handled and used. Jurisdiction appeared to be deferred to so many countries that really no country was in charge, including the United States, and hence the problems were permitted to continue and BCCI was relatively unsupervised.

8.   The tips were not a high priority. It was difficult to believe a bank this large could have the problems alleged in the tips. It was a function of not believing the tipsters enough to act. Also, the whistle-blowers could have supplied additional information.

3.2   Check Kiting or Aggressive Cash Management and E.F. Hutton

<u>Use Transparency 24 to show the complexity of Hutton's cash flow in the check kiting</u>.

<u>Answers and Key Discussion Items</u>

1.   Hutton was able to take advantage of banks that did not have computer on-line banking systems. Hutton was thus able to earn interest from others on funds that did not truly exist. If anything had happened to Hutton's financial soundness, these banks would have collapsed from not being able to cover the amounts the banks assumed Hutton had for their balance purposes. The scheme was not something Hutton could have disclosed to the banks or the public. It was not balanced because it was to E.F. Hutton's benefit with all the risks assumed by the unwitting banks.

2.   The scheme may not have been one to cheat others out of their interest, but rather a scheme designed to earn Hutton more interest at the expense of others. Also it is not clear that it was simply the branch managers who were making these decisions. There appeared to be a culture at E.F. Hutton that permitted them to take advantage as much as they could. They were encouraged to pass along the techniques.

3.   The memo was written after the discovery of the Hutton processes in New York, although Hutton employees in general might not have been aware of the New York discovery. The action that needed to be taken was to stop the activity. However, Bralove was confronting a system that was apparently widespread and a part of Hutton culture. If Bralove had taken action, the outcry and eventual penalties may have been less.

4.   The difficulty in changing the Hutton system came because of the attitude of branch employees that "that's the way it's always been done." Recall for the students that this statement is almost always a certain way to tell that you are involved in an ethical dilemma. Historical precedent does not justify an unethical act. However, supervisors who change longstanding precedent without the support of upper management often encounter resistance and back-biting that can be damaging to them and their careers.

5.   It is possible that the pressure to increase earnings can lead employees to make poor choices, as was done here. It appears, however, that the activity was started long before the earnings pressure existed. The culture of the company seemed to suggest that it was acceptable to take advantage of the less sophisticated.

3.2 Check Kiting or Aggressive Cash Management and E.F. Hutton (cont'd)

Legal Issues

Experts still disagree as to whether Hutton violated the law or just engaged in poor ethical judgments. In a way, "everyone does it" is an accurate reflection of Hutton's conduct. We all use the concept of float; paying bills on time knowing the money is not in the account but realizing the money will be there by the time the check clears your bank. Confront the students with this ethical dilemma. What if the funds don't come? Who is harmed?

3.3   Medical Billing Errors and Practices

<u>Use Transparency 25 to show a summary of all the creative medical billing tactics</u>.

<u>Answers and Key Discussion Items</u>

1. Given the nature of medical costs and the proposed reforms for medical care and insurance, Ms. Young would no doubt attract positive attention from consumers of medical care and insurers for her efforts. However, some physicians, labs and even some patients who benefit from code creeps, unbundling, exploding, etc. might be quite hostile toward her and her efforts. Ms. Young's motive is a noble one: be certain that there is accurate billing in all medical procedures.

2. Even if Ms. Young commissions a study and makes billing procedure corrections, she will not be able to change the behavior of physicians who submit insurance bills. For changes here, she may have to conduct seminars or demonstrate why accurate and moderate billings are the best practice for the medical community in the long run.

3. Everyone is harmed by the upcoding and other creative processes. Costs to insurers and hospitals are always passed along to the ultimate customer. We all pay for medical care and insurance when costs continue to rise because of these creative billing methods. Some patients are helped in terms of extra compensation but if their insurance was not written to cover a procedure, is it fair to obtain coverage through deceit?

4. Discuss with the students why there is a tolerance of error and expanded bills when an insurance company or another deep pocket is involved. Why is it less ethical to lie in a sales transaction than it is to lie in an insurance submission? Is it because the system is unfair? Is it because everyone does it? Is it because that's the way it has always been done?

5. Patients may not be complaining because they are unaware, or because they are temporary beneficiaries of this billing system. However, over the long term, this type of conduct will harm all consumers and providers in the medical care system. A new system of limitations may have to be adopted because of the uncontrollable costs submitted under this lenient system of reimbursement. Cost shifting is debated for its ethics and problems in economics. We cover the costs but what happens to supply and demand as a result?

3.4   MiniScribe and the Auditors

<u>Use Transparency 26 to show the types of employee cooperation in the fraud at MiniScribe</u>.

Answers and Key Discussion Items

1. The MiniScribe case is an illustration of the types of extreme managers will go to when pressured for results as they were in the case with the threat of being fired or, at a minimum, experiencing personal humiliation in meetings. The signal from top management was to get results with no limitations on how to get those results.

2. Under the Velasquez test, Coopers & Lybrand was not morally responsible because its auditors had no control over the fraud committed by the management. Coopers & Lybrand was not a participant in the acts noted on Transparency 26. They were duped themselves and would not be morally responsible. Moral responsibility would require some knowledge on their part. The auditors may have been negligent in failing to spot red flags regarding possible fraud, but oversight and mistakes do not equate with moral culpability. Moral culpability is different from financial culpability, and they were indeed held financially responsible for the losses.

3. It is troublesome that none of the employees came forward to question wrapping bricks as disk drives. However, the pressure that management felt from upper management may have been felt by the workers as well, and hence they were willing to do whatever was necessary to secure their employment. Again, the Velasquez standard would not hold them morally responsible because they were only following orders.

4. Assuming the internal auditors had access to all books and records and knew of the tactics in Transparency 26, they would be morally responsible because they had the authority to stop the activities.

5. Auditors, under AICPA and FASB, are not responsible for detecting fraud by management unless they agree to assume that responsibility. Management, as in this case, can withhold whatever information it chooses and change numbers in work papers and engage in various forms of deception to ensure that the auditors do not even have red flags to lead them to question management. It seems unfair to hold them liable when they were tricked. The message may be that auditors should be above being tricked.

3.5 The Manager's Turn at the Cash Register

Answers and Key Discussion Items

1. Paula is stuck in the awkward position of having her word against the manager's. She needs a compromise here. She should go to the regional manager with her suspicions and suggest that some observations be made to detect the sweethearting. She should emphasize that she has only overheard a conversation and has no proof. The best thing for Paula and the regional manager to do is to obtain some proof. There need not be a confrontation of Hunt at this time. Paula needs to make the point that the shortages may die down for awhile until Hunt becomes more secure and is able to resume his sweethearting activities. Emphasize that Paula is likely to be blamed unless some action is taken.

2. Technically, no. Hunt's conduct is not Paula's responsibility, but she is likely to be caught up in the web and possibly suffer.

3. Hunt is stealing. His actions fit either the crime of embezzlement or larceny. Paula is assisting by not reporting him.

4. Paula needs to understand the long-term consequences of succumbing to Hunt's pressure now. She will be under that pressure from that time forward and the question will exist as to why she succumbed to his pressure if she was indeed innocent. Paula is not a legal accomplice, but she could help.

5. Paula should not rely on Hunt or his word. This is a man who is stealing from his employer. Whatever action Paula takes cannot be dependent on Hunt's behavior or assurances.

Legal Issues

Paula needs to report the crime to either the regional manager or the authorities. She may be used to help document her accusations. She becomes an accessory after the fact if she agrees to Hunt's proposal.

3.6 Phar-Mor Earnings

<u>Answers and Key Discussion Items</u>

1. Conflicts of interest
    Taking things that don't belong to you
    Saying things that aren't true
    Giving or allowing false impressions
    Engaging in personal decadence
    Interpersonal and organizational abuse

2. Rapid growth
    Executives without accountability
    Executives with great spending discretion
    Auditors lacking sufficient access
    Earnings/growth pressure

3. Yes, this was an alter ego situation where the funds and property of the company were not seen as separate from individual control and funds. The officers felt the money could be spent, wherever and however.

4. Board should have been notified. Outside auditors should have been notified. Officers should have been threatened with outside notification.

5. Outside auditors or board members (audit committee). The existence of two sets of books means that fraud/lack of ethics is pervasive among executives. Internal reporting will not help.

6. Creditors
    Shareholders
    Employees of closed stores and their families
    Other stores (credibility problems when they attempt expansion)
    Communities where closed stores are located
    Suppliers
    Accounting firm
    Lawyers
    Insurers

3.7 The Ethics of Derivatives

<u>Use Transparency 27 to show extent of derivative losses</u>.

<u>Answers and Key Discussion Items</u>

1. a. Those affected by your decision:

        Shareholders
        Creditors
        Competition
        You
        Your career
        Your family
        Pension holders
        Pension fund managers
        Employees (retired and otherwise)

    b. Kant: How would you want to be treated? If it were your
        pension fund, would you want this risk and exposure? Probably
        not.

        Laura Nash: Could you disclose this to those affected? No, it
        would be uncomfortable for you to disclose the level of risk
        you were engaging in.

        Blanchard/Peale: Is it legal? At the time, yes. Is it
        balanced? No, it risks the pension fund to maximize earnings.
        One might not feel comfortable about the choice.

        Front page of the newspaper: Treasurer bets pension fund;
        Gibson loses in gamble of pension fund.

2. Many have theorized that for Citron (whose compensation was not
    determined by returns), it was an ego problem: earning as much as
    possible while minimizing in one's mind the astronomical risk and
    exposure if the investments did not work. For Procter & Gamble and
    Gibson, derivatives seemed an easy means for high returns.

3. Leeson's motivation was career progression, and his financial
    rewards were determined by his portfolio's return. The higher the
    return, the more he earned, and the greater his recognitions and
    promotions.

4. Often managers look the other way when returns are high and things
    are going well. They should, perhaps, ask questions, but fail to.

    In fact, managers should follow a philosophy: If it seems too good
    to be true, it probably is and that would be the time to ask
    questions.

3.8 Leslie Fay: The Consequences of a Poor Ethical Culture

Answers and Key Discussion Items

1. The pressure to make quarterly earnings was so intense that the officers were willing to engage in deception, fabrication, shifting of sales, etc. to meet the earnings figures.

2. Employees may very well have been aware of the fraud, but with an ethical culture in which the officers were involved, it wouldn't have done any good to speak up. In a culture such as this one, employees would be afraid to bring such matters to anyone's attention.

3. Changing the signals to officers would have helped. The intense focus on earnings and pressure to meet goals set the stage for the deception.

4. The message would be:
    Earnings the Right Way
    Earnings Through Sales and Satisfaction
    Integrity Without Compromise

5. There are conflicts of interest. Legal counsel for a business (which owes its business and account to the company) is not a good source for audit committee members. The ties suggest "good ol' pal network" and "you scratch my back...".

    Note: At the time of the discovery of the earnings misrepresentation, Leslie Fay's stock was at $13 per share. In June, 1995, the price had dropped to 13/22. Leslie Fay continues to attempt to struggle out of bankruptcy.

3.9   Union Carbide and Bhopal

<u>Answers and Key Discussion Items</u>

1. Yes, the plant should have been operated using all those U.S.
    safety standards that guarantee safe operation of the plant. The
    company need not comply with the details of the paperwork, but all
    those safety requirements that exist in the United States should be
    followed for their plants worldwide. There are many reasons for
    such a posture. First, there are consistent policies throughout
    the world. Second, employees are not sent conflicting signals
    about what is or is not right or permitted under company policies.

2. It is almost inconceivable to think of the costs to Union Carbide
    had the accident occurred in the United States. Further, Union
    Carbide's reputation with the public, its shareholders and its
    regulators was severely damaged. Union Carbide is still recovering
    today from the Bhopal experience and its former CEO is still wanted
    in India for trial.

3. Union Carbide's costs were not just financial: costs were public
    relations, public trust, loss of customers.

4. Those who made the decision to operate the plant at a lesser level
    of safety and did not follow through on training, modifications and
    repairs at the plant are morally responsible for the accident. The
    workers who were at the plant at the time of the accident are not
    morally responsible because they had no decision-making authority.

5. While the seizure of the assets may seem to violate U.S. due
    process standards, it was apparently an act of desperation by the
    Indian government in its attempts to deal with Union Carbide.
    Point out to the students that one of the interesting costs of
    having an accident in a foreign nation is the ability of the
    governments to take far harsher and quicker action than could be
    done in the United States. The punishments are rapid and not
    generally preceded by due process. This danger is often incentive
    for applying safety standards in international operations.

6. A change in ethical culture would help. Safety first with world-
    wide standards for operation. No plant operates without inspection
    and training. Safety needs to be redefined as a focus, not as
    something to be tolerated.

3.10   Product Dumping

Answers and Key Discussion Items

1. Is it legal to dump products? Yes, so long as the other country
    has not banned them. Is it balanced to dump products? No, you are
    selling products without a full disclosure of their hazards and
    their fate in your own country. How will this action be depicted
    in a newspaper? As it sounds: dumping bad products on those with
    little knowledge in countries with little consumer protection and
    no liability system for recovery for harms.

2. The inventory write-off or write-down needs to be analyzed over
    both the short term (20% income reduction), and the long term
    (damage to reputation; possible accidents in those countries and
    liability; public relations damages). The write-down can be
    explained as a one-time event. Wall Street and investors are
    sufficiently sophisticated to understand this.

3. In some cases, the evidence on safety is disputed. Some officials
    believe the product is safe and others do not. Perhaps selling the
    product internationally is possible with new disclosures attached
    about the debate regarding its safety. It is not the selling of
    the product itself that is unethical. It is the selling of the
    product without disclosure of its previous history here.

4. Full disclosure is a compromise on products with safety issues. If
    the problem of defect is known, and one still buys the product,
    there should not be an ethical problem. When the information is
    withheld, it is unfair and unethical. Further, the purpose of
    information is a free market.

3.11 The Taboo of Women in Management

Answers and Key Discussion Items

1. Burns & McCallister's policy may be one to help women succeed. If their proposals will not be reviewed if they present them, they are destined to fail in international work. B & M needs a compromise position. Women should be offered positions in the countries in which accounts can be lucrative, but should have the cultural drawbacks explained to them. B & M doesn't have two standards of operations. The reality is that they cannot change a society's culture by placing women in positions of negotiation and responsibility for accounts in these countries.

2. The issue of discrimination in foreign countries is resolved: U.S. firms can't discriminate against employees there.

3. The idea is to allow women to progress both nationally and internationally. Burns & McCallister's record is not a stand-still one. Women should be permitted to progress in Burns & McCallister's growth areas as well.

4. B & M can work to gradually change the culture. These changes may come about by having women present in their offices in these countries, having them work on proposals and having them have some contact with the client so that the barriers begin to erode. Change does not come about if B & M cannot successfully bid and stay in the country. Opinion is more so -- as firm progresses, women should enjoy an equal opportunity to join in on that progress and success (and earnings).

5. A statement, "if we don't do it, somebody else will," comes to mind. If we don't do business in his country without women, somebody else will do the business and we will have lost revenues. Again, the position that B & M takes may not require complete withdrawal, but simply a gradual indoctrination in these countries. As the borders come down in international trade, it will be important for all countries to accept the business culture and attitudes of others; including the fact that women are key players in business proposals and negotiations.

6. Many firms sacrifice earnings in international markets until ethical concerns are resolved in the areas of human rights, child labor, women's rights, etc.

3.12 Toshiba and the Soviets

Answers and Key Discussion Items

1. Yes. The milling equipment could be sold legally as milling equipment.

2. Kumagai is like many employees who witness wrongdoing. It's none of their business. Their job security and income is important to them. They do not want to be labeled a whistle-blower.

3. All employees who make the decision to come forward with accusations should be certain of their allegations. That certainty comes preferably from documentation. It increases credibility and makes the process easier for the employee who is making the disclosures. In a way, it is the ethics of whistle blowing: make sure you know whereof you speak.

4. Given the end of the cold war, the case seems to be less intense today. However, at the time the equipment was sold, there was the distinct possibility that the equipment could have been used to damage intelligence efforts or offer superiority in war.

5. Moral responsibility if war and loss of lives resulted would rest with those who made the decision to deal with the Soviets. Kumagai was just following orders but, as has been noted in other cases, it still is difficult for those employees to live with their actions when they know they are wrong.

6. In a way, the ethics of Shoichi Saba manifested themselves too late. He did accept full responsibility for the sales and resigned rather than harm his company. His resignation and acceptance of responsibility demonstrate a mature individual ready to bear the burden of Toshiba's unethical choice. However, he should have been willing to threaten to make that same resignation to protest sale of the equipment in advance of the sale.

Legal Issues

The sale of the equipment was not technically a violation, but knowing of its use would make it a violation. It was a fine line that Toshiba crossed.

3.13 Cheap Labor: Children and the Fifty-Hour Work Week

Answers and Key Discussion Items

1. Have the students envision a 12-year-old's body, activity and perspective. Cites to literature may help.

2. Yes, U.S. standards could be imposed. Children can work limited hours, only in certain jobs and under certain conditions.

3. Work could be combined with a mandatory school schedule to help children advance and progress.

4. Levi Strauss will not enter China because it does not want to be in a position of being forced to use child labor.

5. The area of third party ethics (the ethics of one's supplier) is one that is enjoying increasing attention from institutional investors. Businesses must screen the activities of their contractors and suppliers as well.

3.14   The Adoption Agency and Señor Jose's Fees

Answers and Key Discussion Items

1.   The payment to Señor Jose would be considered a bribe in all 50
      states and under federal laws. This type of payment is illegal in
      the United States. This case deals with the fine line, as defined
      in the Foreign Corrupt Practices Act, between bribery to achieve a
      desired result and "grease payments" or those fees paid to just see
      a matter through the system, regardless of the results.

2.   A grease payment may be perfectly legal in another country. The
      ethics of the payments are complicated by the fact that without
      them, business cannot be done. For example, in this case, there
      can be no adoption, certainly a noble pursuit, unless there is the
      payment. A question to ask the students is whether the end in this
      case, the successful adoption of the little girl, justifies the
      means used, the grease payment.

3.   There are many parents who have gone through with adoptions
      requiring such payments. Children who would otherwise have lives
      in poor conditions are given the best opportunities in life. Many
      employees at agencies that arrange international adoptions feel
      that their work results justify the means needed to accomplish
      them. Ask the students if they agree with that posture.

4.   Have the students personalize the example: Would you break the law
      to help a child?

5.   Have the students personalize it: Would a government raid make you
      uncomfortable?

3.15 Facilitation or Bribery: Cultural and Ethical Disparities

Answers and Key Discussion Items

1. It is arguable that the conduct in all the offices violates the law. Money and/or benefits (directly or indirectly) are being given in exchange for favorable results.

2. No, a business should not adopt a culture-by-culture code of ethics. It is confusing to employees. Further, the company's potential for capitalism, investment and growth is undermined by systems of bribery.

3. None are ethical. Moreover, the conduct is probably illegal.

4. Simple standard: our U.S. code of ethics.

5. Yes, the variety in standards generally results in the firm migrating to the lowest standards.

3.16   Johns-Manville and the Asbestos Exposure

<u>Use Transparency 28 to provide a chronology of events in this long case.</u>

Answers and Key Discussion Items

1. The decision of attorney Greenstone benefitted him and his clients, but affected the ability of others to obtain the information that he had with respect to Manville's liability. Greenstone acted in the best interests of his immediate clients.

2. Dr. Lanza probably should have reported the correspondence and at least implicit requests regarding the reports of his results, to a scientific body or the federal government or used the information to obtain further funding for clarification, if any, of his results.

3. Sumner Simpson was in a decision-making position in which he could have made a difference in the sequence of events with respect to asbestos exposure. Full knowledge of the consequences of his actions make him fully accountable for the deaths and illnesses arising after the time when he could have directed a change of course.

4. Dr. Gardner had two choices: accept the funding with the conditions and obtain the opportunity to study asbestos exposure or turn down the funding and lose the opportunity to study the disease. The first choice presents a conflict of interest for it compromises Dr. Gardner's autonomy and taints the results of his work regardless of what those results may have been.

5. Dr. Smith should have considered his Hippocratic Oath and his responsibilities to his patients as opposed to the responsibility to Manville.

6. Manville, in the interest of profits in the immediate sense, missed several opportunities. First, instead of living in denial and an atmosphere of secrecy, they could have had workers take appropriate precautions such as masks. In addition, they could have been working on a substitute that would have been available once the studies confirmed the dangers of asbestos and they would have had a market niche. The decisions of Manville were very much short-term decisions that ignored the long-term implications and liabilities of continuing with asbestos.

7. Manville did not benefit by waiting so long. What company manager or officer would make the decision to assign 25% of its profits forever? What manager would make the decision to assign most of its assets and stock to a trust to compensate victims?

The decision to not liquidate Manville was made with the idea that an ongoing concern could better foot the bills for asbestosis that are expected to continue as more workers and others exposed to it develop the disease.

8.   There appeared to be no substitute for asbestos.   However, a niche was possible rather than the ethical breach.   Find a product without the asbestos hazard and make it.

Notes: Have the students evaluate the actions of Senator Gary Hart in proposing the federal legislation to benefit Manville.

Have the students evaluate the decision of the auditor to not issue a clean financial opinion which forced Manville into Chapter 11 bankruptcy.

3.17   Electromagnetic Fields (EMF):   Exposure for Workers and Customers

Use Transparency 29 to show chronology of events in this "field".

Answers and Key Discussion Items

1.   The evidence is not conclusive at this point but there is sufficient question, as at a similar stage in the asbestos development, for additional precautions, education and further research.

2.   The companies that should be concerned about the liability from EMF would be:
electric utilities (for employees and customers)
governmental entities that decide on placement of power lines
manufacturers of electric equipment (warnings on use and fields)
manufacturers of power lines and power line poles
property owners with self-electrical generation
military operations
radio stations

3.   Regulation in the future will focus on power-line sites, warnings on products, limits on EMF fields on products, limits on employee exposure to EMF, hour limitations in EMF fields.

4.   Landlords and other property owners will have issues of value and liability with respect to the location of lines on or near their properties. The issue of EMF will affect the value of land near EMF fields.

5.   Many utilities are following a policy of "prudent avoidance." That is, they are trying to control or limit exposure. If a line can be placed away from human contacts, it is done so. The location for facilities for employees is made away from substantial EMF fields. Many utilities are conducting long-term epidemiological studies of workers and those located near strong fields to determine health effects, if any.

6.   Warnings would be imperative at this point on blankets and water beds. The evidence in this regard, particularly with respect to these products, is too strong to not take the precaution of furnishing a warning. Remind the students that there might be a hesitation in these cases as in asbestos because of the fear of a loss of earnings. Ask the students to predict the outcome of the companies over the long term if the warnings are not given. The result would be a steadily increasing stream of litigation and high, possibly destructive costs, for these companies.

7.   Monitoring employees; rotating work duties; reconfiguring wires to minimize EMF.

8.   Yes, reconfiguration is a low-cost preventive measure. It should be done.

     Note: Raise with the students the ethics of plaintiff suits and whether product liability cases are filed too often regardless of the level of harm.

3.18 Video Display Terminals and the Miscarriage and Cataract Cluster Studies

Use Transparency 30 as a summary of the series of events in the VDT/miscarriage /cataract studies and resulting regulation.

Answers and Key Discussion Items

1. In this case the response of many employers has been that of the travel agent headquarters, "We'll wait until the lawyers tell us there is a problem, " and "Everybody else does it." Have the students discuss the parallels between this case, asbestos and EMF. A pattern emerges from the cases:

> Some question is raised about the safety of a product;
> Conflicting studies appear;
> The credibility of the researchers is questioned;
> Companies affected attempt to keep the issues quiet;
> A long period goes by before any action is taken, more injuries occur and eventually the outcome is regulation and/or litigation.

The travel agency should make some small and relatively inexpensive changes such as frequent breaks, rearrangement of the display terminal configuration and so on. The travel agency might consider implementing the San Francisco requirements. The point in these three cases (asbestos, EMF and VDT) is that the companies had early opportunities to make ethical choices and waited until litigation or regulation forced them to do so.

2. Low-radiation VDTs are an example of a market niche that would be successful if people were aware of the option and could make choices.

3. Employers should be taking appropriate action with all types of ergonomic issues from VDT exposure to carpal tunnel syndrome. As the U.S. economy moves toward a complete service economy, office workers will develop a full set of workers' compensation issues. Employers should be proactive in addressing these potential problems.

4. Most employers would probably not discuss it, but probably should. Full disclosure, options, protections.

5. The San Francisco ordinance protections are a relatively inexpensive set of preventive measures.

3.19   Airline Workers and Radiation

Answers and Key Discussion Items

This case has developments similar to those in the asbestos, EMF and VDT cases. A study suggests problems and the response is largely non-existent.

1.   The vice president should explore some "prudent avoidance" options. Can flight paths be changed? Can employees be rotated off the worst exposure flights? Can employees wear monitors to determine whether the problem is as significant as the report concludes?

2.   The employer's ethical obligation in cases like this is not to avoid the issue or hope to conceal it. The decisions are often made on a cost vs. risk analysis basis. However, this form of analysis ignores the ethical principle of rights. Is the avoidance of the issue or non-disclosure of it the way the vice president would want to be treated if he were a flight attendant? Costs are being used to justify inaction in an area that carries great potential for injury to workers. The value of a human life is ignored or balanced with fuel costs.

3.   Pregnant flight attendants should enjoy the Johnson controls protections, but should be told.

4.   Again, the fear of the results and impact on earnings from disclosure seems to prevent honesty. However, the promise of honesty is ignored in terms of market potential. For example, an airline could adopt a prudent avoidance policy and reroute to minimize exposure and then advertise to capture the flying public and frequent flyers with the promise of lower exposure.

5.   Withholding the report is dishonest. The employees will gain access to it whether you release it or not. The positive feelings from affirmative disclosure will help in the resolution of the issue. The negative feelings that will result from disclosure from another source will prevent certain solutions as an element of employee distrust enters.

6.   An "either/or" test should not be used here. Why not offer passengers a low radiation route as a market niche? Not all honest actions should be viewed as costing money. Often they bring a business a niche.

3.20   Domino's Pizza Delivers

Answers and Key Discussion Items

1.   No, there are no guarantees with drivers. Incentives to deliver on time made speed and recklessness almost a part of the job.

2.   Yes, the public outrage over safety sacrifices for pizza delivery was growing.

3.   The jury verdict was a strong public message to Domino's: stop the focus on time at the expense of safety.

4.   Have the students personalize the costs: job, verdicts, etc.

5.   It is taking something that doesn't belong to you; saying things that are false; taking unfair advantage.

3.21   Chrysler and Its Cost of Closing

Answers and Key Discussion Items

1. There are differing schools of thought in ethics regarding the obligation of employers who close down plants to the workers from that plant and the communities in which they are located. One group imposes an obligation on the employer to leave the town whole. This obligation requires placement of the workers and economic redevelopment of the community all at the employer's cost with some contributions from governmental entities.

   Another school of thought sees such additional obligations as a double tax to shareholders. Not only must they bear the cost of the cutbacks and economic downturn, they must now ensure that the workers and the community do not have to share in such losses. This view advances the notion that workers are always insulated from financial losses and economic downturns and may not have the appropriate incentives to retool.

2. Obligations to restore the workers and communities add costs to downsizing and prevent flexibility in making allocation and resource decisions. An additional cost is added to becoming more efficient and the incentives may make it easier to remain inefficient.

3. The rights of shareholders are often ignored in the interest of protecting the employees and communities. On the other hand, the communities give the employers the right to use the air and water sheds and the opportunity to benefit from the support of the government resources and often tax breaks.

4. Yes, Chrysler defined its duty as first and foremost to its shareholders. Businesses do have a primary obligation to their investors, but Chrysler did take on more investors here (community).

5. Chrysler's withdrawal may have ultimately benefited the community.

6. Mr. Iacocca's focus would be on Chrysler's earnings. There are ethical risks with such a focus.

3.22   The Closure of the Stroh's Plant Upon Merger

Answers and Key Discussion Items

1.   Stroh's may have been engaging in Albert Carr's business bluffing.
      They were doing the "right" thing but perhaps for the reason that
      the backlash from the closure might affect product sales in the
      state. The result of the placement program is a positive feeling
      in the state toward Stroh's.

2.   The early announcement of a plant closure can have an impact on a
      company's stock in the marketplace. The shareholders' rights are
      affected by the protection of the employees and the community.
      Morale is also affected as employees prepare for outplacement or
      unemployment. Productivity declines during this period.

3.   There is a balancing of employer, employee, shareholder and
      community interests in these plant closure cases. See the
      discussion of the various ethical views on closure on p. 89. At
      some point there comes a time when a local economy can no longer
      absorb the outplacement from plant closure and the community needs
      to focus on economic redevelopment efforts to change the focus of
      its economy as opposed to relying on departing employers to absorb
      the cost of their departure.

4.   Yes, the outplacement program was a way to buy back a possibly
      alienated Detroit beer-drinking market.

3.23   GM Plant Closings and Efforts at Outplacement

Answers and Key Discussion Items

1.   This case is distinguished from the previous plant closing cases because in this case the company had extracted promises from the government in exchange for its promises with respect to operations in the area. These promises result in a greater obligation on the part of the employer and less flexibility in terms of its business decisions because of its financial obligations and otherwise to the local and/or state governments.

2.   Have the students focus on the right of a business to make decisions that will stop the losses it is experiencing. Have them evaluate whether this case is one in which the government and GM almost had a joint venture. Have them discuss whether the government knew there was always the risk that the product made at the plant might not sell.

3.   Ask the students whether there should always be insulation for business plans and decisions that are not successful. Does ethics require that you take away the risk of doing business and have the shareholders absorb that risk for everyone, including employees and government entities involved with the business in a joint venture?

4.   Some courts are beginning to require businesses to repay tax and other benefits if they pull out of a town, reneging on a plant operation agreement.

Legal Issues

The federal plant closing law requires advance notification of closure. There are no financial obligations associated with the law. The purpose of the law is to permit a time period for employee preparation for the lay-offs and closure.

3.24   EFS, The Union, and Its Creditor and Suitors

Answers and Key Discussion Items

1. There is a delicate balance to be maintained in situations where a company is struggling. The company needs the flexibility to negotiate and workers have the protections of the WARN act. It is easy to see that if EFS had gone ahead and given the notice of closure, its ability to negotiate may have been, affected. On the other hand, it is important to see the workers perspective about the possibility that they may not have a job soon. But notifying workers of a closure is different from notifying them of ongoing negotiations. The workers can draw whatever conclusion they want, but they would know that there are some risks associated with the company at that point.

2. Perhaps a buyer or creditor would want the plant to remain open as a condition of the sale or line of credit. The announcement might cause them to assume that the hopes for such were over or that the company is in such desperate straits that it may not be a good credit risk or purchase. Again, ask the students if EFS wasn't trying in good faith to keep the plant open but things just didn't work out.

3. All groups (employees, shareholders and creditors) are stakeholders in the company. But, without satisfied creditors and shareholders willing to invest, there is no company for employees. The WARN act places the needs of workers above the other two groups and carries risks for the company's survival when it is involved in negotiations such as those for EMF.

4. The compensation of employees beyond employee benefits raises questions about public policy. Unemployment benefits are legislative benefits determined by representative government to be in the best interests of all. Requiring companies to pay more than those benefits imposes duties we would not support legislatively. Paying more is insulating employees of a business that is at market risk from that market risk. Shareholders pay twice; once for their losses and again for the losses of the employees.

3.25   Herman Miller and Its Rain Forest Chairs

Answers and Key Discussion Items

1. The woods used for Miller's traditional Eames chair were part of
    the chair's distinction. The woods were also part of what Miller's
    carpenters were used to working with. However, Miller and Foley
    were looking at the environmental impact of the use of those woods
    and behaving in a socially responsible manner. Further, Foley may
    have been ahead of his time. It is likely that there would be
    future restrictions on imports of the woods and Miller would be
    forced to make changes at that point. Foley may also be hopeful
    that the voluntary change is something that helps the company in a
    public relations and marketing sense.

2. It was troublesome to the board of directors that Foley made his
    "environmental" decisions with costs attached at a time when the
    company's earnings were off. However, the board was looking at the
    short-term profit picture and Foley was anticipating Miller being
    around for a long time and coping with environmental concerns
    before being forced to do so by regulation. Further, Foley's
    actions did pay off as sales increased and Miller gained national
    recognition for its responsible positions.

3. Albert Carr, a business ethicist, maintains that businesses take
    socially responsible and ethical actions only when it is in their
    best interests to do so. The appearance of the decision may be
    noble, as in this case, an environmentalist company, but the bottom
    line in the decisions is the bottom line. Carr would support the
    decisions because they brought the company financial results.

4. Miller made the decision to do all that was technologically
    possible and not just comply with the law. Positive law as a
    standard for ethical behavior is not always sufficient. Miller did
    as much as it could and probably earned the respect of local and
    national regulators as well as its customers and potential
    customers.

5. The issue here is: is it wrong to publicize the fact that you are
    doing the right thing? is such publicity in the interest of the
    shareholders, employees, creditors, etc. Yes. The advantage of
    behaving as a responsible company is being able to tell about it.
    There is nothing wrong with detailing the program. The company
    made ethical choices and has the right to let it be known.

3.26   Green Marketing as a Business Bluff

<u>Answers and Key Discussion Items</u>

1.   Milton Friedman would support green marketing. It is a decision that is in the best interests of the shareholders that just happens to be ethical. To the extent that we prevent people from doing beneficial things because they don't have the right reason, we are preventing businesses from making rational choices. The most good is done for the most people regardless of motivation.

2.   No. The response of the market to a company that makes correct choices is to be anticipated. The fact that the market responds to an ethical choice should not prevent the company from making that choice.   We are assuming a certain level of honesty in the company's green marketing; that in fact their tuna is dolphin-free and their detergents are biodegradable. Companies should not be permitted to benefit from dishonest claims that capitalize on environmental consciousness.

3.   To the extent companies are not truly committed to environmental issues and make claims that they are, they are being dishonest. If they have truly made the commitment to the environment and environmentally conscious products, their marketing can focus on these issues as well as quality, service and other marketing tools.

4.   This question focuses on doing the right thing for the wrong reason. If the result is that firms are environmentally conscious and goals are accomplished without legislation or regulation, should we prevent firms from doing something simply because they are not noble?

3.27   Exxon and Alaska

<u>Use Transparency 31 to give a summary of the extent of damage done by the oil spill</u>.

<u>Answers and Key Discussion Items</u>

1.   Exxon's attitude about the oil spill was very much criticized by government officials, local residents and the media. Exxon did not recognize the magnitude of harm, was not appreciative of the urgency of the clean-up work and seemed reluctant to commit the resources necessary for a good job.   Other subsequent spills demonstrated Exxon's attitude that clean-up efforts or even prevention efforts were not a high company priority.

2.   Cutting back on staff and maintenance was a means of reducing costs. Over the short run, these decisions saved the company money.

3.   Hazelwood bears some moral responsibility for the accident because he was drinking. Just as someone who drinks, drives an automobile and injures someone in an accident is held accountable under DUI laws and civilly liable in tort, Hazelwood is accountable for his individual action in drinking and then reporting for duty. Exxon's policies may have caused the excessive drinking, but Hazelwood made the choice to drink and drive, so to speak.

4.   Exxon management also bears some moral responsibility for the spill. The cutbacks in staff caused undue pressure on the crews. An error in operating the ship or in personal judgment (drinking) was bound to occur in such demanding circumstances. Maintenance procedures and the structure of the boat itself all contributed to the accident and its extent. These decisions regarding personnel and maintenance were made by Exxon management.

5.   Exxon needs a commitment to environmentally-conscious operations. Following this accident, many oil firms began upgrading their ships with double-hull protection so that an accident would pierce only one layer of the tanker and a spill would not automatically occur. Exxon needs to base its decisions on long-term issues with respect to its operations as opposed to short-term cost-cutting measures that ignore the environmental and personnel impact. Exxon also needs to understand public expectations with respect to its product and the need to raise its environmental consciousness.

6.   No, follow-up articles have cited Exxon's conduct as a means for creating a public relations nightmare and losing regulatory and customer good will.

3.28   The Disposable Diaper Dilemma

Use Transparency 32 to show lists of the pros and cons of disposables.

Answers and Key Discussion Items

1. Arthur D. Little does have a conflict of interest in its work. The largest maker of disposable diapers is sponsoring its work. There will be a question regarding its credibility because of the source of funding. P & G should have found alternative ways of having a study conducted. Arthur Little should have been more conscientious about accepting the assignment and developed ways to ensure autonomy. No matter how effective the study is, the question of Arthur Little's independence will always cloud the result.

2. Regulation has already begun in the field and would include everything from a complete ban on the diapers to requirements that cloth be available to requirements regarding decomposition times for the diapers. Taxation of disposables is also possible. Companies that sell the disposable diapers need to recognize these possibilities and begin taking independent action that is responsive to the environmental concerns raised about the disposable diapers.

3. The increase in costs should be measured not over the short run, but the long run. The hospital may be making a decision that will be made for them if regulation continues. The decision may assist regulators is seeing that self-regulation is sufficient.

4. Alternative solutions include the development of a diaper that is disposable but environmentally sound. Such a product would be a market niche that could eventually turn into the sole market item. The hospital could consider offering a choice to mothers. There could be disposables and cloth and the mothers could choose while in the hospital. Such a program might convert mothers who would otherwise refuse to consider cloth.

5. It is important to note that businesses must still sell products. If people want disposables, you can't sell them cloth. This is an environmental issue where the commitment is just not there. Conviction disappears when messy diapers appear.

3.29   The Unclear and Unresearched Cancer Connection

Answers and Key Discussion Items

1. The Oak Ridge problem is a typical one in a community dependent upon a particular industry or plant for its economic livelihood. There is slow recognition that there is a health problem associated with operations of the plant or industry because the workers are dependent upon the plant. Other examples include the coal industry's black lung and insulators' asbestosis. The harms may be documented, but the workers are unwilling to accept those studies because of economic dependence.

2. The appropriate action to be taken is follow-up studies. The process of living in denial only postpones the eventual outcome, good or bad. Martin Marietta should sponsor studies to find out if the clusters are significant. They may be able to take preventive steps or discover that something else is causing the clusters.

3. Dr. Reid could go to worker safety agencies such as OSHA and have them determine whether there is any significance to his findings. Dr. Reid could turn to other communities with similar plants and determine the outcome, their courses of action and so on. If all else fails, Dr. Reid could suggest that one of the patients hire an attorney for possible recovery. The discovery process in litigation could make more information public.

4. Yes, in economically dependent towns, many workers are willing to accept a particular type of disease as a natural consequence of the right to work. A good issue for the students is whether this is fair. Should a company be able to take advantage of economic dependence? Should the workers be told of the risks?

5. Acceptance of possible disease does not exonerate a firm, particularly in those instances in which they could have taken precautions to minimize the exposure or disease or could have given better warnings.

3.30   J.C. Penney and Its Wealthy Buyer

Answers and Key Discussion Items

1. Taking things that don't belong to you
    Personal decadence
    Conflicts of interest
    False impressions
    Interorganizational abuse

2. Those harmed include:
    shareholders of Penney's
    Penney's customers
    other buyers
    other vendors, suppliers, manufacturer's reps
    Penney's employees
    Locklear's family(ies)

3. Again, he was doing well. Why rock the boat? Why question?

4. It is an "everybody does it" philosophy; doesn't make it ethical.

5. Yes, both have engaged in act; both are unfair to others.

6. The advantages: no line-drawing; no benefits; all quid pro quo is removed.

7. Poor products; pricing issues; bad choices in lines; product liability.

3.31   Cars for Cars: Honda Executives' Allocation System

Answers and Key Discussion Items

1. Quid pro quo; self-interested executives; lack of honesty; lack of
    loyalty; lack of commitment.

2. The money and goods were economic rents that belonged to Honda.
    They should have gone to Honda.

3. Because they were fiduciaries who breached their duties of loyalty
    to the company. Their judgment was impaired.

4. You probably would lose your job for such a confrontation, but
    given what went on, you will lose your job anyway AND testify.
    Confront the individuals. Take a position. Remind them of their
    legal responsibilities and liabilities.

4.1   Joe Camel -- The Cartoon Character Who Sells Cigarettes

Answers and Key Discussion Items

1. The cartoon character makes Camel cigarettes and all cigarettes more attractive to young people than they would otherwise be. The character is charming, wears his baseball cap as they do (backwards) and makes a lasting impression on young people. Smoking is depicted, via Joe, as something charming.

2. The ad agency does bear some responsibility for the ad campaign. It is unlikely that the agency will be able to develop a campaign as effective and attention-getting as Joe Camel. RJR is in the business to sell cigarettes and the ad agency either does it or is replaced. Suggest to the students that perhaps RJR should sponsor some types of education programs designed to discourage young people from smoking. Would this work or would it just be tokenism that would never counter the efficacy of Joe Camel?

    The ad agency needs to make its decision as to whether it is comfortable with the impact of the campaign. If the company's ethics are in question because of its ads, the ad agency is equally in question for developing it.

3. There are many pension funds (Harvard included) that have made the decision not to hold investments in cigarette companies. These decisions are based on the fact that their focus on health and well-being cannot be reconciled with an investment in a product that has been established as detrimental to health and, in many cases, deadly. Ask the students if they would personally hold tobacco company stocks. Point out to them that it may just be a matter of time before the stocks of these companies begin to decline with the increasing focus on health and studies linking tobacco use to disease. RJR recently spun off its stock; investors can own a choice of RJR food stock or RJR tobacco stock.

4. A positive association with a logo is a positive association with the product. A positive image makes use of the product more likely. It is a weak argument to say that the identifiability of the product does not translate into additional use of the product.

5. Self-censorship can reverse a regulatory trend. By limiting the use of cartoons on cigarette ads, producers could avoid what will inevitably come: government regulation of cartoon/cigarette ads.

    Note: Point out to the students that many people have raised objections to the Surgeon General's focus on such "trivialities" as ad campaigns. Ask them if they agree that the focus on these ads is trivial.

4.2   The Sexist Beer Ads

Answers and Key Discussion Items

1. Ads with attractive women in them have two things in common: (1)
    they are very common; and (2) they are very effective. An issue
    for the students to discuss is whether there are other ads that are
    equally or more effective that may not emphasize sexuality. Review
    for the students some of the most effective ads over the last 30
    years: "I can't believe I ate the whole thing." (Alka-Seltzer);
    "Where's the beef?" (Wendy's); Little Caesar's Pizza ads today;
    Coca-Cola's "I'd like to teach the world to sing,"; Oreo cookies;
    Rex the Beer Dog; etc. None of these ads involved a focus on
    sexuality but were effective in both the selling and award-winning
    senses. Successful ads do not require a focus on sexuality.

2. Regulation of sexism in ads would be difficult if not impossible
    because of definitional problems. This area of responsibility is
    truly an ethical and self-regulation one. The Canadian guidelines
    have faced definitional and application difficulties. Even if the
    regulations are put into place, enforcement become arbitrary and
    difficult.

3. Nudity in alcohol and other advertising available to the general
    public is inappropriate. Again, the advertisers and agencies need
    to focus on successful ads, not sexual ads.

4. The idea in advertising is not to have ads that are objectionable
    or generally unobjectionable. The idea for ads is to sell
    products. Those who are offended by the ads are not going to buy
    the product. The disturbing trend in advertising is to assume that
    sexuality is a prerequisite to a successful ad. History and
    experience tell us differently and companies need to focus on
    successful ads that sell products.

Legal Issues

Advertising does enjoy some First Amendment protection. Regulation is
permitted to prevent deception, misrepresentation and disparagement of
competitors. However, absent these problems, ad content is a matter of
taste, customer appeal and goals of the advertiser. This form of broad
First Amendment protection is appropriate because regulation of other
factors could prove to be arbitrary and difficult to define.

4.3   Alcohol Advertising: The College Focus

Answers and Key Discussion Items

1.   The brewery officer needs to consider that there can be tremendous backlash in the adult market for its focus on college-age drinking. Also, the officer should consider the possibility of increases in the drinking age because of irresponsible advertising. Also, the officer should accept the social responsibility of not having the company take advantage of the lack of wisdom and discretion that accompanies youthful drinking. The issues of moral responsibility arise when young people cause accidents as a result of drinking.

2.   The ads could have a more general focus, but the spring break campaigns are directed at college-age drinking. There are certain portions of the advertising that would not hold appeal for a general audience. The additional focus is not the issues. The problem is the unusual appeal for college students and their temptation to overdo it.

3.   The government certainly has precedent for censoring ads completely and also controlling content. Cigarettes are no longer advertised on television. The possibility for alcohol ad bans clearly exists because of the same harm argument made with respect to smoking. The standards for controlling youth appeal might be difficult for the government to define and a ban might be an easier regulatory control.

4.   Companies often undertake responsibility campaigns to counter the effect of their ads in a general sense. The campaigns are pointed to as being socially responsible. But many experts maintain there is comparatively little time and money spent on responsible drinking in comparison to the general ad campaigns of the companies.

5.   All breweries deny that the ads are designed to encourage underage people to drink. However, the ads are geared toward young people, feature young people and represent the alleged intrigue that accompanies drinking.

4.4   The Obligation to Screen?   The Obligation to Reject? *Soldier of Fortune* **Classifieds**

Use Transparency 33 to highlight the types of questionable ads from *SOF*.

Answers and Key Discussion Items

1.   A policy many firms have adopted with respect to classified ads is that no questionable or ambiguous ads are accepted. Background checks on all ads are too expensive. But you could screen out by type of ads.

2.   The conflicting moral standards in the case are the First Amendment rights of publication and the issues of responsibility with respect to those publication rights. There are also physical difficulties of trying to screen all the ads and those who place them.

3.   There are conflicting loyalties in making the decision with respect to *SOF* ads. There is the loyalty to your employer and the conflict with the moral standard of not having the ads bring about harm to innocent people who become victims of the connections made through the ads.

4.   *SOF* made the decision to run the ad and ads like it even knowing that there were previous criminal investigations resulting from ad connections. It was a risk *SOF* agreed to assume. Although <u>SOF</u> had no direct knowledge of any problems with the ad or those associated with it, the nature and character of the ad and the magazine make such events likely. *SOF* is not held to any legal liability in the case but does have some moral responsibility for what occurred.

5.   The court's decision is a utilitarian one. The court is trying to balance the need for advertisements with the rights of individuals to be safe from the harms that can occur when connections are made through the ads. The court acknowledges the risk but finds there is no effective way to screen for that risk. The utilitarian analysis fails to take into account the natural law concept of the value of human life and the concept of rights.

Utilitarianism often dictates who will recover and who will not. We can impose burdens of protections in some cases but not in others. For example, in Arizona, water and utility companies are exempt from liability for injuries or deaths caused by people falling into the state's man-made water canals. Those same deaths or injuries that result in private swimming pools or ponds would be actionable. However, the water and those utilities are the lifeblood of Arizona and have been given additional protection in the interest of doing the most good for the most people.

6.   The Sandra Black murder makes the power of the ads very clear. It
     shows that people who would not otherwise become involved in
     harming others become involved in such because of the connections
     the ads bring. *SOF* has had presented to them, through the Sandra
     Black murder, a much more vivid picture of the power of their ads.
     The ad policy should at least be changed to require a screening or
     refusal of ads similar to the Hearn ad.

7.   We have made the decision to impose liability when the conduct is
     foreseeable, preventable or outrageous enough.   We make
     distinctions based on a balancing of interests: liability vs.
     injury and danger.

8.   Yes, as suggested in answer 1, it avoids the heavy cost of
     screening but eliminates worries about connections and liability.

4.5   Black Death: The Vodka with a Twist

<u>Answers and Key Discussion Items</u>

1.   Mr. Lines sounds as if he will continue the campaign as planned. The students need to examine the campaign from the perspective of parents and the influence of the ads. The ads focus on someone who is idolized for his bad behavior. Excesses are part of that behavior. This music personality is being used to attract those young people who are enthralled with the rebellious image of the singer. Further, drinking the vodka, whether they are of legal age or not, is a means of showing their own rebellion which they see as a desirable trait in the successful Slash.

2.   The use of Slash in the campaign is a brilliant marketing decision, but it is not socially responsible. The campaign will be successful and will sell vodka. The issue is, over the long term, will the company feel as comfortable about the campaign as they do now? Will all of alcohol advertising be affected if campaigns such as this one continue?

3.   One of the purposes of advertising is to provide information. Information is a key component in the free market system. However, advertising has long been regulated for content, type and location. Alcohol advertising has not had much scrutiny because the industry has been (until the last few years) responsible in its ads and used discretion. Continuing abuses will result in further regulation.

4.   There is some First Amendment protection for advertising subject to constraints such as misrepresentation and public policy (limits on ads for children, location of ads, etc.). It would be difficult to establish a clear policy for eliminating Slash ads. However, the fact that such a policy would be difficult does not mean there would be no regulation. It is possible, for example, the ATF would just establish a policy of no celebrity endorsements in alcohol ads. Industry abuses will bring strict regulations.

5.   Slash perhaps has as much responsibility for the ads as the company. He and other celebrities need to recognize the influence that they have and that they need to use that influence carefully. There are dangers to the purchasers and others injured as result of the purchasers who might, for example, drink and drive.

6.   Often, at least temporarily, companies enjoy great gains from ethically questionable behavior. The company's performance and results, however, must be judged over the long term.

4.6   Malt Liquor Ads: Crack, Gangs and Ghettos

Answers and Key Discussion Items

1. The clear, although denied, references to drug-related terminology
    is not a balanced advertising approach. The marketing strategy may
    be very effective, but the social responsibility of making
    reference to a growing and disturbing social problem is in the
    interests of the company for only the short term.

2. These companies and others have used the ghetto approach in recent
    years to attempt to tailor products and campaigns to these target
    areas.   These campaigns have met with great public outcry from
    those inside and outside these areas. They are seen as a means of
    capitalizing on a lack of education, sought-for identification and
    self-esteem. The campaigns have nearly all been withdrawn because
    of public objections over the ethics of the sponsoring companies.

3. Again, the decision is made based on its marketing efficacy.
    However, that factor is not the sole determinant of whether a
    campaign should go forward. These campaigns often prove costly
    because the public outcry forces their withdrawal after much
    expense and the company carries a taint of the lack of social
    responsibility particularly in these campaigns that focus on the
    plight of urban America.

4. Many institutional investors are selling stock in firms that sell
    alcohol or have subsidiaries that do. Their perception is that it
    is not possible to sell beer ethically.

5. A ban on TV ads has precedent and will eventually come about. It
    is an easy solution. Just recently, baseball broadcasters agreed
    not to show cigarette billboards in ball parks during TV coverage
    of the games.

4.7 Telemarketing Trips: The Great Hype

<u>Answers and Key Discussion Items</u>

1. It is possible that under some state fraud statutes, there have been violations of the law. Another possibility is bait and switch. The "free" trips come-on is deceptive and could be subject to federal regulation as well.

2. Yes, there is deception. The issue that remains is the test of deceiving a reasonable person vs. actual deception. States vary on which test they follow. A reasonable person might not be deceived because of the old adage that you can't get something for nothing. However, the test of actual deception could bring a number of people in for complaints because they may have actually believed the marketing program.

3. Sheila has no moral responsibility because she is just doing what she is told. Sheila obviously has not had the "catch" in the program explained to her. She knows something is amiss because of the number of callers. In looking out for her own interests, Sheila needs to realize that Itinerary may not be around for very long if its methods of doing business continue. If she wishes to stay employed, she should leave and find other work.

4. Yes, those third parties that gain information about such a scam should undertake an investigation or notify authorities to do so. These types of scams cost the credit card companies as well because the customers exercise their rights to dispute the bills and refrain from paying until the dispute is resolved. Financially and ethically, it is in the best interests of a third party to conduct an investigation once the complaints are received.

5. The federal laws are a response to ongoing abuses in telemarketing. Now all telemarketers are restricted in their operations because of unethical conduct that became pervasive in telemarketing.

4.8   Bungee Ads: A Big Jump

Answers and Key Discussion Items

1.   The ad does compare products but it uses poor taste as opposed to just shock value. The ad minimizes the value of human life.

2.   The humor is definitely dark humor. From the public positions taken after the ad appeared, it is clear that the viewing public does not think death should be used as a means of illustrating the differences among products. The result is too extreme to be acceptable.

3.   The ad was perhaps too clever and sophisticated to be acceptable. But running the ad and receiving the resulting outrage brought more publicity to the companies, the sport, and the individuals than they could ever hope to gain through just straight advertising.

4.   The harm from the ad is the impact it has on our feelings about the sanctity of human life. The message of the ad is that the loss of a life need not be taken seriously. In these times of violence, the additional diminution of the value of life contributes to an ongoing societal problem.

5.   Ask the students to express their views on the ad.

6.   The ad was withdrawn because of the significant public, television station, and regulatory objections. Given the extent of the protests, continuing to run the ad would alienate customers. The ethical choice is thus the financial and economic choice.

4.9 Aggressive Marketing of Prescription Drugs: Forms of Direct Sales

Answers and Key Discussion Items - Part I

1. The increased sales goes to the Laura Nash questions: What is your intent in doing this? What are the likely results? The campaign may have been intended from the outset as a marketing ploy.

2. In a way the donations suppress criticism; it's hard to go after a donor or not at least look at the donor's product.

3. The recipients of these gifts need policies on contributions to help them maintain their independence.

Answers and Key Discussion Items - Part II

1. Users of prescription drugs need medical advice -- ads cannot provide that information.

2. Yes, ads on hair loss, etc. appeal to a "we'll try anything regardless" group.

3. Patients come in demanding the drug, not seeking medical advice or a determination of their condition and whether the drug would work.

4. Yes, as in other industries, too much with too little disclosure leads to a ban on ads.

4.10   The Obvious Idea and A Parting of the Ways

Answers and Key Discussion Items

1.   The step itself is generic. The idea of the use of a step in an aerobic workout is unique.

2.   Reebok and Sports Step did not carefully negotiate their contract regarding the step. The terms of their agreement were not specific enough with respect to the types of market and how far-reaching their joint venture would be. The home market was probably not intended to be covered. The two should be permitted to pursue their markets independently.

3.   The two parties are paying the consequences of an unclear contract. The two should be permitted to go their separate ways but a negotiated end should be attempted prior to litigation. Neither side is making a poor ethical choice. They are dealing with an ambiguity. Both benefitted from the original relationship and both are now striking out in the same market.

4.   It's possible that the problems have resulted from one side taking unfair advantage of the other side. Miller did not have the business knowledge and skills, and the result was to her disadvantage.

Legal Issues

One of the issues that clouds the "step" market is whether the idea was protectable. The idea of a step is certainly not unique. The idea of using a step as an aerobic workout was unique. Perhaps an issue here is whether Ms. Miller has been adequately compensated for her work.

4.11   Ragu Thick and Zesty

Answers and Key Discussion Items

1. Ragu is an aggressive competitor, but Ragu has crossed the line and appropriated the efforts of Hunt's. The appropriation of "Thick and Zesty" and the attempts to confuse the two sauces with the use of similar ad photos is not comparison or aggressive advertising; it is appropriation of an idea and an attempt to palm off one product as another or at least create confusion in the consumer market.

2. Ragu has violated the moral standards of honesty. Its product is being touted as the same as Hunt's. Indeed, Ragu is borrowing the Hunt's ad theme and other similarities to make its product the same in appearance. Ragu is appropriating the efforts of a competitor.

3. No ad executive should feel comfortable with the new Ragu name because the name is an appropriation of Hunt's work and ideas. It is just wrong to use the name.

4. No, product confusion is not an appropriate method of competition. Palming off, an attempt to use another's good product and name to sell your own product, is a tort and Hunt's would be permitted to recover damages for Ragu's actions. The amazing thing about Ragu's poor ethical choices is that they were made at a time when Ragu enjoyed a monopoly in the market. Hunt's was a new entry in a market in which Ragu enjoyed a 65% share of the bottled sauce market.

5. Ragu is always free to compete with a better product. However, instead of distinguishing its product or developing a better one, Ragu chose to rely on the work of its competitor and compete through confusion. The choice was dishonest and only a temporary measure. Ragu will need to refine its product to compete.

Legal Issues

The tort of palming off is the use of confusion in advertising and labeling to take advantage of another's good name and make sales because of that. That tort has occurred with Ragu's conduct in this case.

4.12   The Little Intermittent Windshield and Its Little Inventor

Answers and Key Discussion Items

1.   The decision to go forward with an idea because the person who had
     the idea is a "little guy" and probably would not go forward with
     litigation is an unethical choice. The company would not want to
     have its ideas appropriated like this so it is treating others
     differently than it would like to be treated. Also, the approach
     is not balanced.   It was a taking of someone else's idea and
     property and it was wrong.

2.   The intermittent system was an original idea, a helpful addition to
     an auto, and a means of distinguishing one's product in a very
     competitive business.

3.   Many small inventors are learning to file their ideas with
     independent third parties before presenting them to large
     corporations. This pre-filing enables them to establish that they
     did indeed have the idea and that the company later appropriated
     it.   In one case, an inventor videotaped his presentation to the
     company to provide documentation in case the idea was used.   It is
     a sad commentary on U.S. businesses that a small inventor risks
     circumvention when an idea is presented to a large company trying
     to avoid paying for the idea and the work in its development.

4.   An executive could not correct the past decision to bypass Kearns,
     but could make the decision to treat him fairly now and offer to
     settle with him as opposed to carrying through with the litigation
     with the hope that he would drop out eventually. A settlement is
     the honest thing to do based on the poor decisions in the past to
     appropriate Kearns' ideas and work.

Legal Issues

It is infringement to use another's idea without compensation. The
issue in this case was whether the idea was obvious and would have been
developed independently by the car manufacturers' engineers.
Apparently, the courts have found the idea would not have been developed
as quickly as the car manufacturers alleged and Kearns expedited the
process for them.

4.13   V-A-N-N-A: It Belongs to Me

Answers and Key Discussion Items

1.   Yes, Vanna's image, a role she has made famous, has been used to commercial advantage without her consent and without compensation.

2.   Samsung is enjoying the attention an ad that plays on Vanna and "Wheel of Fortune" will get.

3.   Satire is on "Saturday Night Live". This satire is used to sell products which makes it different (more of an appropriation).

4.   Yes, permission, which as the case decision subsequently demonstrated, was needed. Both ethically and legally, Ms. White should have been asked. Ms. White is also entitled to damages.

Note: The ninth circuit ruled in Ms. White's favor.

4.14 Caterers and the Duplication of Overhead Recovery

Answers and Key Discussion Items

1. All firms assign a percentage of overhead as part of their costs in service contracts such as these catering contracts. The issue is whether the overhead assessment is a fair estimate of the actual overhead costs. The computer time is another common contract cost in a service contract; the issue is the fairness of those computer charges. Not passing along the 15% discount is an example of one billing practice where Cindy is being dishonest in that she is not reflecting the actual cost of the soda. Billing for soda when it was not actually furnished is dishonest and wrong. Hoping the customer will catch it does not mitigate the fact that it is dishonest.

2. All of the billing practices from the overhead and computer charges to the soda issue are unethical. In Cindy's defense, these types of practices are very common in the food vendor business, but just because everyone else does it does not mean that the practices are ethical. Cindy's approach is not balanced and, although she is successful now, she may be setting a pattern of billing that could cost her customers or, at a minimum, cost her credibility with her customers. Once a customer discovers these types of errors in billing (and they do through their internal audit functions), they are suspicious in the future and all bills will be carefully scrutinized if they continue to use Cindy at all. Cindy's attitude is very short-sighted. Her successful business does not entitle her to be dishonest.

3. Cindy is correct. It is standard industry practice for food vendors to overbill. Unfortunately industry practice does not make it ethical or a wise business choice.

4. As noted above, Cindy could lose customers. She is viewing the situation incorrectly. Why doesn't she cut her prices by billing honestly and perhaps attract more volume? She has independent success and does not need to rely on these tactics.

5. Vera could make the suggestion in number 4. She should also explain the function and role of internal auditors in the customer firms and the consequences to Cindy of discovery of the billing practices. Vera could put together some data with the help of professors to make her case for an ethical billing system.

4.15   Nursing Homes, the Elderly and Video Cassettes for "Home Viewing"

Answers and Key Discussion Items

1.   MPLC is trying to protect its copyrights on the motion pictures.
      The MPLC is entitled to this protection and the protection is
      dependent upon self-enforcement. If action is not taken to prevent
      non-home uses, the owners stand to lose their protection.

2.   As sympathetic as the hospices and nursing homes are in their needs
      and limited uses, they are violating the rights of MPLC. The
      nobility of the use does not change the fact that the screening
      could be construed as a public screening and a violation of the
      copyright protections.

3.   Often videos are shown to church groups, sometimes they are shown
      to groups of children at day care centers. School have been known
      to run movies on rainy days when recess can't be taken.

4.   No one is harmed except the owners of the copyright. It is an
      infringement and unless there is self-enforcement, allows others to
      do the same thing. The MPLC needs to establish an exception or
      develop a policy such as Disney and Columbia so that they do not
      become the "bad guys" in this scenario. The nursing homes and
      other situations similar to them can use the videos for a limited
      cost. In this way, the rights of MPLC are protected and the needs
      of these group homes are met.

5.   "Everyone else does it" is not a justification for unethical
      conduct. The fact that the nursing homes and hospices have people
      who could not get to a movie creates a sympathetic picture but does
      not make their conduct any less ethical. They are infringing the
      copyrights of others. There is a compromise solution for the
      problem.

      Note: In June, 1995, the MPLC notified blood banks that movies
                 could not be shown for donators to watch while they gave
                 blood. The Red Cross was surprised. Why would the MPLC
                 "go after" blood banks?

4.16   Pharmaceuticals: Ethical Pricing of Life-Saving Cures

Answers and Key Discussion Items

1.   Pharmaceutical firms must be sensitive to the life-saving/life-giving nature of their industry. As such, the ability to charge and obtain higher prices should not be used in a monopolistic way. Public outcry could force government pricing or price controls.

2.   The shareholders want a return, but they also want the company to continue. Good pharmaceutical CEOs learn to balance short-term and long-term goals.   Temporary high short-term prices and profits might bring on destructive price regulations.

3.   Yes, effective self-regulation could halt regulatory process and steps.

4.   Yes, government pricing can't address issues of why pricing is high, exceptions, etc. Inflexible regulation contributes to market withdrawals, etc.

4.17 Salomon Brothers and Bond Pricing

<u>Use Transparency 34 to illustrate how Salomon was able to control the U.S. Treasury's bond market.</u>

<u>Answers and Key Discussion Items</u>

1. There was documented harm in the Salomon case. Many who had anticipated being able to cover their purchases were unable to do so. Bond traders and their clients suffered tremendous financial losses. Also, the general integrity of the bond market suffered because Salomon cornered the market. There was question as to whether it was a level playing field.

2. Competition, opportunity, ease of infiltration, pressure for earnings.

3. Much was written about the sufficiency of the Salomon Brother penalty. Many said criminal charges should have been brought and the penalty was insufficient. Others, as noted in the materials, viewed it as nearly half the penalty paid by Drexel Burnham for its ongoing involvement in the junk bond market that involved much more in terms of dollars and investor losses.

4. The failure to disclose the practices by anyone within Salomon who was familiar with them is typical of organizational misconduct. Employees are aware of the wrongdoing but the peer pressure, the strength of group think, the feeling that everyone else does it and the need to retain a job all contribute to the lack of disclosure at either the internal or external levels.

5. Michael Irelan is a good illustration of how unethical behavior does affect individuals even though it seemed to the Salomon traders that their conduct was detached and remote. His reputation has suffered permanent damage and his professional life is destroyed.

6. Salomon is paying the costs for ethical violations. Charles Williams had to be brought in because of the climate at Salomon and the need for a strong public statement to correct past misdeeds. Firms with an ethical culture can work to prevent misdeeds and avoid having to hire expensive officers to correct the past and its poor choices.

7. Yes, Buffet is making a case for the "front page of the newspaper" test.

8. No, hindsight always demonstrates how obviously wrong choices and actions (and lack of actions) can be.

5.1 Intel and Pentium: What to Do When the Chips are Down

Answers and Key Discussion Items

1. Ethically <u>and</u> legally, Intel should have disclosed the flaw. The inventory should have been used for those who were not concerned about the flaw and would buy for a discount. Intel was gambling with its reputation, trust, consumer confidence, buyer faith, etc.

2. Yes, and now looking back most Intel executives and experts agree that an immediate recall would have been best.

3. No, the product was flawed. Legally, whether you needed it for math computations or not, the product was flawed.

4. Consumer trust was sacrificed. Intel will take years to shake not that they made a mistake, but the fall-out from the way they handled the mistake.

5. Business history would be persuasive in your meeting with Grove. You would offer the following:
    Tylenol and its miraculous recovery following a recall;
    Jack-in-the-Box and its E-Coli disaster for not responding quickly enough;
    Exxon and its PR problems from the appearance of a lack of remorse;
    Dow Corning and its bankruptcy over product flaws that may not truly be there;
    Johns-Manville and its bankruptcy from liability for asbestos damages;
    A.H. Robins and its bankruptcy for the flawed Dalkon Shield; and Ford and the Pinto fiasco.

    Point out that the failure to spend a little to correct resulted in financial and PR disasters for these firms.

6. Not a life-threatening product issue, so you might stay to try to change things. Document your position.

7. The issue of computer component manufacturer liability for flaws will be a topic of legislative discussion.

8. See the list above. Add to it Sears, ATVs, EMF and VDTs. Many refer to the 5-part plan as "Watergate PR" named after the burglary of Democratic National Headquarters by men tied to the Nixon White House. It is a common pattern and it is important to emphasize to the students: IT DOESN'T WORK!

Legal Issues

There was warranty protection under the UCC for customers.

5.2   Joseph Horne Company and the Dillard's Premature Takeover

Answers and Key Discussion Items

1. Horne's damages were something more than a failed takeover. Horne's, perhaps naively, allowed too much infiltration of its organization and experienced too much loss of authority along with too poor management of its orders and merchandise. Dillard's perhaps because of its experience, may have gone too far in conducting its due diligence and may have become too involved in Horne's operations.

2. Dillard's is a large company with extensive experience in takeovers. Horne's is a local company with no experience in takeovers. Dillard's was able to take over the books as part of its due diligence examination, but was also able to assume a management role prior to the actual takeover. Horne's was probably naive in terms of the extent to which Dillard's could take over in performing its due diligence. Horne's was anxious to have the takeover and may have been willing to do more than it was required to do with respect to the books, records and management control.

3. Horne's did have to surrender access to its books and records, but did not have to surrender management control of purchasing and other functions. The due diligence portion of a takeover is a means by which the offeror (Dillard's) can examine the books and records to verify the financial information furnished by the takeover target (Horne's).

4. Dillard's had a duty of trust imposed by its experience and the tentative nature of the takeover. It was not proper to take over the functioning of Horne's nor interfere with its management structure until the deal was completed. Due diligence does not authorize assumption of responsibility for management of the firm. While Horne's could have objected to Dillard's conduct at any time, it apparently was not experienced enough to know that such conduct was unusual prior to closure.

5. Many business people argue that they hire experts: lawyers, accountants, to do just that -- find the technicalities to minimize cost and maximize returns. From an ethical perspective, the long-term views should be: how long do I want this relationship to last? What will my reputation in the industry be?

5.3   Hidden Car Rental Fees

Answers and Key Discussion Items

1. The policies with respect to CDW are dishonest. The customers should be informed of the possibility of other protections. The charges for CDW should be explained up front. The car rental companies' policies with respect to CDW were deceptive enough to bring about litigation and regulation. A voluntary change would be the balanced and ethical thing to do.

2. Advertising need not spell out CDW charges but could include a phrase to the effect that there could be additional charges. Other industries do it ("tax and license not included" for the car industry). The point in this case and many others like it is that either the companies can make the disclosures ethically and voluntarily or they can be required to do so through regulation.

3. The agents should be instructed to be certain the customers understand that CDW is not required. Nor should the agents do anything to mislead the customers into thinking that they should purchase CDW. The agents will not know whether the coverage is necessary for a particular customer. But they can be instructed to say, "You may have coverage through another source such as your car insurance, but that is impossible for me to tell you."

4. Many companies fail to see that by choosing an ethical path, they may be able to develop a market niche. For example, a company that was able to advertise a flat rate (CDW included) would probably win the hearts of many customers. The change could help in a competitive sense. Such changes also might prevent detailed regulation on disclosures and, as was noted, FTC actions for deception.

5. Yes, the disclosure of car seat, mileage and gas charges. Rates on additional drivers. Rates on younger drivers. Deposits and accident payments. To the extent a firm makes changes voluntarily, it is able to keep going when regulation inevitably arrives. Further, it builds trust of its customers and an ethical culture within the firm.

Legal Issues

The car rental firms have probably violated FTC standards in advertising. The car rental prices are a form of bait and switch because the lower prices advertised don't actually exist due to additional charges for CDW, gas, mileage, etc.

5.4 Thinning Diet Industry

Answers and Key Discussion Items

1.   The ethical constraints you might feel as a diet counselor would include the information you have that the weight doesn't stay off in most of the cases. The client is paying money for something that will not work permanently. In some cases there has been damage to health as a result of these programs. As a weight counselor you should provide the information for the client to check with a physician periodically and to consider a long-term maintenance plan.

2.   Most people do just want to lose weight quickly for personal reasons or because of a special event. Perhaps it is human nature to return to old habits such as the eating habits that existed prior to entering the diet program. Ask the students if most people don't understand that risk going into a diet program. Do the programs need to explain that the percentage of permanent success is low? The FTC guidelines require companies to disclose their clients' average weight loss and not simply highlight their best success stories in advertising. The additional disclosures require a statement to the effect that not everyone loses as much and that permanent weight loss figures would be different.

3.   The diet industry capitalizes on human nature. There is a tendency to overeat and a need to lose weight quickly when the motivation strikes. Ask the students if it is wrong to take advantage of human nature.

4.   The FTC believes the ads are misleading and made the changes noted above so that everyone is aware of the actual weight losses and the problems with permanency of those losses.

The FTC regulations and disclosures are simply the result of companies taking advantage of human nature. The companies went too far in their ads and approaches and regulation was required to impose ethical standards in advertising and operations.

5.   Weight Watchers is adopting an ethical posture that will quite possibly give it a market niche given the ethical void in the industry that prompted the FTC regulatory crackdown.

5.5   The Sure Sale of the Paper Bags

Answers and Key Discussion Items

1. There was an element of honesty and reliance in the parties'
    ongoing relationship. The failure to purchase the remaining bags
    changed a multi-decade pattern of behavior for the two parties. If
    that pattern was going to change, there should have been some
    notice given. There was an obligation of honesty and fair dealing
    between the parties and those moral standards were violated.

2. Yes, the parties had a pattern of conduct on which they both
    (justifiably) relied.

3. Mayer was saying that the company would honor its commitments as it
    had done in the past. There was no cause for concern with respect
    to the bags.

4. There were no alternative uses for the bags and the pattern was to
    have sufficient bags on hand. There was no resolution other than
    buying the bags.

5. Even though there was not a formal contract covering the bags or
    the holding of the bags in inventory, a pattern of behavior and
    reliance had been established. If that pattern was to be broken,
    there needed to be notice to allow both sides room for planning.
    Ethical obligations arose here well beyond the legal obligations of
    a contract.

Legal Issues

A pattern of dealing between two parties can become the parties'
standard of performance. Any deviation from that pattern requires
notice.

5.6   The Cluttered Apple Powder

<u>Answers and Key Discussion Items</u>

1.   The parties thought they understood the terms of their agreement.
      But they were selling and buying two different things. Tree Top
      was selling standard industry apple powder. But Schulze and Burch
      was buying apple powder that would work in its processing machines
      and not clog up the equipment with stems and other items
      traditionally found in industry apple powder.

2.   Arbitration should really not be the issue here. The issue should
      be the intent of the parties and their good faith in performing.
      The issue is whether Tree Top should have furnished clutter-free
      apple powder. The issue was really not negotiated. However, Tree
      Top should examine the issue over the long term. If the case is
      settled between the two, Schulze and Burch will probably continue
      as a long-term and loyal customer. Litigation will produce costs
      and arbitration will produce a settlement, but the relationship of
      the parties will be lost.

3.   The product did ruin the equipment and is about to ruin the
      relationship. Ask the students in a case such as this whether it
      matters who is right or wrong. Shouldn't the desire be to have a
      satisfied customer, not a customer who is forced to bear the costs
      of a misunderstanding because of a legal interpretation?

4.   Tree Top's reputation and a possible long-term source of apple
      powder purchases are being lost in the legal battle. So often
      litigation is used as a means of resolving business disputes that
      are better resolved by the parties in a way that preserves their
      relationship (ethically).

5.   Tree Top must ask: Regardless of my legal obligations, do I want to
      continue to do business with this customer? Do I want to preserve
      the relationship? How would I want to be treated? Is my approach
      balanced? Will I be as comfortable with my decision over the long
      term as I am now?

<u>Legal Issues</u>

Tree Top probably did all that it was legally required to do under the
contract. It did not agree to furnish a particular type of apple
powder. However, the legal resolution may not be the ethical
resolution. Is it balanced? How does it make me feel? Will I feel as
good about this over the long run?

5.7   Sears and High-Cost Auto Repairs

Answers and Key Discussion Items

1. The employees were under an incentive system that indeed gave them every incentive to sell more than a customer or car needed. Their judgment was affected by the bonuses and rewards built into the Sears compensation system.

2. Repairs for safety reasons are not unethical recommendations. Repairs recommended when the brakes are fine or the service will not be needed for some time are unethical. The case revealed the fact that cars that had just been repaired were being re-repaired at the recommendation of the service advisors. These recommendations were unethical and illegal.

3. Sears reputation has been damaged. Its earnings were down for the quarter following the announcement of the California investigation. Sears is currently reeling from an attempted re-focus of its efforts. The company suffered tremendous public setbacks because of the repair scandal.

4. Brennan is acknowledging both legal and moral responsibility for the repairs. Sears has agreed to compensate the victims and Brennan accepts responsibility for the compensation system that led to poor ethical judgments on the parts of the service advisors.

5. The motivation for the overcharges is irrelevant. They were wrong whether recommended dishonestly or in the interest of incentives. Reasons are not relevant when the result is that the customer was taken advantage of.

6. Honesty. Fair treatment. Correct conduct in the future, changing the company's ethical culture and incentive system if necessary.

7. Abuses. Incentives tied solely to sales and revenues motivate employees to cut ethical corners.

5.8 Tylenol: The Product Safety

Answers and Key Discussion Items

1. The key is to find out if the studies are correct. Depending on findings there, you might want to issue warnings and offer physicians and pharmacists information on the problem. The important thing is to follow the PR rules covered in the Intel/Pentium case (5.1).

2. The product is a good one. It is needed and can be used effectively. That there are other things that shouldn't be mixed with it does not take away from the product. The information should just be disclosed.

3. Have the students discuss the following issues as they address the question of warnings:

   a. Consumer trust
   b. Company reputation
   c. Physical harm to customers
   d. Long-term reputation of the company
   e. Public relations issues
   f. Honesty

5.9   Ford and Its Pinto

Use Transparency 35 to show the costs analysis for the redesign of the Pinto.

Use Transparency 36 -- it is a summary of the Ford internal memo on the value of human life as used in Ford's evaluation as to whether to redesign the Pinto.

Use Transparency 37 to illustrate figures in the Pinto debate as well.

Answers and Key Discussion Items

1. $18.66.

2.   Management's position was that the "fixes" would take too long. Ford needed a small car out on the market to compete with the foreign car manufacturers. Further, the fixes were not worth the additional costs given the analysis that had been done on accidents and the cost to Ford of the accidents and the compensation for victims.

3.   Mr. Copp, under the Velasquez test, was one who carried out orders, but did not have the ultimate decision-making authority with respect to the Pinto.   He would thus not be held morally responsible. However, Mr. Copp did possess certain strengths by virtue of his position in which he could have revealed the information or stood firm with respect to the redesigns.

4.   No, there was no violation of any safety standards or other laws. It was simply an ethical decision to leave the design as it was.

5.   There was tremendous demand at the time for small, fuel efficient cars. Ford was trying to deliver the car as quickly as possible. But, using one of the Laura Nash questions, it is difficult to believe that the buyers would have wanted the car that quickly had they known of the defect in design with respect to crashes.

6.   All autos are dangerous and we all assume some risks. But, as was decided many years ago in the *MacPherson* case, we only assume a reasonable risk in accidents.   We do not assume risks that manufacturers had knowledge of and could have corrected or minimized.

7.   Copp, as noted above, had valuable information and could have used that information to change events either inside or outside the company.

8.   The resurgence in popularity of the car should cause Ford to take
     some actions with respect to warnings.   Particularly given the
     nature of stock-car racing, warnings about the gas tank and its
     possible rupture should be given again.

5.10   A. H. Robins and Its Dalkon Shield

Answers and Key Discussion Items

1. One of the moral standards is the right of women to have birth
    control devices available to them. Another moral standard is that
    of manufacturing products that do not result in injury or death.
    A.H. Robins was trying to get an effective birth control device on
    the market quickly. In so doing, Robins may have ignored another
    fundamental right which is the right to full information so that
    rational choices can be made. The product was sent out for
    insertion without full instructions on risk, length of insertion
    and so on. The Robins case is no different from the Manville, Dow
    Corning, VDT and EMF cases. A problem is noted early on, at a time
    when changes can be made. In the interest of rapid product sales
    or continuing sales, the notes of caution are ignored. Yet the
    outcome is the same: harm to individuals that is often
    irreparable.

2. The same moral standards apply. The fact that the shields have not
    been banned in other countries does not change the ethics of the
    decision. Some argue in a utilitarian sense that the need for
    birth control outweighs the harms from the device. However, that
    argument ignores the fundamental human rights perspective and the
    need to make choices based on full information.

3. Robins was able to sell a very popular and effective birth control
    device. Its earnings were substantial and, women were happy with
    an effective birth control device. However, the initial warnings
    on the product safety proved to be foreshadowings and the result
    was a litigation and liability nightmare for Robins. It was not
    only the destruction of a reputation, it was the destruction of a
    company as well as the destruction of the birth control industry in
    the United States. There has been no new birth control device
    developed by an American company since the time of the Robins'
    bankruptcy.

4. Those who are morally responsible for the injury to the women are
    those who made the decision to go forward with the product with
    knowledge of the concerns about the wick problem. Ask the students
    if they would have done more than Crowder did and whether Crowder
    should be morally responsible. Ask the students if they have seen
    a pattern in these cases where one individual tries to warn of the
    problem and is disregarded. Ask them how they would feel if they
    were in that same position and they faced cases like these and
    their outcomes and harms to individuals.

5. The question of the amount of lawyers' compensation in this mass
    product liability/class action suit is an ongoing ethical debate.
    How much is enough? Do the users have sufficient say in their
    cases? Are the users compensated adequately?

5.11   Suicide is Painless

<u>Answers and Key Discussion Points</u>

1. There are conflicting moral standards at issue here. One is the
    First Amendment protection for writers, books and information. The
    other is the value of human life. Yet another moral issue is
    whether an individual should have the right to choose unilaterally
    to end his or her life. There is also the danger of moral
    responsibility for suicide committed by someone who is not
    terminally ill but rather, mentally ill and prone toward suicide.
    Ask the students if they would carry the book but would not have it
    displayed in the shelf. Does having it be a book customers would
    have to ask for make a difference? Could this policy prevent
    someone from being attracted to the option of suicide if they were
    "browsing"?

2. The issue of the nursing home access is more of a liability than an
    ethical issue. The home has responsibility for the persons placed
    in their care. The bookstore's liability is not direct. The
    nursing home director may want to make the decision based on legal
    liability as opposed to ethical issues. Family members can always
    make the book available. The residents could always talk to their
    physicians about it. But, making the book available in an open
    forum like the library may impose liability on the home.

3. This scenario did in fact occur with respect to the book and
    litigation is pending because the family's feeling is that the
    young man was making progress and would have overcome his
    difficulties if he had not had access to the book. Some argue that
    freedom and access to full information are important. Their point
    is that selling the book is no different from selling a gun or a
    knife or drugs that are then taken in fatal quantities. However,
    the students might want to consider the distinction that the book
    may make an act that would otherwise not be contemplated because of
    its pain and horror seem relatively easy to do. The other
    purchases may come because of a predisposition that the purchases
    did not motivate. The book may serve as a motivator.

4. The right to choose the time of death is a delicate issue about
    which there are many views. Our views have evolved over the last
    twenty years. For example, many states have "living will" statutes
    that permit individuals to decide in advance whether they desire
    life support systems. There has been support for the right to
    refuse treatment and food when those decisions are made
    consciously. Other views that incorporate religious values would
    dictate that the moment of death be a time that is not self-
    induced. The issue then becomes what is or is not self-induced:
    the decision to refuse life support? the decision to refuse
    treatment? The Hemlock Society represents a viewpoint that
    supports the right to choose the quality of life through a decision
    on the time of death.

5.12   A Toy to Die For

<u>Answers and Key Discussion Items</u>

1.   Larami needs to realize that its toy carries potential dangers. The marketing of the toy may need to be changed. The design of the toy may need to be changed. Larami may have to develop ways to prevent or discourage the use of liquids other than water in the gun. A suggestion would be a type of plastic that disintegrates when any harmful chemicals are inserted. Another suggestion would be the marketing of a disappearing ink that would give buyers the thrill of a fired shot without harm to the individual or clothing.

2.   A moratorium might be appropriate until Larami can develop alternatives. Larami needs to see the consequences of misuse of the toy. Such misuse could lead to costly lawsuits and tremendous damage in terms of public reputation. The desire to continue with sales as usual may be fueled by the felt need to capitalize on a very popular trend. However, often the ethical choice makes things better for the firm. For example, a moratorium could (because of supply and demand) make the product more in demand by the time Larami reintroduces its safer, more colorful model.

3.   Larami may want to restrict marketing or perhaps provide neighborhood interaction in certain areas. Sponsoring a safety event or contest may be the best way to discourage the types of dangerous behaviors that are beginning. Contests that are safe and challenging could serve to turn the use and image of the product around.

4.   Some toy stores did make the decision to pull the guns. Some would argue that absent illegality, the guns can be sold. A compromise might be appropriate where the store sells the guns but undertakes a warning program or sells them only to young people who are accompanied by an adult for the purchase.

5.   Larami apparently had no knowledge of the potential misuse of the product. In this first case, there would be no moral responsibility. After this point, however, Larami does have knowledge of the potential dangers of its product and absent mitigation would be responsible for future injuries.

5.13 Nestlé Infant Formula

Answers and Key Discussion Items

1. Nestlé, as an unassailable proposition, had a brilliant marketing program for infant formula. However, social responsibility and the moral responsibility for the right of these young children to life, dictated that Nestlé take other factors into account before using the marketing program. Once the boycotts began, the harm to children was obvious. It was morally wrong to continue the program unchanged. An executive with authority to do so should have changed the program.

2. Nestlé has suffered a twenty-year taint on its reputation because of the decisions made in the infant formula marketing program.

3. A marketing program that satisfies not only WHO and AAP but the ethical constraints as well is one that begins with the premise that in these third world nations, mother's milk is best and should always be the first choice. "If you cannot nurse . . . " is the next line in a marketing program that would be socially responsible. Also, a marketing program must involve some education because mothers need to understand the risks they run of drying up if formula is used.

4. Those who made the decision to go forward with the program and were aware of the cultural, physical and educational problems that would produce watered-down formula and malnourished babies are morally responsible for the deaths and developmental problems of those children.

5. The moratorium is voluntary but it is only a matter of time before regulation is imposed that would prevent distribution of samples. The potential for harm is great when the samples are used and the mother's milk dries up or decreases. The lack of knowledge about lactation can cost infants' lives. The moratorium is not required by positive law, but it is mandated by ethical constraints.

6. A discharge pack from a hospital with formula sends a signal of hospital approval. There is no disagreement among the experts about breast milk being best. As a hospital administrator, you may be making rationalization easier and actually be affording the opportunity for formula.

7. Some ads do read "Breast is best." Many companies are exercising great ethical discretion in the marketing of their products. Such an approach has the additional business benefit of building trust among mothers.

5.14   The Tobacco Industry

Answers and Key Discussion Items

1. The strategies for "Uptown" and "Dakota" are targeted toward specific and vulnerable groups. Their success rate is evidence of the target success. The strategy is to appeal to groups that seem to be most vulnerable to adopting the smoking habit. This type of strategy is no different from marketing BMWs to lawyers (they seem to be vulnerable) with the exception that the product sold has been linked to various types of lung diseases and cancer.

2. Freedom of choice is a moral value too. Cars are dangerous, but we still sell them. Have the students compare and contrast other potentially harmful products with tobacco such as alcohol, sugar, lard.

3. Harvard, Johns Hopkins, and NYU have taken the position that they do not wish to profit from a product that brings so much harm to its users. Universities with medical schools must be particularly sensitive to health issues. They are not required to divest but it seems inconsistent to have a commitment to health care while earning on investments in products linked to so much of the health care problems. Ask the students if there aren't other similar products. What about the danger of autos? What about butter? Products such as potato chips?

4. The statement of Harvard read as follows: "We have made the decision that in spite of its dangers, tobacco should still be available and be legal and that there should be freedom to choose." Some U.S. surgeon generals have advocated the elimination of advertising to stop some of the teenage association with smoking, its ads, and characters (like Joe Camel). Restrictions or bans on advertising have been accomplished before (TV ban on cigarettes) and could easily be adopted for other media forms.

5. Passive smoke represents an interesting dilemma because it is not an issue of choice. If we allow smoking, we are requiring those who do not smoke to subject themselves to a documented risks. There is a certain infringement of rights involved when passive smoke is considered. Freedom of choice cannot violate the rights of others.

5.15   Suicide Attempts and the Anti-Depression Prescription

Answers and Key Discussion Items

1.   The situation in which a company is faced with a question of safety
     about its product is not unusual.   There are at least six other
     cases in this text where the same thing has happened.   The problem
     is generally the company's response to the question.   The source of
     the question is discounted, the results refuted, and the product
     touted as safe.   Those responses might be appropriate if the
     allegations were also investigated to determine whether there is
     indeed any substance.   The irony is that many times the safety
     issues can be resolved and the product cleared, but there often
     seems to be a hesitation to do so.

2.   Eli Lilly's strategy is one of defending its product and it is a
     moral thing to do, assuming that Eli Lilly has the documentation to
     support its position and that it is simply not denying any of the
     allegations made.   On the contrary, this means of providing support
     appears to be quite public and the court documents will contain the
     information about the drug and will be subject to the scrutiny of
     defense lawyers, juries, and the trial process.

3.   There are several conflicting interests here.   This drug has been
     very helpful and very effective for many people.   But there are the
     questions about its safety.   A warning label would be a compromise
     of these rights.   Doctors would know close supervision was in order
     and could prescribe the drug based on specific patient needs and
     problems.

4.   The posture on the disclosure orders seems unwarranted given
     Lilly's confidence in the drug.   The resistance to disclosure costs
     the company some credibility.

5.   Once there is knowledge of reactions to the drugs (not allegations
     of reactions, but documented reactions to the drugs), those who
     continue to market the drug without appropriate precautions and
     warnings are morally responsible for the actions users of the drugs
     take that are similar to the reported reactions.   The decision to
     go forward without appropriate precautions and limitations ensures
     that there will be reoccurrences of the documented reactions and
     harms.   Foreknowledge of these problems requires assumption of
     responsibility in the moral and liability senses.

Answers and Key Discussion Items

1. The product is either too dangerous or the nature of the product causes a lapse in judgment for the people using the product. It appears that the three-wheel product cannot carry sufficient warnings or require sufficient responsibility for guaranteed safe use.

2. The companies must do more than comply with the bans. They must be certain that ATV owners of the three-wheel model have knowledge about the ban and that the appropriate warnings and information be given to them. There is potential liability for the companies beyond their ethical obligations.

3. The sales efforts for the four-wheel models are different from the previous three-wheel sales. The four-wheel vehicles are more stable, warnings are increased and appropriate limitations on age and speed maximums make the vehicle what it was intended to be: a vehicle for enjoying the terrain but not hot-dogging.

4. There are some who would have supported a recall. But there are the rights of the individual owners who would elect to keep their vehicles. Freedom of choice is an issue in the recall. Perhaps more effective than a recall would be a recall of the customers only for the purpose of training or warning.

5. The cost of a recall (in this case requiring replacement of three-wheel vehicles with four-wheel vehicles) would have been astronomical. On the other hand, the cost of civil liability for accidents on the three-wheel vehicle may exceed the costs of the recall. As a compromise, although not required by positive law, the companies might want to consider a substantial trade-in allowance for a new four-wheel vehicle. Again, this would be costly to the companies but would it be as costly as compensation for the certain injuries that will occur with the three-wheel vehicles?

5.17   Tylenol: The Product Rescue

Answers and Key Discussion Items

1.   The risk was very small that there would be any further Tylenol poisonings.

2.   No, the shareholders' interests were examined for the long-term. In the short-term, the shareholders had to accept a write-off that was substantial. But, as history has shown, the write-off helped restore consumer confidence and restored Tylenol to its previous market share and then some. Ethical choices are not mutually exclusive.   Ethical   choices   benefit   both   customers   and shareholders.

3.   Most did continue with their capsule sales, assuming that the public wanted those sales. Again, the firms would miss the opportunity for a market niche. The caplets would be what consumers were looking for and would feel comfortable with.

4.   Burke's decision was one for Tylenol's future. It was a difficult decision in terms of present costs but it ensured that Tylenol could return to the market position it once held. The interests of consumers and shareholders were the same: make a good product and be certain that it is safe. The formula translated into what consumers want and hence profit for the shareholders.

5.   The decision to abandon the capsule makes Tylenol the odd market entry. Unfamiliarity can cause a drop in the market share. In this case the caplet was the answer to consumer fears and the down side of not having what the customer wanted was minimized.

6.   In this case, as in many others, taking care of the moral responsibility of producing a safe product, was the same as ensuring long-term survival and earnings for the company. The balancing is not difficult once a manager establishes that ethical choices are often the same as good financial or marketing choices.

7.   Yes, the manufacturers should have made the decision to do the tamperproof packaging on their own. However, they followed the prisoners' dilemma notion: you are always better off doing nothing.

8.   With the Tylenol case, Johnson & Johnson did follow its credo. However, its more recent response on the liver issue has not been as forthcoming or as consistent with its credo.

Note: In June 1995, the FDA announced that companies could elect not to have tamperproof bottles. Apparently the bottles were adult-proof as well.

5.18   Halcion: The Sleeping Pill of Presidents

Answers and Key Discussion Items

1.   There is a compromise for the CEO. The CEO needs to be certain
      that there are adequate warnings on the pills and that doctors are
      informed about the possible reactions to the drugs. The drug has
      been helpful to many, and consumers want the freedom to choose
      along with their doctors' advice. Those choices should be made
      with full information.

2.   No, it would not be wrong to jeopardize the sale of Halcion if it
      can be established that there will be significant harms to
      individuals using the drug.   It is not an all or nothing
      proposition. The compromise is to provide the warnings. There may
      be some decline in sales but perhaps those declines eliminated the
      users who would have reactions and perhaps recovery from Upjohn.

3.   Ask the students if they would feel comfortable using the drug.
      Would they take it under supervised circumstances?   Is the
      recommendation that the patient be supervised, at least initially,
      a sound one?

5.19   Preventable Potholes

Answers and Key Discussion Items

1. Ask for the students' view on doing something cheaper than another
    company knowing the product won't last as long. Isn't there a need
    for cheaper alternatives in markets? For example, many people buy
    Yugoslavian Hugos knowing of reliability problems, but it is very
    cheap and provides them with transportation for at least a few
    years.

2. Quality in service and product is an ethical component of a
    business. The lack of quality will cause a business to lose
    customers and eventually end the business. The lack of quality is
    costly in a financial, ethical and survival sense.

3. No, it would not be difficult to run a business by underbidding and
    sacrificing quality. It is done all the time. Many businesses
    survive, at least temporarily, by underbidding and them scrimping
    on the product or service. The cost is non-renewal of the contract
    and a message to others in the industry regarding the workmanship
    or service.

4. Yes. He could offer to do a stretch of road to demonstrate the
    difference in the lasting quality and let the work flow in after
    this graphic demonstration.

5. Moral responsibility for accidents caused by poorly maintained
    roads is a tough causal connection to make because of the other
    factors that enter into accidents. It could be argued that
    accidents and property damage to cars and personal injuries caused
    by potholes would be attributed to the firms who do shoddy
    workmanship and are aware of the road risks. The link is more
    difficult to establish.

5.20 Credit Card and Buying Privacy

Answers and Key Discussion Items

1. Customers whose names are sold without their knowledge have had their privacy violated. There may not be a positive law against such sales of lists and names, but there is the moral constraint of privacy.

2. The credit reporting agency has an even greater obligation of privacy because the information it has is so sensitive and cannot be disclosed without the permission of the debtor. It is more wrong for credit reporting agencies to sell the lists than the creditors.

3. There are those who would not be offended by the sale of their names in a list. Indeed, some would like to have their names on certain mailing lists. Their preferences need not be ignored but this waiver of the right of privacy should be done voluntarily and with full knowledge.

4. No, the lists can be sold without violating the law. However, positive law standards are not the sole measure of ethical behavior.

5. The firms should take a proactive position and ask those on their lists their preferences with respect to the sale of their names in list firm to certain marketers. The ability to choose takes away the ethical issues of violating privacy.

6.1 The Clean Opinion and the Failed Merger

Answers and Key Discussion Items

1. The decision the Brigham auditors made was one that did not disclose the possibility of a problem. In hindsight, many auditors' decisions are examined and evaluated according to the outcome, generally the evaluation takes place when the outcome is bad. Auditors are attempting to balance the needs of company to continue as an ongoing concern with the needs of the shareholders to be adequately informed about the status of the business. Disclosure to shareholders and investors often results in negative market and creditor reaction and the auditors' disclosure becomes a self-fulfilling prophecy.

2. Often a senior management official can control the information available to an auditor to hopefully guarantee a clean opinion. Auditors should be aware of management's interest in the pending event and take appropriate steps for verification of management figures and the work of those who report to the interested management people.

3. One of the questions audit committees of boards of directors ask outside auditors is their percentage of income derived from the work at that firm. The question is asked to be certain that the auditor is not issuing a clean opinion solely for the purpose of retaining the firm as a client.

4. Hindsight bias is a phenomenon that influences the evaluation of conduct after the fact, knowing the results. It is easy to say the auditor made a mistake once the outcome is known because steps and actions can be traced to build as case leading to those results. However, the real question should be, not knowing the results, did the auditor conduct an appropriate audit?

5. Disclosure could hurt the ability to raise capital and get credit. Again, the auditor walks a fine line between the interests of investors and shareholders.

6.2   Of Golden Parachutes and Antitakeover Protections

Answers and Key Discussion Items

1. There is much debate about the validity of parachutes. Some argue that the officers are more willing to stay if they know that a takeover will not bring a loss of a job. Others say that the presence of the parachutes prevents management from evaluating an offer for a takeover since they stand to benefit even if the offer goes through.

2. Poison pills are also subject to great economic debates. Is it in the best interests of the company to prevent takeovers? Will it be better for the shareholders to let the market determine the company's value?

3. Some objections include the possibility that management will become sedentary because there is no need to worry about a takeover. The antitakeover clause prevents someone from taking over who might have legitimate ideas to move the company forward.

4. The community might have an interest in local ownership and the community may have contributed to the development of the company. A takeover might not permit the community to see a return on its investment.

5. Many shareholders take whatever position gives them the most money. Other shareholders invest for the long term and would be unwilling to sell their shares in anticipation that the value of the company will increase.

6.3 Ice-T, The *Body Count* Album, and Shareholder Uprising

<u>Answers and Key Discussion Items</u>

1. It is free speech, but the sensationalism of it all does make
    money. Freedoms also bring responsibilities -- some discretion
    must be used to enjoy the First Amendment protections we have.

2. No, and in fact, the head of Time Warner's record division was
    terminated in June 1995. Levin should have been more sensitive to
    public backlash and to institutional investors' concerns.

3. Time Warner does not want to be seen as a censor. Perhaps it is
    not morally responsible for the artists' works. But Time Warner <u>is</u>
    responsible to its shareholders for earnings, stock value, etc.

4. Yes, any screening of speech is carefully watched and controlled in
    a constitutional sense as a slippery slope.

5. Shareholder objections <u>should</u> influence corporate conduct. As
    Milton Friedman phrases it, managers of the corporation are simply
    agents of the company and are accountable to them. If you can't
    sell shares, there is no company.

6.4 Compensation-Fueled Dishonesty: Fraud to Get Results

Answers and Key Discussion Items

1. It has been said that there are two reasons for dishonesty: need and opportunity. The opportunities for dishonesty are available and the high stakes/high pay atmosphere makes many Wall Street employees feel the need to make more and more money. The compensation system of a company does set its ethical tone: how much people make and how they make it are two forces that influence workplace conduct.

2. In many situations like Jett's at Kidder, Peabody, supervisors want to believe in super performers. They do not ask the hard questions. The advice many ignore in unusually high earnings periods is: if it sounds too good to be true, it probably is.

3. Firing those who question practices; fear of losses and reporting them; under reporting to cover future losses. Earnings were everything.

4. They were fired so no one would rock the boat. No one wanted to believe anything was wrong and everyone was enjoying high earnings individually based on Jett's and Kidder's supposed performance.

5. Never questioning is "That's the way it's always been done." Firms need to have an "always question" attitude, whether there are high earnings or losses. Not questioning creates an ethical culture that says earnings count, how you got there is irrelevant.

6. A hotline; an ombudsperson; more emphasis on the corporate compliance program; all would help. The programs at Kidder seemed to be symbolic; name only. The obvious commitment of the CEO and board would also help.

7. Jett, his family, friends
    Kidder investors
    Kidder employees and their families
    GE investors
    GE employees
    All who do business with Kidder and GE

    There is an economic ripple effect of all who lost money and jobs as a result of Jett's deceit.

6.5   Levels of Executive Compensation: How Much Should the Boss Make?

<u>Use Transparency 38 to show a chart of various CEOs' pay.</u>

<u>Answers and Key Discussion Items</u>

1.   There are two schools of thought on executive compensation.   The first school, an economics-based one, is that CEOs should be paid whatever the market will bear.   A second school of thought maintains that CEOs are paid too much and their pay should be tied to the wages of the employees and the performance of the company.

2.   The argument has been made that large CEO salaries are subsidized with taxes because they are deductible.   There have been Congressional proposals to place a cap on the amount of CEO pay that would be deductible.

3 and 4.   Many follow the philosophy that CEO pay should be tied to maximums above worker compensation and that the payment should not go up unless the company's financial health is improved.

5.   Currently the compensation committee of the board of directors of a company establishes officer pay.   Their independence has been called into question in recent cases since these directors are often doing business with the company.

6.   Institutional investors have been demanding more say in board matters and have raised objections about CEO pay.   However, there are some questions about having outside investors set the management pay incentives in a company.   These investors would then be involved in micro-managing the company which is not the role of either the board or the shareholders.   The issue arises also at what point do the shareholders simply sell their shares and move onto other companies that pay officers within reasonable bounds? Traditionally, the market has functioned as shareholders move from stock to stock depending upon the performance of the company. Shouldn't these investors express their dissatisfaction with the pay system via the market, with sales?

7.   Yes, these directors are not independent and have conflicts of interest in maintaining the happiness and presence of existing management.

8.   Yes, there would be interference but it is bound to come.

6.6 Hidden Bonuses: Stock Options for Officers

Answers and Key Discussion Items

1.   Options were designed as an incentive for executive performance that brings about an increase in the value of the stock.

2.   Some have raised the point that there are only so many hours in a day and a CEO can work only so hard. Rewards that go beyond any additional effort simply encourage the CEO to try to remain put and perhaps not take the company forward or take some risks that might not be beneficial to the company over the long run. Shareholders are harmed.

3.   Beginning with the proxy statements for Spring 1993, there will be disclosure of the options for the top five executives of the company in the proxy materials.

4.   As noted in Answer #1, there is only so much a human being can do. Rewards beyond that are not producing results for the extra money.

5.   Yes, but the increase in value may only be temporary at the long-term expense of the company and its shareholders. A CEO could make earnings sing long enough to enjoy tremendous gains on options at the expense of the company's future earnings.

6.   It is not always in the best interests of a company to have present earnings at the expense of the long-term. In the Tylenol case, if the write-off had not been taken, the earnings would have remained level, but the company's revenues over the years would have decreased.

6.7   The Boy Scouts of America, U.S. West, and Gay Rights

Answers and Key Discussion Items

1.   U.S. West was simply contributing to a longstanding organization
that promotes the values of honesty, patriotism and integrity. The
BSA policy is one example of many policies many organizations have
that might not be consistent with corporate policies. The issue
becomes will donations be made on the basis of the donee
organization's goals and accomplishments or on its policies?

2.   Freedom of choice in philanthropic giving is an important standard
whether it is a corporation or an individual. A corporation runs
the risk, however, of offending customers through its choices of
donees. Milton Friedman would say that the corporation should
engage in philanthropy only to the extent that such contributions
help the company make more money. To the extent that customers are
lost through philanthropic giving, the giving should stop.

3.   Public outcry may not restrict corporate giving but it may
eliminate it because of the company's fear of alienating customers
and receiving adverse publicity about its donees.

4.   Levi Strauss is experiencing the backlash from the withdrawal of
funding. On issues such as the BSA ban on homosexuals, companies
cannot win. There are as many customers that would support the ban
as there are customers who would object. The result is that the
giving or not giving alienates customers. The company is then not
serving its main purpose which is to earn a profit and the
philanthropy must be abandoned to avoid the controversy.

6.8 Dayton-Hudson and Its Contributions to Planned Parenthood

Answers and Key Discussion Items

1. No. In both this case and the U.S. West case the companies cannot win. They have encountered issues in which public opinion differs and public outcry on both sides is strong.

2. On issues this sensitive, tying marketing to contributions is a fatal mistake. Under Friedman's notion, the company's voluntary giving is costing it customers and should be avoided.

3. If the contributions are consistent with the firms' values, they may not be consistent with a group of customers' values (as in the Levi's/BSA dilemma). These donations are lose/lose propositions and need to be avoided. The downside is the impact on organizations that rely on corporate funding for survival.

4. The ethics of the situation are that attacks be answered or the firm loses customers and money; a violation of its duties to its investors.

6.9   Giving and Spending the United Way

Answers and Key Discussion Items

1. In light of the purpose of the United Way, the nature of its donors and the problems of too many needs and too little funds, Aramony's salary and expenses were not balanced and did not take into account how the $12,000 per year wage earner would feel about these levels of expenses as he/she makes a $500 per year payroll contribution.

2. The Board was responsible for the supervision of the expenses and had the authority to halt the expenditures.

3. Aramony may have been behaving as other CEOs of large multi-national organizations behave, but his distinction came from being the head of a charitable organization as opposed to a for-profit corporation.

4. Compensation in for-profit corporations should be whatever the market is. Salary, benefits and perks should be set along the lines of industry. CEOs of non-profits must be particularly sensitive to their fish bowl existence and recognize their vulnerability on the issues of salary and perks. People don't want to donate funds to organizations that they perceive spend lavishly.

5. Chao faced and faces the decline in donations, the tarnished reputation of United Way, public outcry and local chapter uprisings and withdrawal from the national United Way. In short, Chao faces the task of restoring a non-profit's reputation lost through questionable spending. Her task is a fundraiser's nightmare.

6.10   The NAACP: Unauthorized Settlements

<u>Answers and Key Discussion Items</u>

1.   NAACP ousts director over funds dispute
      NAACP director pays off on harassment charges on the QT
      NAACP director ousted over funds and harassment allegations

2.   No. The allegations involve workplace conduct and performance of
      an officer. Board approval is required.

3.   Because the board must decide what its follow-up conduct will be
      with respect to the director.

4.   No, the payment settled a potential lawsuit and it involved the
      conduct of its highest-ranking officer.

6.11   The Chicago Inner-City School Experiment

Answers and Key Discussion Items

1.   Yes, Friedman would support their actions so long as the CEOs could show that there would be a return to them in their businesses, which would be better-trained employees and a savings in training costs.

2.   The comments from the shareholder should be addressed with information about training costs, the inadequacy of the public school systems and the business's need for adequately trained workers. The sponsorship of the school should be addressed as a quantitative issue; one that will produce higher returns for the company over the long run.

6.12   The Rock Music Warning Labels

Answers and Key Discussion Items

1.   There are not controls on how the albums are distributed or sold. Young, impressionable teenagers have access to them. Without the appropriate levels of wisdom and discernment, their activities and attitudes may be influenced by very popular groups whose attitudes and beliefs may not reflect ethical values. These lyrics sometimes cause the adoption of behaviors that would otherwise be foreign to the young people. Rock groups have significant power to influence young people and the use of explicit lyrics is an abuse of that power (when there are no warnings about content and the ability of parents to screen).

2.   So long as the labels are universal, all those who have objections to the lyrics appear ready, willing and able to accept the voluntary compromise. The only drawback would be the unwillingness of the artists or the record companies to participate.

3.   The songs with explicit lyrics often do well. The question is whether you are willing to assume moral responsibility for the consequences of the lyrics, as in the Reno case where there is a suicide.

4.   As a record producer, you would probably be unable to do much more than to put on the labels. Asking that the albums be set apart in stores may actually fuel the sales as opposed to controlling them. If you decide to produce the records, there is little control that can come once they are "out there."

5.   If you are aware of the suggestive nature of the lyrics and the influence that rock music stars can have on young people and their particular vulnerability, there would be some moral responsibility. The courts have not held record producers or the groups legally liable but the question of moral responsibility is one of prior knowledge.

6.13 Insurance for the Drive-By Victim

Answers and Key Discussion Items

1. Sheila is concerned that the insurer is making money from the misfortunes of those who live in areas that have succumbed to gang influences. The sale of policies in these areas seems to be a cold and detached method of making money.

2. The marketing director has a point. The compensation for the inevitable is helpful for the family. In a way, the policies provide for the expenses associated with the loss of a loved one.

3. The distinction is that the sales people in inner-city neighborhoods can capitalize on the fear element in the sales.

4. The comfort level for selling the policies would rise if it could be established that the insurer is also undertaking social programs in the area to decrease the drive-by shootings and improve the quality of life in the neighborhoods. By so doing the company would be increasing its profits (fewer claims) and also accomplishing a social goal not being addressed by government agencies. The sales could be a win/win proposition. The company pours back funds into the insured neighborhoods.

6.14   Saturday Night Specials: The Weapon of Choice

Answers and Key Discussion Items

1. The causal link between the sale of guns and crimes is more
    difficult to draw even in the moral responsibility sense.   Some
    people buy the weapons to defend themselves and their homes.   There
    is a constitutionally protected right to keep and bear arms.   This
    right was given even knowing that weapons might be used immorally
    and irresponsibly at times.   On the other hand, it is clear that
    the availability of cheaper weapons makes access easier and may
    create more of an ability to commit crimes because of the strength
    of being armed.

2. The gun dealers are in the same position.   There is a protected
    right of owning guns.   The issue is whether the dealer is
    responsible for the ultimate use of the weapon.

3. The low cost factor for the guns is the focus of concern because
    ready availability almost insures that those with lesser means will
    be able to afford weapons they would otherwise not have access to.
    The problems with the sales of the guns indicate social problems
    caused by their ready availability.

4. The Jennings family's moral responsibility might be reduced because
    the impact of a price increase on the market would be to reduce the
    availability and possibly impact the crime levels.

5. Many sporting goods stores choose not to carry the weapons on a
    voluntary basis.   Other owners screen purchasers of their guns.
    Waiting periods are helpful in deterring conduct.   The store owners
    have options apart from not carrying the weapons.   They often
    assume a posture of social responsibility in the sale of this
    merchandise.

6.15   The Killer Novel

Answers and Key Discussion Items

1. The First Amendment only places restrictions on obscenity as
    defined by the U.S. Supreme Court or the local community as upheld
    by the U.S. Supreme Court.   Merit is not the equivalent of a
    positive impact on society.   Indeed, in some cases the nature of
    the subject matter may be to have a negative impact on society and
    encourage behavior that would otherwise be dismissed from the
    rational mind.

2. Yes.   The editors were expressing an ethical concern about the
    impact of the book on sexual violence and women as victims.

3. Mr. Ellis can always publish his book himself.   Publishers are not
    required under the First Amendment to publish books.   As any good
    or bad author will tell you, publishing commitments are the
    publisher's choice.

    Ask the students if they would have made the choice knowing that
    the book is selling well.

4. "If we don't do it, someone else will," does not mean that a
    correct ethical choice was made.   The publicity will help its
    sales.   Ethical choices are not always the short-term profitable
    choices.   However, Simon & Schuster may attract other authors and
    buyers because of its position that it would not otherwise be able
    to attract.

6.16   Killer Video Games

Answers and Key Discussion Items

1.   Video games need <u>not</u> be violent to make money. The violence
      provides a splash and intrigue, but may not serve the company well
      for the long-term.   Non-violent games have staying power and
      attract a broader customer base. Tetris, a simple geometric game,
      is as big a seller and very popular among adults.   There is no
      violence, only moving squares and classical music.

2.   Parents have a responsibility for supervision, but as the letters
      point out:

      a.   Parents can't control fads that permeate society;
      b.   Parents can't control access except in their own homes; and
      c.   The presence of the game numbs society and not responding is
            consent or at least tolerance.

6.17   The "Killer Cards"

Answers and Key Discussion Items

1.   The cards are a glorification of criminals and gruesome crimes.   It
is difficult to imagine anything beyond a profit motive in the
decision to make the cards.

2.   The cards are a tribute to the worst society has to offer and send
terrible signals to children who will buy the cards as they would
baseball cards.   They trivialize the brutality of the crimes and
criminals.

3.   If the manufacturer won't stop making the cards, merchants should
refuse to carry them.   Someone else will sell them but it is a
quick profit that ends quickly.   Justification that everyone else
does it or someone else will do it is not sufficient to establish
an ethical choice.

4.   Parents cannot supervise children in an environment so infiltrated
with bad influences.   The cards will be out there no matter how
much control a parent has and children will see them and be
influenced by the statements that they make.   Please note
discussion on Case 6.16, too.

Answers and Key Discussion Items

1. The concern about that doll is that it would glorify, encourage and make look glamorous teenage pregnancies because the doll looks so young and the "ease of delivery" so appealing.

2. Some see the doll as a means of educating children about the birth process and family responsibilities. There is a father doll to go with the mother and child.

3. Parents always have the ultimate control over what comes into the home but friends will still have the dolls and conversations, questions and some idolizing will occur.

     Note: Have the students consider the latest concern about the talking Barbie doll that says, "Math is tough." The concern is a characterization of women, i.e. that they can't do math. Ask the students whether objections have gone too far or the toys have gone too far.

6.19   The Toys Parents and Teachers hate

Answers and Key Discussion Items

1.   The toys represent socially irresponsible behavior. They are a
     brilliant product line with great potential that disregards the
     ethical issues and long-term implications of marketing such a line
     of toys. The possibilities of boycotts of Kenner and the backlash
     from the sales have not been adequately reviewed.

2.   If the toys are manufactured, the failure of store owners to sell
     them can still spell their demise. On the other hand, often the
     refusal to sell the toys translates into added sales.

3.   The ads are something that could be the subject of future
     regulation since children's television ads have already been
     subjected to certain minimum FTC standards. Good choices by
     station managers will ensure that future regulations are kept to a
     minimum. Toys such as this involve line-drawing. Someone has to
     be willing to draw the line when we have crossed into the anti-
     social arena. If everyone goes along with the toy, we have only
     made a toy manufacturer rich from a poor ethical and socially
     irresponsible decision.

6.20 The NFL, Arizona, and the Martin Luther King Holiday

<u>Answers and Key Discussion Items</u>

1. The NFL used an economic form of duress to achieve a social goal. Ask the students if this role of the NFL was appropriate.

2. Again, the economics of the Super Bowl were used as clout for the achievement of a social goal. Does the end goal (so to speak) justify the means?

3. Outside intervention in intrastate political issues has increased substantially over the past decade. Ask the students if this economic duress from outside the state is appropriately used to influence decisions within a state.

4. The NFL's position is both. Ethical decisions are not always poor business decisions. Sometimes the ethical decision carries business benefits with it.

5. Economic boycotts have always been used as a political force (Boston Tea Party). But, it is their use by those outside the state who will not vote that raises concerns about the validity of votes and political process.

    Note: Arizona hosted the Super Bowl in January 1996.

6.21   Beavis, Butt-head, and MTV

Answers and Key Discussion Items

1. MTV, by placing the program on in prime time without warning to parents, shares some responsibility for the mishaps.

2. As noted in the *Mortal Kombat* case, parents do have a responsibility to supervise, but the standards of society decline as more and more is tolerated, despite parent's ability to say "No".

3. MTV did a great service with the program move and disclaimer, but the question can still be raised, "Why do we need this program?"

4. Have the students discuss why the program is popular. What is its purpose?

5. "The proud sponsor of `Beavis and Butt-head'" is not a noble label. Sponsors risk boycotts on these types of controversial programs. Beyond the ethics of sponsorship is the risk of loss of sales and earnings from a boycott.

Answers and Key Discussion Items

1.   Infinity may hang its hat on First Amendment issues, but it is still in business. It must be able to sell air time, it can't face boycotts and it can't risk astronomical fines. To that extent it has a business obligation to monitor and control Stern. An ethical responsibility for those you employ exists as well.

2.   Yes, and Simon & Schuster has some restraint (see *The Killer Novel*). The First Amendment does not mean that every manuscript must be published. Social, moral and financial considerations are part of every publication decision.

3.   The shareholders are probably very pleased with Howard Stern. However, do the shareholders and management recognize the short term focus of this one-time publication and short-lived radio figure? Can they recover? Can they focus on strengths?

4.   Have the students debate the merits of a Sternless world.

6.23   Retailers and Weapons: Self-Imposed Bans

Answers and Key Discussion Items

1. Although the decisions by these two major retailers may have been prompted by the potential liability for selling guns, there are other reasons that could have played into the ban. For example, some customers are happier if weapons are not sold in the stores in which they shop. Also, the chains enjoyed a great deal of free publicity from their decisions. The moral responsibility for another's death because of the sale of a murder weapon could also be a great relief to the store in a public relations sense.

2. The realistic-looking toy guns created problems for law enforcement officials. Although the employers (municipalities and so forth) of the police officers involved in shooting the youngsters with the toy weapons would be first in the liability line, it is possible that in the scheme of deep pockets and product liability, the families and victims could return to the retailers and manufacturers of the realistic-looking toys.

3. Yes, the decision earned all the stores a great deal of positive publicity. In a nation that faces the problem of weapon use, it was a terrific story to see a retailer respond by doing what it could do to cut down on the possibility of senseless deaths. It was an ethical and moral choice for the retailers, but it also brought them great economic benefits in terms of publicity and customer appreciation.

4. Have the students discuss the issue and what information they would want: how much business is involved? what is the potential liability? are we creating an additional societal problem with the realistic-looking guns?

5. Guns are still a legal product; the issue is whether it is ethical to continue to sell such weapons. Guns can be used for lawful activities such as hunting. A ban on selling guns is an easy way to avoid the complexities of the paperwork as well as the liability for the failure to adequately screen gun purchasers. Another choice would be to screen carefully all potential purchasers, honor waiting periods, be careful on screening applicants etc. Some retailers, such as Sears, felt they could not do an adequate job on the paperwork and abandoned selling weapons so they did not make a mistake.

6.24 "It May Be Immoral, But Not Illegal. The Bottom Line is Money."

Answers and Key Discussion Items

1. The Daniels follow a positive law standard. If what they are doing does not violate the law, then it is okay to do. The Daniels do not consider moral issues in their business.

2. They make the argument that no retailer can control what is done with a product purchased at a store and that no one can anticipate every act performed with a good purchased from a merchant.

3. The Daniels have indeed found a market niche and are doing quite well within that Niche. There are still protected rights for gun purchases and the Daniels believe their role is part of making sure the guns are always available despite current trends away from permitting gun sales.

4. Have the students review some of the quotes from the Daniels and decide whether they are there to fulfill the Second Amendment or for profit and gain.

6.25 E. Coli, Jack-in-the-Box and Cooking Temperatures

Answers and Key Discussion Items

1. Jack-in-the-Box did not follow the formula for handling corporate and national crises:

   a. Be forthcoming with information;
   b. Respond immediately;
   c. Recall, recall, recall;
   d. Do not blame others;
   e. Do not say it is not a big issue;
   f. Do not attempt to cover-up; and
   g. Do not discredit the media or the victims.

2. The change should have been made voluntarily and sooner as an ethical choice because of the potential loss of human life and certainly illness and also because of the relatively low cost of implementing the temperature increase as opposed to paying out for the loss of life and illness as well as the long-term damage to the chain for the bacteria-induced illnesses.

3. The misplacement of the memos tells us that compliance with the law was not systematic at Jack-in-the-Box. The company should have made regulatory compliance a top priority.

4. Yes, the harm to individuals is so extensive and there is a great potential for loss of life. The cooking temperature decision was absolutely a moral decision. It was treated, however, as an expense and time situation.

5. The sales have declined and the chain is trying to recover. Despite a new advertising campaign, the chain continues to struggle.

6.26 "Dateline NBC": Pick Up GM from the GM Pickup Story

Answers and Key Discussion Items

1. The explosion devices made the story much more compelling and more interesting to watch. It made a good teaser for the story to see the exploding pickup.

2. It is significant that outsiders disclosed the embellishment because the culture at NBC was such that no one there would have disclosed that there was a staging of the accident. The culture in the news organization was such that either no one saw a problem with the embellishment or such that no one would dare to bring the problem to the attention of those who were in charge.

3. It was the appearance of the accident that was emotional and upsetting. Even if the rockets did not cause the explosion, the depiction of what happens to the trucks in accidents was not accurate.

4. Yes, the firm was involved in the litigation of the case for plaintiffs. It was in the firm's best interests to have the accident look as awful as it possibly could.

5. Have the students review the pressure you would feel if you noticed the rockets and felt it was wrong. Ask them who they would approach first. What would they say? How would they follow up? Would they discuss standards of fairness? Would they discuss the implications for NBC and Dateline if the rockets were disclosed publicly?

7.1 His Honor: The Gambler

Answers and Key Discussion Items

1. Taking things that don't belong to you: using government time for personal reasons; using government facilities and employees for personal business; not using vacation time for personal business and trips.

    Conflict of interest: awarding contracts to those making payments to his various companies; placing pressure on people to invest in exchange for award of contracts; increasing payments to companies for no additional work; awarding referrals to friends and investors.

2. Court employees are like many who witness misconduct in the workplace. They don't want to rock the boat. They don't want to be perceived as a tattle-tale, whistle-blower, etc. They feel it is none of their business. They count on others to bring it to someone's attention. It is, however, one of the categories of ethical violations to fail to bring to someone's attention unethical behavior: condoning unethical conduct.

3. So many people were beneficiaries they wanted to keep the system in place. There were inadequate internal controls in place. There were an insufficient number of in-depth audits. If the judge did well, all others did well. Many wanted to perpetuate his scheme of operations.

4. The following problems existed that allowed the Mirretti problem to go on for so long:

    a. Lack of internal controls;
    b. Lack of systematic and detailed audits;
    c. Inadequate division of award of contracts and bidding;
    d. Lack of supervision of judges and their management of matters beyond the courtroom; and
    e. Lack of reporting mechanism or system for employees to report wrongdoing when they are supervised by the wrong-doing employee.

7.2   The Book of Newt: Conflict of Interest

<u>Answers and Key Discussion Items</u>

1.   Yes, Mr. Gingrich does have a conflict of interest. He will vote
     on major issues affecting his publisher and its parent. Turning
     down the advance does not solve the problem of the marketing of the
     book and ongoing royalties. As hard as it may be to face, public
     officials need to wait until they leave public office to write
     books and accept royalties and/or advances. Even without a direct
     conflict, Mr. Gingrich has the appearance of impropriety in that he
     is in a partnership with a major corporation regulated (in some
     cases heavily) by a body of which he is the leader.

2.   All members of the house also have cars and vote on auto industry
     issues.   The distinction is whether you are being paid by the
     companies and voting on legislation that impacts them, not whether
     you use their products.

3.   Have the students discuss how they feel about these books and the
     conflicts.   To balance the political scales you might remind the
     students that when Mr. Al Gore was a senator he accepted an advance
     for his book, *Earth in the Balance*.

7.3 A Club in My Name

Answers and Key Discussion Items

1. The funds from the settlement were intended to help children in the state. They were not intended to be used to develop name recognition for elected officials. The donations were not made the attorney generals from their pockets -- they were from a lawsuit settlement.

2. Is it bad form to use charity to develop name recognition? Although much good comes from what it done, the introduction of political benefit into a good cause is an appearance of impropriety.

3. The front page of the newspaper test would have helped. Gaining mileage from a donation for which other attorneys general are not raises questions about motive and propriety. It is a terrific topic for newspaper mileage.

7.4 Bath Iron Works

Answers and Key Discussion Items

1. There are two reasons given for wrongdoing during the course of employment: opportunity and need. Mr. Haggett probably did not need to see the file given the long, successful relationship of Bath Iron with the Navy. But the opportunity was given with the file left on the desk. The temptation was too strong.

2. The competitive process is undermined which harms the Navy and those who pay for the Navy (the taxpayers). To the extent no one feels the process is fair, competitive benefits and bidders are lost.

3. Mr. Haggett probably resigned to demonstrate to the Navy that it was his transgression and not a reflection of the standards of the firm. He needed to isolate himself from Bath Iron Works. It would be difficult to regain trust so long as he remained at the company. Also, Haggett probably did not want to incorporate any notion of cheating into the culture of the Bath Iron Works.

4. The temptation to peek when information is so accessible would be tremendous. It is still not ethical. It should not be done. The long-term personal, professional and business damage is too great.

5. Yes, Haggett's conduct would have set a compromised ethical tone for the company. One can envision employees saying things such as, "It's no worse than Haggett," or "Haggett did it. Why can't I?"

Legal Issues

There are civil and criminal penalties for interference in the government bidding process.

7.5 Stanford University and Government Overhead

Answers and Key Discussion Items

1. Mr. Kennedy's attitudes did evolve as the case evolved. His initial statements conclude that whatever was done was insignificant and therefore justified. His last statement (March 23, 1991) is one that recognizes that while the accounting practices may have been legal, they were not necessarily ethical.

    Mr. Kennedy also resigned as a result of the Stanford problem. He became so identified with the problem that he needed to leave to restore Stanford's credibility. Mr. Kennedy's initial reaction to the accounting issues and his attitude of "little amounts not being issues" cost him deeply in the crisis. It became more than just unethical booking of costs; it became the unethical booking of costs and justification of it by a president who saw little wrong in a scenario that outraged others.

2. This case is an illustration of practices that were legal. It is also an illustration of practices that had "always been done this way" by Stanford and other universities. Accounting overhead was a nebulous concept that was used to maximize the government funds to the university.

3. Casper has set an ethical tone for Stanford by saying that everyone must observe, question and evaluate what is being done. He is suggesting that "the way things have always been done" be questioned. He is suggesting an open, honest and above-board atmosphere.

7.6 The Degrees-for-Grants Program

Use Transparency 39 to show similarities in writings and contract work.

Answers and Key Discussion Items

1. To the extent that the degrees were not earned, those students who actually earned their degrees are harmed. Also, those who rely on this academic measure of learning will assume that the steps required for the award of these degrees were followed. The University's credibility is also harmed as a result.

2. An employee who noted the similarities should first clarify the situation. Perhaps the degree work and the contract go hand-in-hand. Perhaps the university is benefiting from the work of the students and not vice-versa. Any employee raising ethical issues should be certain about the facts. The immediate supervisor is the first step. If there are no results, then the employee should turn to an independent party within the university or the next immediate supervisor and keep progressing until a response or clarification is obtained.

3. It would be very tempting to be able to earn a degree with relative ease. However, the degree holder would always be glancing back to be certain no one exposes the true nature of the degree and the work for that degree.

4. The Institute and the University appeared to be so inextricably intertwined that the contracts for the Institute were bound to have some effect on the relationships and the quid pro quo that resulted from the contract decision-makers also pursuing degrees.

7.7 Orange County: Derivative Capital of the U.S.

Answers and Key Discussion Items

1. Government has a greater interest in the public trust and is a fiduciary for public funds and the public. Their investment interests should be more conservative.

2. County employees
   All those who had funds in the account from personal injury victims to wards of the state to school districts
   Families of employees
   School children
   Teachers
   School programs and suppliers
   Airports, parks and other public facilities
   Taxpayers
   Bond traders in general
   Accountants, lawyers and investment bankers who handled the portfolio and the investments

3. Immediately after the bankruptcy, there were articles on how investors were now nervous about any other municipal bonds. Municipalities had to change their portfolios or offer assurances that they were not in the same situation as Orange County. The cost of municipal bonds went up.

4. No. You would not expose your funds to the leverage and risk that Citron exposed the Orange County funds to.

5. Yes, those who invested assumed the standard conservative government approach to investment, not this form of leveraged gambling.

6. Yes, the brokers should at least be brought in to answer questions about how candid they were about the risk and whether they advised the leveraged position and offered any advice on the potential for earnings and the problems in terms of risk.

True/False Questions

F   1.   A conflict of interest is unethical only if those involved actually change their decision based on the benefits to be derived.

T   2.   An illegal act is an unethical act.

T   3.   Using positive law as an ethical standard means simply compliance with the law.

F   4.   Those firms with higher compliance with the law earn less than those with greater numbers of violations.

T   5.   The element of balance in the Blanchard/Peale ethical model requires an examination of the issue from the perspective of the affected party.

T   6.   A valid ethical barometer is the reaction of family and friends outside the business setting to your proposed decision.

F   7.   An agreement by an agent to accept a 10% commission from a seller who will sell goods to the agent's employer is ethical so long as the agent would have chosen that seller anyway.

T   8.   A real estate agent who recommends a management firm to an apartment complex buyer without disclosing that the agent owns 50% of the firm has committed an ethical violation.

F   9.   A commercial broker who accepts fees from both the seller and the buyer of the business without disclosure to either has not committed an ethical violation if both parties are happy with the transaction.

T   10.   A member of the city council who is employed by a waste management firm would have a conflict of interest in voting on the city's award of a contract for the handling of the city's waste.

F   11.   A physician conducting a study on a new prescription drug manufactured by a firm in which he is a 10% shareholder does not have a conflict of interest so long as his stock ownership is disclosed in his report on the drug.

T   12.   A physical fitness expert retained by a fitness magazine to evaluate walking shoes has a conflict of interest if she has an endorsement contract with one of the shoe companies that manufactures the shoes she will be evaluating.

F   13. Giving preferential treatment in contract bidding to the daughter of a member of the company board is not a conflict of interest.

T   14. Physician referrals of patients to laboratories for work-ups when the physicians own all or part of the labs, but do not disclose such, is a conflict of interest.

F   15. A major donation by one of your long-term suppliers to a non-profit organization run by your spouse should not create perception problems so long as your purchasing decisions are based on the merits.

F   16. Having loan applicants pay for the expenses of bank officer travel for purposes of evaluating collateral is not a conflict of interest.

T   17. Purchasing agents accepting a pleasure trip from a supplier when no bids are pending is still an ethical violation.

T   18. Payments of royalties from drug sales by a pharmaceutical firm to the university where a researcher conducting studies has validated the firm's claims is a conflict of interest.

F   19. Hiring an employee from a competitor firm who has brought with her proprietary information is ethical so long as the employee has not breached an employment contract with that competitor.

F   20. Leaking proprietary information to the media is not an ethical breach.

T   21. The failure to disclose that your college degree was withheld because of outstanding parking fines and violations is unethical.

F   22. Taking information from a confidential file accidentally left on your desk is not unethical.

T   23. The failure to speak out when an ethical or legal lapse occurs within your firm is in itself an ethical violation.

F   24. Lie detector tests can be properly used as employment-screening devices.

F   25. Drug testing for employees who handle deliveries for a company is unconstitutional.

F   26. Employers can prevent women of child-bearing years from working in positions where exposure to risks could harm a fetus.

T   27.   Employers could be held liable for injuries to fetuses experienced as their mothers worked in jobs where, with full knowledge, they were exposed to known fetal hazards and risks.

T   28.   The employment-at-will doctrine contains an exception for whistle-blowers.

F   29.   The duty of loyalty between employee and employer makes whistle-blowing unethical per se.

T   30.   The sale of a product with known, but undisclosed dangers, is unethical.

T   31.   Removing records from the workplace to prevent access by regulators on a pre-announced inspection is both illegal and unethical.

F   32.   The Equal Pay Act follows a comparable worth theory.

T   33.   "Everyone else does it," is a signal of an ethical pitfall.

F   34.   "The lawyers have okayed this," is a signal that the decision/action is legal and ethical.

T   35.   Labeling infertility surgery as "diagnostic surgery" in order to allow the patient to recover the costs from an insurer is unethical.

T   36.   The failure to follow U.S. safety standards in foreign operations constitutes an ethical lapse.

F   37.   Product dumping does not present ethical problems in those countries without product liability recovery systems.

T   38.   Selling component parts that could be used to construct weapons to a nation against which an embargo on direct weapons sales is in place would be an ethical breach.

F   39.   "Grease" or "facilitation payments," which are legal under the Foreign Corrupt Practices Act can be considered ethical.

T   40.   A company executive exerting pressure on a scientist and her university to delay disclosure of study results harmful to the company and its products would be unethical.

F   41.   Downsizing itself is unethical.

F   42.   Compliance with the Worker Adjustment and Retraining Notification Act meets the standards for ethical conduct in downsizing.

T   43.   Ethical choices often prove costly to firms in the short term.

T   44.   Ethical advertising requires an examination of unintended impact and effects of ad content.

T   45.   It is unethical to introduce a product with deceptively similar packaging to that of a major competitor.

F   46.   An industry practice that permits bill-padding is ethical.

F   47.   Taking advantage of a party in a contract situation due to the party's inexperience, and not due to any lack of disclosure on your part, is ethical.

T   48.   The failure to disclose relevant information about a product or service is unethical.

T   49.   Long-term relationships create ethical and legal obligations between the parties through conduct and accommodations.

T   50.   The failure to correct a known defect in a product is both an ethical lapse and a basis for a negligence claim.

T   51.   A decision not to sell realistic-looking toy guns is an example of an ethical choice not mandated by law.

F   52.   The failure of an auditor to disclose the possible obsolescence of a firm's major product is a judgment call and not an ethical issue.

F   53.   Decisions on corporate charitable contributions carry no ethical implications.

F   54.   Corporate takeovers and mergers are unethical per se.

T   55.   Executive compensation disclosures include information about conflicts of interest between directors and CEOs.

T   56.   If I worked in purchasing in my company, it would be unethical for me to accept season tickets for my city's NBA team from the company that has supplied catering for the company's training sessions.

F   57.   If I discover that a fellow employee is reporting falsely his overtime hours, it is best for me to say nothing and ignore the situation.

F   58.   If I discovered that I unintentionally violated a federal environmental regulation, I should just wait and see if anything happens before taking any action.

F   59.   If my supervisor asked me to cover for him by lying about his whereabouts, I should agree to do it but remind him that I can't make it a habit.

T   60.   Your company's policy on company vehicles is that no family members may use them or ride in them. It would be unethical to use a company car to drive you and your spouse to a movie.

T   61.   You are taking a graduate level course in management that will help you in performing your duties at work. Each week you must submit case analyses to your professor. Using work time to complete the analyses would be unethical.

T   62.   With respect to #61, using your work computer and paper to complete the case analyses would be unethical.

T   63.   Attending a class on company time would be unethical.

F   64.   A supplier has just been awarded a large contract by your company. As an employee in purchasing, you were largely responsible for awarding that supplier the contract. The supplier's sales representative has just called and would like to take you to lunch to thank you for the support. Going to lunch with the sale representative does not present any ethical problems.

F   65.   Accepting gifts from suppliers and vendors is not a problem so long as no bid decisions are pending.

F   66.   You are a building inspector for the county. A friend of yours is a plumbing contractor. Under county regulations, all steps in plumbing construction from the initial dig to the final installation of sink and bathroom fixtures requires an inspection sign-off. Your plumbing contractor friend has just called and wants to take you to dinner for your birthday at a five-star restaurant. Because you are friends anyway, the dinner presents no ethical problems.

T   67.   Your company has several outdated computers sitting in a storage closet that no one is using. You have taken one home and set it up for personal use. This is unethical conduct.

T   68.   You work for a school district as a facilities coordinator. You drive to the various schools in the district and supervise construction and remodeling and assess various building needs. When you are traveling around to the various schools, you use a district vehicle that is clearly marked as such. One day you stop at the country club and have lunch before heading to the next school since the country club is on the way. You also stop at the bank drive-thru teller to do some personal banking business. Both the lunch and the bank stop are ethical breaches.

F   69.   Your supervisor has told you that he wants to "get rid of Jane." Jane is a Hispanic female co-worker who is very bright and capable and hardworking. Your supervisor has asked you to document everything Jane does and says that will help build a case for termination. You should do as your supervisor tells you.

T   70.   Alice is a co-worker who is going through a divorce and has two small children. Alice's husband is not paying the child support the temporary court order requires. As a result, Alice is broke until she can get her court hearing. Alice has been able, through diverting checks returned to the company, to take about $2200 from the company to "temporarily help her cover her bills," as she has explained to you. You must report Alice's embezzlement.

T   71.   The mayor owns property next to one of the proposed sites for the city's new baseball stadium. The mayor has a conflict of interest and should not vote on the location of the stadium when the city council takes action on the site.

F   72.   Although you are not part of your company's engineering group, you have discovered a major flaw in the company's new paper-thin solar calculator. The calculator adds when the subtract button is pressed if there are more than 3 figures to the right of the decimal point. Since it is not your area, you should do and say nothing.

F   73.   With respect to #72, it is not necessary for the company to take any action to correct the problem or refund money for those who already own the new calculator.

T   74.   You are in marketing for one of the three U.S. auto manufacturers. You have just received a notice from your seat belt buckle supplier that the buckles shipped to you and used in the cars made between June 94 and September 94 are defective. The defect means that the buckles will come undone if pressure is placed on the belts at any speed over 10 miles per hour. You must encourage your firm to issue a recall.

T   75.   Alice is a secretary in your department. Alice is also a member of the American Guild of Organists. Alice has been placed in charge of the Guild's national convention. Each time you pass by Alice's desk or go to her to have some work done, you notice she is on the phone discussing or working on the convention. Alice's work on the convention during work hours is an ethical violation.

F   76. Your supervisor has had a calendar with pictures of naked women on the inside panel of his desk for several months. A secretary spotted the calendar and commented to your supervisor that it was not appropriate for an office. Your supervisor took down the calendar and has asked you to back him up if any complaints are filed. He has asked you to say that you never saw the calendar. It would not be unethical for you to do as your supervisor requests because he has removed the calendar.

T   77. A newspaper reporter is interviewing you about your experiences in working for a member of Congress. You have indicated you have information about his private life but will not share it. The reporter responds, "Tell me, just between you and me." You share the information and a quote from you on the private life of the member of Congress appears in the newspaper the next day. The reporter was unethical in violating a trust.

F   78. It would not be unethical for you to accept two employment offers in case one fell through.

F   79. It would not be unethical to continue interviewing for positions after you have already accepted employment with a particular firm.

F   80. Selling products banned from sale in the United States in other countries is not an ethical violation.

T   81. You work for a construction firm that is submitting a bid for the construction of a new company headquarters building for Smithco. A friend you have known since high school works in Smithco's capital budgeting area and has full knowledge of all the bids from all firms. It would be unethical for your friend to share that information with you before you submitted your bid.

T   82. With respect to #81, it would be unethical for you to hire your friend to get him to bring the information to your company.

T   83. Your unit has not been able to meet its sales goals for your quarter. Your assistant has suggested that you ship out enough goods to meet the quarterly goals by simply overshipping quantities on customer orders. When the goods are returned, you would simply take the returns in the next quarter after you have had more of an opportunity to meet goals. Your assistant's suggestion is a breach of ethics.

T   84. With respect to #83, suppose you learn that other divisions within the company have always engaged in this form of earnings shifting. The practice is still an ethical breach.

F   85. With respect to #83, a customer who agreed to help you with your shifting would not be engaged in unethical behavior.

F   86. Your college of business is sponsoring a case competition. All teams must watch the other teams compete. The order of presentation is by luck of a draw. The team that is the last to present left during one of the presentations, went to the computer room and redid its Powerpoint slides and restructured its presentation based on what other teams had presented. This team has done nothing wrong.

F   87. Ethical codes for companies cannot apply internationally.

F   88. Bribes to government officials are only unethical if the culture of a country does not believe they are unethical.

T   89. Intentional breach of a contract carries a legal remedy, but it is also unethical.

T   90. Conduct may comply with the law but still be unethical.

T   91. The failure to disclose material information in negotiations is an ethical breach.

T   92. Following positive law is not the full extent of ethics.

F   93. It is not your responsibility to report a co-worker who leaves the office early each day without taking time off.

F   94. Using things of minimal value that belong to your employer for personal reasons (such as paper, paper clips, pens) is not an ethical violation.

T   95. You should disclose to your employer if a relative of yours has submitted a bid for work with your company.

T   96. It is an ethical violation to disclose personnel information about your co-workers even to your family.

F   97. If you are fired from your job, you can use any information you gained while employed to help your next employer.

F   98. You need not disclose in your employment application those positions you held which will not result in good feedback about you if your supervisors there are contacted.

F   99. Violation of company rules is not considered an ethical violation.

T   100. Employee hotlines exist to help employees who feel they cannot communicate concerns through the lines of authority.

Multiple Choice

1. Which of the following phrases does <u>not</u> signal a potential ethical pitfall?

   a. "That's the way it's always been done."
   b. "If we don't do it, someone else will."
   c. "Your job is to be a team player, not ask questions."
   <u>d. **All of the above signal an ethical pitfall.**</u>

2. Which of the following is not an element of the Laura Nash's model for evaluating ethical dilemmas?

   <u>a. **Is it legal?**</u>
   b. How would I feel if I were on the other side of the fence?
   c. How will my actions be perceived?
   d. Could I discuss my decision with my boss, CEO, family, friends?

3. Under the Blanchard/Peale model, which of the following statements is correct?

   a. If it's legal, it's ethical.
   <u>b. **If it's illegal, it's unethical.**</u>
   c. If it's balanced, even if it is illegal, it is ethical.
   d. None of the above.

4. Which of the following statements is correct with respect to the correlation between ethical practices and earnings?

   a. There is no correlation between ethical practices and earnings.
   b. There is a short-term correlation between higher earnings and ethical practices.
   <u>c. **There is a long-term correlation between higher earnings and ethical practices.**</u>
   d. There is both a short-term and long-term correlation between lower earnings and ethical practices.

5. Ben Small, a sole practitioner, has just decided to form a law partnership with his lifetime friend, Harvey Steptoe. They agree to name the firm Steptoe and Small and to split all profits. Ben is also a director for a publicly-traded telecommunications firm, NewVector, Inc. Ben has just learned that Harvey is lead counsel is a lawsuit against NewVector. Ben continues to serve as a board member and participates in sensitive discussions about the lawsuit. Ben does not disclose that Steptoe is his partner. Ben's feeling is that he and Harvey are as honest as the day is long and neither would compromise their duties to NewVector and client, respectively.

    a. <u>Ben has a conflict of interest and must either resign as a director or leave the partnership.</u>
    b. The pledge of both Ben and Harvey is sufficient to cover the ethical issues on conflict.
    c. It is Harvey's obligation to take action, not Ben's.
    d. None of the above.

6. Randy White is the executive director of a non-profit preschool for special needs children. Part of Randy's responsibilities include fundraising for the preschool. Because of his experience and success in operating specialty pre-schools, Randy is sought after as a consultant at locations around the country to assist in the start-up and operation of such facilities. Randy does so quite frequently. Randy does not take vacation time for this work, and his consultant fees (which range from $750 - $1500 per day) are kept by him as personal income. Randy uses his secretary at the preschool to book his travel arrangements and prepare his consultant reports and bills for these outside engagements.

    a. Randy's activities are ethical so long as disclosed.
    b. <u>Randy is using the time and resources of his employer in an unethical manner.</u>
    c. Randy's activities are ethical whether disclosed or undisclosed.
    d. There is no conflict of interest in Randy's activities.

7. Beth Williams is an exercise physiologist who serves as an expert consultant for Women's Walkers, Inc., a shoe company specializing in manufacturing walking shoes for women. Dr. Williams is paid an annual consulting fee along with additional fees for drafting reports and making media and public appearances for the company. *Executive Woman*, a national magazine, has asked Dr. Williams to serve as one of three experts on a panel that will evaluate the full market range of women's walking shoes. Dr. Williams will be paid a consulting fee by *Executive Woman* as well.

    a. <u>Dr. Williams has a conflict of interest and should decline the *Executive Woman* offer.</u>
    b. Dr. Williams can participate in the *Executive Woman* panel so long as her affiliation with Women's Walkers is disclosed.
    c. Dr. Williams can participate in the *Executive Woman* panel if she waives her fee.
    d. Dr. Williams is an academic with no conflict of interest and can participate in the *Executive Woman* panel.

8. Which of the following is not a conflict of interest?

    a. A doctor's referral of a patient to an x-ray lab that he owns for a full work-up without disclosing his ownership interest.
    b. A purchasing agent's failure to disclose a 22% ownership interest in a supplier that would be chosen anyway.
    c. A bank officer's solicitation of a charitable contribution for a non-profit organization of which he is a member from a customer with a large line of credit up for renewal in 30 days.
    d. <u>All of the above are conflicts of interest.</u>

9. Jeff Sanders, head of finance for Components, Inc. has just interviewed Laura Dern, an employee from the finance department of InChip, Components' chief competitor. Laura has explained that she has been passed over one too many times for a promotion at InChip and is thus in the job market. As Laura is leaving she whispers to Jeff, "Look, I have no contract at InChip that obligates me in anyway. I can begin immediately. Further, I have been able to obtain copies of our newest computer chip designs. You'll have them before InChip even begins production."

    a. Jeff should hire Laura on the spot without any worries about ethical breaches since Laura is not under contract.
    b. Jeff's hiring of Laura may constitute an ethical breach, but would not constitute illegal conduct.
    c. <u>Jeff should not hire Laura, and must analyze the issue of whether to disclose Laura's conduct to InChip.</u>
    d. Jeff should not hire Laura and need not worry about Laura's conduct and its impact on InChip.

10. An application for graduate school admission at Arizona State University includes the following request for information:

Please list all institutions attended since graduation from high school.

Marie Davis, a returning student, is applying for admissions to the Masters in Architecture program. Marie attended the University of Arizona for one semester in 1976. Marie had a substance abuse problem and did not attend many of her classes. She left the University of Arizona before classes ended that semester. She did not take her final exams and earned 15 credit hours of "E" for that semester. After 8 years, the policy of the University of Arizona is to expunge the records of non-matriculating students. Marie's record was expunged in December 1994.

a. Marie need not disclose her attendance at the University of Arizona.
b. **Marie should disclose her attendance at the University of Arizona.**
c. Since Marie did not matriculate according to the University, she did not attend the University of Arizona.
d. None of the above.

11. A radar detector:

a. if purchased legally, is not an unethical device.
b. if used only in those states in which they are permitted is an ethical device.
c. is a legal and ethical tool for circumventing speed limits.
d. **None of the above.**

12. The sale of a product with a known defect or with knowledge of its potentially harmful impact on users:

a. is illegal.
b. is unethical.
c. exposes the manufacturer to strict and negligent product liability.
d. **Both b and c.**

13. Which of the following employment tests would be illegal?

a. **Pre-employment lie detector screening**
b. Drug testing for delivery van drivers
c. Handwriting analysis
d. All of the above are illegal.

14. Which of the following is an exception to the employment at will doctrine?

    a.   More than 10 years employment
    b.   A recent evaluation of performance that is generally favorable
    <u>c.</u>   <u>Whistle-blowing activity by the employee</u>
    d.   All of the above.

15. Which of the following would be both legal and ethical acts in an international operations?

    a.   Offering to pay a regulator for a favorable inspection report
    b.   Offering to pay a police officer for not writing a ticket
    c.   Offering to pay a government employee extra to speed up phone service connections
    <u>d.</u>   <u>None of the above.</u>

16. You work in the finance division of a NYSE company. You have just learned that your supervisor has been using information on quarterly returns, prior to the time they are made public, to trade in the company's stock. You:

    a.   need not do anything because the SEC will eventually uncover his activities.
    b.   need not do anything because only officers are prohibited from trading on inside information.
    c.   must confront the supervisor.
    <u>d.</u>   <u>must report the activity in some way.</u>

17. You have witnessed one of your co-workers engaged in behavior that constitutes sexual harassment of one of the department secretaries. The secretary has spoken with you about the behavior and her concerns. She has also said, "Let me handle it." It seems that she is not able to handle it because the behavior has continued. You should:

    a.   talk with her again.
    b.   report the behavior.
    c.   talk with your co-worker.
    <u>d.</u>   <u>Any of the above.</u>

18. You are a sales associate with a large department store chain. You have noticed that a fellow sales associate has been taking high-ticket items home with her. You have checked the sales records and she has not been paying for the items. You should:

    a.   ignore the conduct because it is not your business.
    b.   ignore the conduct because she will be caught eventually.
    <u>c.</u>   <u>confront her with your knowledge.</u>
    d.   report her conduct to the police.

19. A professor for one of your courses has assigned reading materials from various publications. He tells you that the materials are on reserve and that each student should go and copy the materials individually. He notes that for him to copy the materials for students and then sell them or distribute them would be a violation of copyright law. The professor's conduct:

    a. <u>is unethical and violates copyright law as well.</u>
    b. is something everyone does and is accepted behavior.
    c. does not really harm anyone.
    d. is acceptable in an academic setting.

20. You had quite a night last night of partying. Because of excessive drinking, you are unable to get to work today. When you call your supervisor you:

    a. should just say you have the flu.
    b. should just say you are sick.
    c. <u>should disclose the prior night's activity.</u>
    d. None of the above.

21. You are at lunch when you notice one of your firm's delivery drivers sitting at the bar in the restaurant. The driver is having shots of tequila over the course of the lunch hour. He then returns to his truck in the parking lot and resumes deliveries. You:

    a. should stop the driver.
    b. should report the driver.
    c. should take the keys to the truck.
    d. <u>should do all of the above.</u>

Short Answer/Essay

1. Dr. Phil Hayes has received an offer of full funding for his research on a new drug manufactured by Eli Mentin. The drug would be a competitor for Prozac without the questioned side-effects of possible violent behavior. Eli Mentin has, however, attached a condition to the funding. That condition is that Dr. Hayes may not publish his findings until Eli Mentin executives and its attorneys have had the opportunity to review them.

    List the ethical issues Dr. Hayes faces with this offer.

    SUGGESTED ANSWER:

    Dr. Hayes is creating a conflict of interest for himself and possible sacrificing the perceived independence of his work.

    Eli Mentin is compromising the integrity of Hayes' research and potentially withholding information about the product and its safety.

    Eli Mentin's approach is not one of candor and compromises the ethical values of honesty, fairness and safety.

2. Data Processing, Inc. is a service firm that performs word processing functions for law firms, corporations and government agencies. Their facilities consist of 120 office units with a word processor in each unit. Their facilities were formerly a shoe manufacturing plant, and all of the office units are located in one large room. Over the past 14 months, 7 of the 120 word processors have been diagnosed with breast cancer. In six of the seven cases diagnosed, there is no family history of breast cancer. Jane Quinn, the owner and CEO of data processing, has seen a cluster study that links employment as a word processor to a higher rate of breast cancer. Ms. Quinn does not disclose the study to her employees and takes no further action. Discuss the ethical issues.

    SUGGESTED ANSWER:

    Ms. Quinn has knowledge of a potential harm and is withholding information.

    Doing nothing does not solve the problem or minimize risk. At a minimum an investigation is warranted. Safety, fairness, honesty, balance and long-term survival of the employees and the firm are at issue.

3. National Medical Enterprises, Inc. (NME) is a multinational health care enterprise with 143 hospitals on four continents. NME was started by Richard K. Eamer, a tax attorney, in the 1960s. Eamer's development of NME was possible because of the implementation of the Medicare and Medicaid programs. He saw the programs as opportunities for a virtual guarantee of profits.

He began by acquiring six hospitals. He paid for these hospitals with promises to the physicians on staff of stock in his company. After the six hospitals were acquired, Eamer did a $25 million national stock offering and gave the physicians shares of stock in NME.

Eamer adopted a decentralized structure for the company. Hospital managers were simply given a financial goal and complete autonomy in their operations. Eamer traveled a great deal and used a company plane to get to NME-owned condominiums in London and Aspen. While Eamer was not a hands-on manager, he set very clear goals for NME managers. Achievement of established goals was rewarded. Under NME's pay structure, it was possible for managers to double their pay by meeting goals. Eamer was harsh when goals were not met. In meetings he would refer to those executives who had failed to meet established goals as "morons."

Eamer's managerial style paid off in the form of earnings growth of 15% per year through 1985. But, in 1986, earnings growth was off, down to 3%. When informed by his managers of the decline in earnings growth, Eamer announced that NME would now focus on operating and acquiring psychiatric, substance-abuse and rehabilitation hospitals. NME had 62 psychiatric hospitals in 1986, but by 1991, that number had grown to 86. Further, NME occupancy rates for its psychiatric hospitals were 25% higher than any of its competitors. NME maintained an occupancy rate of 84%.

The director of NME's Fair Oaks Hospital in New Jersey, testified at a Congressional hearing that NME executives circulated information on how to maximize insurance payments. Strategies included longer stays and additional tests.

NME's intake manual specified as a goal that one of every two people who came to the hospital for a psychological assessment would be hospitalized. Some adolescent patients were billed for as many as 10 therapy sessions per day. A memo from one senior officer to the various NME hospitals stated that the length of a patient's stay would be determined "not by the patient's individual medical needs, but on the insurance or payor mix."

A controller for an NME hospital in Texas testified that probation officers, clergymen and officers in corporation employee-assistance offices were offered up to $2,000 in referral or "bounty hunter fees" for referring patients to NME. The controller also testified that he was required to make "cold calls" on facilities for purposes of soliciting referrals. He indicated that one of his cold calls was to a nursery school.

Former executives of NME have provided information showing that physicians were given 50-year leases for $1 per year by NME and then referred their patients exclusively to NME hospitals. Many of these physician-occupied buildings operated at a loss. Both Medicare and Medicaid regulations prohibit payment of referrals fees to physicians.

By 1991, occupancy rates at NME psychiatric hospitals were down to 52%. Eamer began selling of the psychiatric hospitals and announced to shareholders than NME would return its focus to its core 35 general hospitals. In announcing the refocus to shareholder, Eamer noted, "Our focus is on the patient. We know everything else will follow."

a. What type of ethical culture existed at NME? Why?

b. What does NME need to change?

c. Do you think NME's strategies with respect to the psychiatric hospitals were ethical?

d. Evaluate the ethics of clergymen, counselors, and probation officers accepting referral fees.

SUGGESTED ANSWERS:

a. NME had a culture very much focused on earnings. Bonuses were tied to financial goals and achievement of occupancy rates. The quality of care and the needs of the patients were strictly sub-issues to the issue of earnings. It was also a culture that came as close to breaking the law as one can. The rent subsidies to physicians were arguable violations of the law. Further, the tolerance for less-than-goal performance was non-existent. In fact, managers were treated as "morons" for not achieving their goals. The focus in this company's culture was so much on earnings growth that the message came across as "earnings at any cost."

b. NME needs to change its "earnings at any cost" approach. Eamer may also need to be replaced as at least a symbol of the company's refocus. Its admissions policies, referral practices and discharge standards need to be set with a focus on the law and patients' needs as opposed to financial goals exclusively.

c. No, NME's standards could not survive the front page of the newspaper test. NME's approach was earnings at any cost. The approach was not balanced and, in some cases, bordered on illegality. NME treated hospitalization for psychiatric needs as a potential sales market to be tapped through sales calls and referrals.

d.   The members of the clergy, the counselors and the probation officers have conflicts of interest. They are to be acting in the best interests of their clients and by accepting referral fees they have an interest in seeing as many of them hospitalized as possible. Further, they would have an interest in their patients going to a certain hospital as opposed to a referral to the facility that would be best for the patient.

4.   Susan Wade is the president of the Illinois Hospice Organization (IHO). IHO is a state organization affiliated with a national non-profit organization, the National Hospice Organization. Both the state and national organizations have members from both for-profit and non-profits hospices. Susan Wade is the director of a non-profit hospice in Illinois. A Chicago newspaper has printed a story about hospices and what they do. Susan was interviewed extensively for the piece. In one quote in the article, Susan expressed her concerns about for-profit hospices. "It has become the sort of franchise of the decade. They're not all bad, but I think the original spirit of hospice is becoming very adulterated. There's one time in a person's life when he shouldn't be looked at as a number, as a piece of an actuarial problem. If your first and last priority is making money, it flies in the face of what hospice is all about. It's the end of the health-care chain. It's the place of last hope for patients. Dollars should not be the issue here."

A chief operating officer of a for-profit hospice has written to Susan complaining that her remarks are libelous and misinform the public about for-profit hospices.

a.   Does Ms. Wade have a conflict of interest?

b.   Is Ms. Wade properly executing her role as the president of the state organization?

SUGGESTED ANSWERS:

a.   Ms. Wade has a conflict of interest in the sense that as president of the state organization she represents all members and should not speak favorably of one type of member and unfavorably about another type. It is not, however, the traditional type of conflict of interest in which she benefits. Ms. Wade works for a non-profit institution and discussing the problem of for-profit will not change whether she has a job. The remarks could have an impact on how many

189

patients her hospice has, but because of the non-profit nature, there is no financial gain to her.

b. As an elected representative, Susan should represent all members and not divide the organization or question the motives of some members. Perhaps her issues that she raised for the newspaper stories could be topics of seminars and debates for the members. But she should not be in a position, because of her role as president, to use opportunities with the media to lessen the standing of some members of the organization.

5. James and Jennifer Stolpa and their five-month old son, Clayton, were stranded outdoors in a snowstorm for 8 days. They were rescued after James left Jennifer and Clayton in a cave and hiked 30 miles in subfreezing temperatures to get help.

During the time they were stranded, the Stolpas ate Doritos-brand corn chips that they had with them in their car. When they were rescued and taken to the Washoe Medical Center for treatment of severe frostbite, they were visited by boxing champ, George Foreman. Mr. Foreman is a spokesperson for Doritos. His visit to the Stolpas earned national press and television coverage that emphasized the Doritos consumption.

If you were an executive with Doritos, would you have sent Mr. Foreman to the hospital?

SUGGESTED ANSWER:

The issues here are that of privacy and propriety. The chip maker would be capitalizing on the injuries and suffering of a family with a fairly peripheral fact that they happened to have Doritos in the car. The family can consent to Mr. Foreman's appearance and the cameras rolling, but it is a fairly intense situation for them. The added sales from eating the same chips the stranded family did may not be as significant as the marketing folks may believe.

6. Henry Rauzi, the controller for Sunbeam, issued an offer to Linda Croce for an entry-level accounting position at Sunbeam at a salary of $34,000 per year. Ms. Croce accepted the offer and gave notice to her employer. When then-CEO of Sunbeam, Paul Kazarian, was informed of the offer, he demanded that Mr. Rauzi rescind it because Kazarian had not approved it prior to it being made. Mr. Rauzi called Ms. Croce at 10:00 P.M. three days before she was scheduled to being work and told her of Mr. Kazarian's action. Ms. Croce had no job and remained unemployed for several months while she searched for a new job.

Evaluate the legality and ethics of Sunbeam's officer's actions with respect to Ms. Croce.

SUGGESTED ANSWER:

Apart from the obvious legal difficulty that Ms. Croce had a contract because she had already accepted the offer, there is the ethical dilemma, even without such formality, of reneging on one's word. There was a meeting of the minds and Ms. Croce relied on the promise in quitting her other job. The fact that an internal error in reporting lines was made should not affect the extension of the offer to Ms. Croce. Ms. Croce had no way of knowing that there were limitations on Mr. Rauzi's authority. Certainly she had no way of knowing that he could not issue an offer. Sunbeam's actions with respect to Ms. Croce were unfair, unbalanced and unethical.

7. In 1991, James McElveen fell 30 feet from a waterfall and broke his back. He was employed by a small business and had no medical insurance. His lifetime friend, Benny Milligan, was with him when the fall occurred. Benny took James to the emergency room. Moved by his friend's severe injuries and pain and suffering and realizing that James did not have insurance, Benny switched IDs with James in the hospital emergency room. James required surgery to fuse his back to avoid what doctors said would have been certain paralysis. The cost of the surgery and hospitalization was $41,107.45. Neither James, employed as a mechanic, nor Benny, employed as a painter, could have paid for the surgery and follow-up care. Benny's employer's insurance paid for the surgery because the hospital took the information from Benny's ID found in James' pockets.

While Benny was contemplating telling his employer, someone notified the insurance company of the switch. Benny, James, and Benny's wife, Tammy Milligan were charged and convicted of mail fraud, wire fraud and conspiracy. Tammy, because of the Milligans' three young daughters, is serving her sentence through home confinement, Benny is serving 9 months and James is serving 7 months. All three were serve three years on probation and pay restitution.

Benny states, "I know what I did was wrong. But I look back on it, and I feel that I had to do it at the time. I don't feel like I'm a criminal in the sense of rapers, muggers and murderers." Benny said he did not understand that a hospital has an obligation to treat someone who is dying. Friends testified that as they were racing James to the hospital they told Benny that hospitals in the area had routinely refused to provide medical treatment.

Benny said he wanted to tell his employer, but he was afraid he would be fired and then be stuck with the bill. Tammy adds that the government is right to demand restitution but wrong to imprison them. James asked the judge if he could go to prison for all three of them, "I would be lost without my friendship with Benny. I probably would be dead."

a.   Benny and James committed an illegal act. Was it unethical?

b.   What punishment is appropriate in the case?

c.   If you were Benny's employer, what would you have done?

SUGGESTED ANSWERS:

a.   It was wrong and illegal to defraud the insurance company. It was taking the costs of the medical care, something that did not belong to James. Although the case evokes a great deal of sympathy, we all pay the cost when someone who is not insured enjoys payment by an insurer. The harm comes in the form of higher payments for all of us. Benny, James and Tammy all had to lie and sign sworn statements that were untrue in order for James' surgery to be covered under Benny' insurance. They committed their acts in the name of something very important, but it was wrong.

Benny defined the problem incorrectly: it was either switch IDs or have his friend suffer. In fact, there were alternatives, but Benny did not think them through. James would have received his emergency treatment at the first hospital. If the surgery was not something necessary to preserve his life, he would have been transferred to another hospital, such as a county hospital, where care is provided without regard to whether the individual has insurance. No one was asking questions about the care. They made assumptions and committed fraud to be certain there was medical care.

b.   While the fact that there was lying and fraud involved cannot be changed, the circumstances, as well as Benny's misunderstanding about the availability of medical care, should have some impact on the punishment for the three individuals. It is proper and fair to require reimbursement. However, Benny's lack of criminal intent should be considered as a factor in determining whether jail time is appropriate. Some other form of punishment such as restitution along with community service or the funding of a program of medical insurance coverage for those without would seem to suit the situation better than imprisonment.

c.   Benny's employer probably had little choice but to report the problem because the impact on its insurance costs was perhaps tremendous because of the extensive nature of the injury and

192

care. The employer could not be expected to lie to the insurer about Benny's presence at work after such major surgery. In short, the employer could not be asked to participate in the fraud. However, the employer could have served as a character witness if Benny was a good and stable employee. Further, the employer might have been more understanding about Benny's motivations. On the other hand, from the employer's perspective, it is difficult to send a strong message to employees about insurance fraud if Benny is retained.

8. Althea Caldwell is the director of Arizona's Department of Health Services (DHS). DHS is charged the administration of the state's behavioral health system and is responsible for contracting with private providers for millions of dollars of mental health care each year for eligible patients.

Ms. Caldwell accepted a $20,000 per year director position for a hospital group corporation. One of the hospitals in the group was one to which state contracts for mental health treatment had been awarded.

One month after accepting the position, Ms. Caldwell asked the state's attorney general for an opinion as to whether she had a conflict of interest.

Does Ms. Caldwell have a conflict of interest?

SUGGESTED ANSWER:

Ms. Caldwell has a classic textbook conflict of interest. You cannot be the state official responsible for awarding conflicts AND the director of a company that owns one of the facilities bidding for those contracts. The $20,000 is a quid pro quo -- a position awarded with compensation with the hope of gaining an edge in the state agency's award of contracts.

9. Stanford University medical researchers conducted a study on the correlation between the use of fertility drugs and ovarian cancer. Their study, published in the *American Journal of Epidemiology*, concludes that the use of the fertility drugs, Pergonal and Serophene, may increase the risk of ovarian cancer by three times. The lead author of the studies, Professor Alice Whittemore, stated, "Our finding in regard to fertility drugs is by no means certain. It is based on very small numbers and is really very tenuous."

FDA Commissioner David Kessler would like the infertility drug manufacturers to disclose the study findings and offer a warning on the drug packages. He notes, "Even though the epidemiology study is still preliminary, women have a right to know what is known. We're not looking to make more of this than there is."

If you were a manufacturer of one of the drugs, would you voluntarily disclose the study information?

SUGGESTED ANSWER:

Given the history of asbestos, the breast implants, the Dalkon shield and other products covered in the text, it is not difficult to spot a similar pattern here. Although the law may not require disclosure, the ethical tests of balance and "how would you want to be treated?" point manufacturers in the direction of disclosure. Full market information requires that buyers make choices based on full disclosure. Without the study information, making those decisions becomes one-sided. The drug firm has more information that is not available to their purchasers. Further, the history of the cases mentioned demonstrates that firms are always better off financially if they make the disclosure and allow the market to function than if they withhold the information and must later defend product liability suits. The disclosure should be made not only from an ethical perspective but also from a financial and litigation perspective.

10. Raymond Randall is an attorney with the Federal Trade Commission. A 19-year veteran with the agency, Mr. Randall was known as a good trial attorney. The FTC charged William Farley, the chairman of Fruit of the Loom, Inc., with violations of the reporting provisions of the Hart-Scott-Rodino Act, when he purchased shares of West Point-Pepperell Corporations prior to a Fruit of the Loom takeover bid. The Hart-Scott-Rodino Act requires investors to notify the government when their holdings in a firm pass $15 million.

The FTC sought a fine of $10,000 per day against Mr. Farley, for a total of $910,000. Mr. Farley did notify the FTC once Fruit of the Loom made its decision to acquire West Point-Pepperell. Randall was assigned the Farley case. The FTC took a position of refusing to disclose to Farley and his attorneys documents relating to the case. Mr. Randall felt that the documents pointed to weaknesses in the FTC case and supported Mr. Farley's point that he notified the FTC once the takeover position was announced. Mr. Randall leaked the documents to Mr. Farley's lawyer.

Mr. Farley's lawyers were concerned that they should not be in possession of government documents returned the documents and resigned from the case because they had seen the documents. Mr. Farley's new attorneys went to court demanding production of the documents. The documents were ordered produced by the court. When the FTC refused to produce them, the case against Mr. Farley was dismissed by a federal district judge.

a.   Did Mr. Randall do the right thing in disclosing the documents to Farley's attorneys?

b.   Did Mr. Farley's lawyers do the right thing in returning the documents to the FTC?

SUGGESTED ANSWERS:

a.   Mr. Randall was engaged in a form of civil disobedience. He knew that the documents were government property and enjoyed the protection of the courts, but he also felt that Mr. Farley was being prosecuted without sufficient evidence. Mr. Randall's principles, values and ethics took control of the situation and he sent the documents as a means of allowing Mr. Farley access to the information. It is important to note that Mr. Randall's action should have been his last choice. Did he go to those within the agency and attempt to resolve the problem? He should also consider his loyalty to his employer and his responsibilities as an attorney before taking the action that he did which was a form of civil disobedience.

b.   Mr. Farley's attorneys acted with the utmost integrity in returning the documents and resigning from the case. They made some difficult choices and not only followed the law but then resigned from the case because they had seen things they were not permitted to see. Their forthright actions probably helped Mr. Farley with the court and provided great credibility for Mr. Farley and his new attorneys as they successfully pursued the dismissal.

ADVANCED INSTRUCTIONAL MODULE
ETHICS

Prepared by Geoffrey P. Lantos
Stonehill College

Overview:

This lecture is concerned with constructing an ethical philosophy, i.e., with understanding the different moral principles, their strengths and weaknesses, and how they can be applied. We also look at difficulties that arise in business firms which hinder people from acting ethically as well as practical difficulties in using the moral philosophies. We conclude by focusing on analysis of ethical decision-making cases. We describe how ethics cases can be analyzed and provide some cases for classroom analysis.

The discussion on constructing an ethical philosophy deviates from most textbook discussions in that it begins at the most general level (often not discussed or only curtly treated): comparing two approaches to moral philosophy - relativism (the dominant approach) and absolutism. Four major sources of absolute standards are described, and the strengths and weaknesses of both relativism and absolutism are discussed.

Next, the six most frequently discussed perspectives for ethical decision making are reviewed. These break out into three major categories: intuitionism, teleological moral theories (utilitarianism, ethical egoism, Christian consequentialism) and deontological moral theories (rights, justice). A suggestion is then made on how to reconcile the different ethical philosophies.

Two areas of difficulty in being ethical in business are then discussed. The first is several pitfalls that hinder organizations from developing moral corporate cultures, and the second is a few practical difficulties that can prevent a decision maker from implementing her moral philosophy.

The lecture ends with Arthur Andersen & Co. SC's suggested approach for solving ethical dilemmas and cases. This approach is very similar in many respects to the methods used for solving traditional business school cases.

Then, several short, easily digested cases are presented along with suggested solutions patterned after the Arthur Anderson case study method. The module wraps up with an appendix which offers some helpful tips for the instructor in leading business ethics case discussions.

Learning Objectives: By the end of this module, the student will be able to:

1. Discuss the differences between a relativist and an absolutist philosophy towards resolving ethical dilemmas, the possible sources for absolute standards, and the advantages and disadvantages of using these two ethical perspectives.

2. Recognize and describe the use of six ethical theories: intuitionism, utilitarianism, ethical egoism, Christian consequentialism, theory of rights, and theory of justice.

3. Explain the advantages and disadvantages of each of the six ethical theories and how to reconcile these different perspectives.

4. Be alert to stumbling blocks which prevent many organizations from establishing moral corporate cultures.

5. Discuss the practical constraints which can hinder an individual from implementing an ethical course of action.

6. Solve a business ethics case using the Arthur Anderson Co, SC approach.

Outline:
I. Constructing an Ethical Philosophy
  A. Two Ethical Approaches/World views
    1. Moral relativism/situation ethics
    2. Moral absolutism/moral idealism
      a. Societal culture and norms
      b. Civil law
      c. Natural law
      d. Divine revelation
    3. Analysis of relativism
    4. Analysis of absolutism
  B. Six Ethical Theories
    1. Intuitionism
    2. Teleological moral theories
      a. Utilitarianism
      b. Ethical egoism
      c. Christian consequentialism
    3. Deontological moral theories
      a. Theory of rights
      b. Theory of justice
    4. Conclusion on ethical theories

II. Areas of Difficulty
  A. Obstacles That Detract From Building Moral Corporate Cultures
  B. Practical Difficulties In Using Moral Philosophies

III. Solving Ethics Cases

IV. Appendix: Methods for Leading Discussions of Ethics

Lecture Notes:

Constructing An Ethical Philosophy

How one goes about constructing an ethical philosophy is the domain of normative ethics, a prescriptive study that attempts to formulate and defend basic moral norms governing moral life. Normative ethics, studied by philosophers, aims at deciding what ought to be done, as opposed to what actually is done (descriptive approaches to ethics, studied by sociologists, anthropologists, and historians).

In order to render a moral judgment on the rightness or wrongness of the action taken in the ethical issue under consideration, one must apply moral standards.   Also known as moral philosophy or ethical philosophy, these are rules or principles people use for deciding if something is right or wrong.   People learn these principles through the process of socialization with family, friends, religious institutions, social groups (including the workplace), and formal education. Ultimately, ethical choices are based on the personal moral philosophy of the decision maker.

Moral standards include, first, moral values (absolute values, common morality, moral common sense), which embody a set of moral rules that most people agree on, at least in a given culture. In this section we will further explore the idea of absolute values, discuss their possible origins, and compare the absolutist approach to ethical decision making with the relativist perspective.

The second component of ethical standards is moral principles (moral perspectives, moral theories). These are particular approaches, some of which are relativistic and others of which can be used both absolutely and relatively to solve ethical dilemmas.   Moral principles present guidelines for business people as they resolve specific ethical issues.   However, there is no one universal moral philosophy applied by all persons in all situations; hence we refer to them as personal moral philosophies or perspectives. We will survey those moral perspectives which are most relevant to business decision making. We will discuss the advantages and disadvantages of each approach in order to aid the student in formulating his own personal moral philosophy, without recommending one approach over another. In fact, often it is helpful to analyze a given ethical scenario using several of these approaches.

All ethical philosophies deal with one or more of three characteristics of the behavior under question: the act itself (the means), the consequences of the act (ends), and the actor's motives or intentions.   Absolutism focuses on the act, teleological moral theories (utilitarianism, ethical egoism, Christian consequentialism) are concerned with the consequences, and intuitionism looks to the actor's motives. Deontological moral theories (theory of rights and theory of justice) can focus either on the act (deontologists) or general moral principles combined with the situation (rule deontologists).

Two Ethical Approaches/World views

There are two general approaches to ethics, i.e., two ethical philosophies or world views: moral relativism (a.k.a. ethical relativism, relative standards, situation ethics or speculative philosophy, based on a humanistic view) and moral absolutism (a.k.a. absolute standards or moral idealism, often based on religious and/or cultural values). Relativism tends to rely on moral theories whereas absolutism relies more on moral norms and values. Often these two approaches will give different answers to the all-important question: "Is it right?" Most observers seem to agree that whereas once absolutism was predominant, in the twentieth century (especially during the second half) relativism has come into vogue. For instance, Alan Bloom, in The Closing of the American Mind, observes that moral relativism dominates college campuses today. In the late twentieth century it seems that the notion of timeless, universal principles of right and wrong has gone the way of buggy whips and pocket watches: rather quaint, but out of date.

Moral relativism/situation ethics. Using relative standards, one denies that there are absolute answers to ethical quandaries which hold true in all instances; rather, the correctness of a particular action depends on the situation. Morals are relative to the individual (e.g., "You must do what's right for you"; "What's right for you might not be right for me"), the circumstances (e.g., premarital sex is fine if two people feel they are in love and the relationship will last; theft is justified if you cannot earn a living wage and meet your expenses; women go on "The Oprah Winfrey Show" and justify their acts of adultery with married men since the mens' wives aren't sexually satisfying them), and society (cultural relativism) (e.g., community standards used in obscenity trials; "the spirit of the age"). Relativists assume that right and wrong are just a matter of what a social group, or even an individual, approves or disapproves.

In other words, "There are absolutely no absolutes" and "The only thing that is absolute is that nothing is absolute." Ethics is autonomous (in Greek "self-law"; you are a law unto yourself; we make up the rules as we go along). Moral values are derived from human experience ("Experience is the best teacher"), i.e., the basis of ethical values lies in the minds of men. The approval of one's peers or classmates can be used to validate one's decision; the "new morality" becomes acceptable.

This is humanism, the idea that humanity can determine what is best for society by its vast knowledge and technological capability; it exalts man and disregards or disbelieves in God. Thus, we have heuristics such as "thou shalt not steal--ordinarily." There are all kinds of exceptions. This humanistic world view subscribes to Protagoras' assertion back around 400 B.C. that "man is the measure of all things." Unfortunately, humans are fallible (even fallen, according to biblical teaching).

Thus, the relativist observes the actions of members of some relevant group and attempts to determine the group consensus on a given action. For instance, the Generally Accepted

Accounting Principles gain their authoritative support from a political process in which interested bodies lobby the Financial Accounting Standards Board in support of their views on acceptable and unacceptable practices; the Principles change over time. Within many professions, such as accounting, law, and medicine, it was until around 1980 considered unethical to advertise. As competition became more intense and as consumers increasingly demanded their right to know, these professions decided that advertising is an acceptable practice after all and concluded that restrictions hindered free competition.

Relativistic rules are bound within a closed system; no appeal can be made to a principle or existence outside the system (e.g., God in an open system). Relativism is founded on the notion in Immanuel Kant's Critique of Pure Reason that we as humans are responsible for the nature and structure of the world. An extreme fringe of relativists goes so far as to say that there is no such thing as objective truth; each of us has our own version of reality. Skepticism denies that truth in moral matters can be known.

Such worldly wisdom leads to such maxims as: "Do unto others as you know they'd do unto you, given the chance," "Everyone does it, so that makes it okay" (vs. your mother's question, "If Billy jumped off the bridge, would you jump off the bridge?"), "As long as we all agree, then whatever we do is right," "Don't get mad, get even," "Go ahead and do it, just don't get caught" (or the variant "...just don't tell me about it"), "Might makes right," "It's a dog eat dog world," and "Whatever you do to me, I have a right to do to you" (vs. "Two wrongs don't make a right").

Moral absolutism/moral idealism. Absolutism is concerned with the morality of the act itself or means, not with the consequences or other circumstantial factors. It judges the act on the basis of moral ideals or absolute universal standards ("traditional values") which hold true over time, place, and person. These permanent, immutable, rules are to be followed regardless of the circumstances, i.e., there are certain behaviors that are plain right and wrong, good and evil, whether prince or pauper, mighty or meek. Moral law is as unchangeable as the law of gravity. There are timeless truths which have worked well in the past and which will work well in the future. Plato insisted that we cannot be good without a timeless idea of goodness. Ethics is meaningless unless based on a solid value system.

For instance, Kantian absolutes are considered "higher truths" (e.g., compassion, honesty, kindness, protection of the weak). These are known as virtues, i.e., elements of moral excellence and righteousness. Aristotle advocated absolutes, whereas Plato admitted we can't always be certain what is right. Aristotle and Plato considered the four cardinal virtues to be prudence (practical wisdom), justice, courage, and temperance.

As a simple business example, the Director of Research for the Beech-Nut Corporation told the Food and Drug Administration that Beech-Nut was selling a blend of synthetic ingredients labeled as 100 per cent apple juice after his superiors ignored his internal memos. When asked why he did this, he replied, "I thought apple juice should be made from apples."

(Note: at this juncture you might want to ask your students, "How many of you think it is possible to know for sure if an ethical value is true or false?" Few hands will rise. Then ask, "How many of you think it's wrong to torture someone for the heck of it?" All hands will rise.)

There are different degree of absolutism. At one extreme, some absolutists claim that moral ideals are rigid, everywhere and always the same. For instance, lying is always wrong, regardless of the situation. At the other extreme, some moral idealists believe that the most general principle of morality is absolute, but that as it is applied in various circumstances, certain lower-level norms may vary. For example, lying is generally wrong, but exceptions can be made to, for instance, protect a person's sensitivities ("little white lies"). A middle ground believes that moral principles and norms are everywhere and always the same, but that the norms have exceptions. For instance, it is wrong to lie, except where a lie will protect human life.

Moral idealism sometimes considers certain rights or duties and standards of justice to be universal (e.g., JFK's Consumer Bill of Rights). These forms of moral idealism will be discussed as a subset of deontological moral theories (rights and justice) below.

In any event, the question naturally arises, "Where do moral ideals come from?" There is a difference between believing in universal moral principles and holding that one knows with certainty where they come from. Such a person might search in several places to answer the questions, "Whose values are valid? What or who is the ultimate authority to judge what is and what is not ethical?" We now look at the major sources of moral absolutes.

Societal culture and norms. Culture refers to the set of values, ideas, and attitudes of a society that are transmitted from one generation to the next, where a society usually refers to a group sharing common institutions and culture. Culture serves as a socializing force that dictates what is morally right and wrong.

Cultural relativism is the idea that cultures vary widely, and morality is relative to a particular culture, society, or community. This concept is very important in today's global marketplace. Anthropologists and sociologists have documented the fact that people in differing cultures, as well as people within a given culture, disagree on what is morally right and wrong (e.g., bribery, sexism, racism). Transcultural relativism means that there are differences in what is considered moral between cultures. For example, the ancient Greeks believed that infanticide was morally permissible, whereas we do not. According to the nineteenth century doctrine of Manifest Destiny the U.S would convert the world to Christianity, capitalism, and democracy. It failed when anthropologists discovered diversity. Cartels are considered illegal and immoral in the U.S. but not in Europe. Intracultural relativism suggests that people within a given culture can disagree on what is morally acceptable. For instance, before the Civil War, many Southerners insisted that slavery was morally permissible while many Northerners did not. And, within the U.S. today, there is a heated debate on the morality of abortion. South Africa displays sharp cultural differences between the white majority and black minority.

Differences in cultural moral values are due primarily to two factors. First, is differing conditions. Thus, a country with many men but few women might consider polygamy acceptable. A second factor accounting for cultural differences is factual beliefs. Hence, a society that believes the volcano gods demand human sacrifice will consider that practice to be moral.

Note that cultural relativism is descriptive, whereas ethical relativism is prescriptive. Thus, cultural relativism says that being ethical is doing whatever society accepts. An implication is that it is impossible to make moral judgments about other cultures. Everything is equally valid; nothing is better than anything else and nothing is worse. We can't judge the morality of a particular culture, we can only try to understand it. According to this approach, Sweden sees abortion as right, and so for Sweden it is right, whereas Ireland sees abortion as wrong, and so for Ireland it is wrong.

However, there are several problems with looking to a given society's morals for constructing a value system. First, cultural diversity might not be fact, especially since cultural and social laws are rooted and grounded in religious traditions which are founded on common moral values. For instance, in every country murder is considered wrong since if it becomes commonplace, society could not survive. Lying is always considered verboten because otherwise there would be no secure social interaction. Fortunately, there is sufficient agreement among societies to permit business to be carried on internationally, although a host of unresolved differences exist. For instance, does American business have a right to impose its ethical standards on foreign firms doing business here? (Most would say yes.)

Second, if there is cultural diversity, diversity does not necessarily mean that both parties are right (despite the conventional wisdom). Some societies believe what is false. For instance, communist USSR (pre-1991) and the U.S. were often portrayed in the media as morally equivalent, even though communism is considered by many Americans as Godless and unnatural, hence evil. Nazi Germany's murder of some six million Jews, although sanctioned by the government, was not moral. The same could be said for the policies of Saddam Hussein's Iraq. If a society becomes overly permissive, does that mean that adultery and fornication are okay? Which country's value system are we going to use? The dilemma is highlighted by the continuing discussions of the Foreign Corrupt Practices Act. If bribing customers and government officials is an accepted business practice in a given country, why should a U.S. company doing business in that country be prohibited from this practice? Because it is wrong. The implication is that it's not always true that "When in Rome, do as the Romans do." This might be true concerning customs and folkways, but it's not always true regarding behaviors in the moral arena. We cannot always rely on society's decisions about right and wrong. Society makes its decisions in its own wisdom and for the welfare of its own members. The idea that moral values vary over time and place contradicts the notion of fixed absolute standards.

Third, moral pluralism often exists. American society is diverse, a combination of various cultures and traditions. It is characterized by diversity, with many ethnic and racial groups. Not only is it culturally pluralistic, to some extent it is morally pluralistic.

Nonetheless, if a society is to properly function, it must have a large core of commonly held values and norms which form the common morality of a society. Respect for human beings, respect for truth, respect for others' property, and other elements of moral common sense are all commonplaces in America, making business possible. In areas of serious disagreements (e.g., capital punishment, abortion) differences must be settled by public debate and perhaps by legislation. But it is not true that when faced with moral claims against me or my business practices, I can dismiss them as simply being your opinions but not mine. Basic moral claims are universal.

Civil law. Laws are society's values and standards that are enforceable in the courts. Laws and regulations are created by government to establish minimum standards for ethical behavior. Laws regulating business conduct are passed because society does not always trust business to do what's right, especially in four major areas. First, are laws regulating competition, i.e., practices that reduce or restrict competition among businesses. For instance, the Sherman Antitrust Act of 1890 prohibits monopolies, and the Robinson-Patman Act of 1936 restricts price discrimination against retailers and wholesalers. Second, are laws protecting consumers, i.e., that require businesses to provide accurate information about goods and services and that they follow safety standards. For example, the Consumer Product Safety Act of 1972 created the Consumer product safety Commission to establish safety standards and regulations for consumer products, and the Magnusson-Moss Warranty Act of 1975 created standards for consumer product warranties. Third, there exist laws protecting the environment. Thus, the Clean Air Act of 1970 established air quality standards, and the Toxic Substances control Act of 1976 requires testing and restricts use of certain chemical substances. Fourth, are laws promoting equity and safety in the workplace. An example of an equity law is title VII of the Civil Rights Act of 1964, as amended, which prohibits discrimination in employment on the basis of race, color, sex, national origin, or religion. An example of a safety law is the Occupational Safety and Health Act of 1970, which is designed to assure healthful and safe working conditions for all employees.

The term corporate compliance suggests that a firm will be law abiding. However, a common fallacy is that, "If it's legal, then it's moral." An easy way to get off the hook is to let the lawyers decide what is ethical. The legalist believes that the law, and hence morality, is whatever the king says it is. However, moral standards aren't established or changed by the pronouncements of particular authoritative bodies. Sometimes the boundary between right and wrong is the same as that between legal and illegal, but sometimes it is not.

First, some laws simply are not relevant to morality, e.g., procedural issues such as how to evaluate a real estate contract.

A second problem with the law as an ethical guidepost is that it is often of limited scope. Some moral situations are not covered by the law since legislators can't anticipate every problem area.

Third, some laws are immoral or unjust because they are the product of fallible humans. It is not excusable to dismiss an action by saying, "There isn't a law against it." St. Thomas Acquinas said, "An evil law is no law," Montesqieu believed that, "We should never create by law what we can accomplish by morality," and Oliver Twist's Mr. Bumble quipped, "The law is an ass, an idiot." Controversial laws include those related to abortion, capital punishment, legalized prostitution and gambling, and speed limits which slow us down to 55 mph on highways that were meant to be driven at 70 mph. George Washington committed an act of high treason against the British crown and yet was considered a morally great leader for what he did. As another possible example, you can ask your students if there should be laws to regulate the behavior of consenting adults (e.g., a prostitute and her client; two friends wagering a bet on a football game). It's legal to lay people off, but is it always ethical? A final problem here is that an action might be illegal but morally compelling. Ethics should judge the law, not vice versa.

Fourth, the law merely provides a floor or moral minimum for business conduct. The law is reactive, telling us what ought not to be done, rather than proactive, telling us what ought to be done (i.e., to exercise various virtues). It simply draws the line, telling us what the majority (or at least a majority of the ruling body) feels is unacceptable conduct. The law can then degenerate into the question, "What can we get away with?" For instance, in the late 1980's the vague insider trading laws were pushed to their limits. In the savings and loan scandals, where one drew the line between constituent service and peddling influence wasn't clear. As the old saw goes, "It's difficult to legislate morality," at least regarding the gray areas (vs. laws against rape, murder, theft, and other areas of common morality which we can all agree on). Laws don't make people moral. Too often people follow the letter of the law but not the spirit of the law. For instance, ask your students, "If a brilliant tax expert could legally cut your taxes by 90 per cent through some legal loophole while completely violating the spirit of the tax code, would you let her do it?" If enough people decide to break the law, of course, the law breaks down. Legislation is often viewed as coercive or restrictive. Business laws usually provide less stringent standards than trade or professional association rules; if they did not then the latter would merely be redundant or unnecessary. Industries and professional associations generally mandate less strict standards than do individual firms; after all, who would want to work for an organization which does not even adhere to standards in its own industry?

Fifth, laws can provide a confusing basis for morality since they are sometimes inconsistent, both over time (e.g. abortion laws) and place (e.g. certain state laws). For instance, product liability laws prior to the 1960's restricted a manufacturer's liability to persons injured using the manufacturer's product because of his negligence or fault. Today's liability laws are based on tort law as a means of social welfare to ensure that victims are compensated for their injuries regardless of whether the party forced to bear financial responsibility for the damage was at fault; the lawyers go after the "deep pockets," i.e., those parties even remotely involved in a transaction, which are best able to pay. Thus, laws can help people determine what is deemed right or wrong by society at a given point in time, but what is legally right today might be vie as unethical tomorrow, and vice versa. Even at one particular time, different courts, or different state legislatures, may take different views. For example, the courts differ on what constitutes a "substantial" reduction of competition.

And, laws differ over places, especially in the international arena. For instance, many Koreans believe that the ideas of one person should benefit all. Thus, the Korean government rarely prosecutes infringements of intellectual property rights (copyrights, trademarks, patents), whereas in the U.S. unauthorized use of these is considered illegal and unethical. As another example, certain infant formula failed to meet U.S. legal safety standards, but local laws in third world countries permitted it. Should it have been sold?

In general, sociological law has no fixed basis. It is arbitrarily determined by what a group of people says is good for society at the time. Thus, even Jesus broke the manmade rules about working on the Sabbath because he believed they contradicted a Higher Law. The major problem with using man-made rules as absolute yardsticks is that they are the product of fallible humans. The standards used are, as we have just seen, in fact relative, not absolute.

Natural law. The concept of nature refers to the proper ordering of the universe. Natural law is a body of laws that derives from nature (and God, if you believe that He is the creator of nature), and the laws are believed to be binding upon human activity apart from or in conjunction with laws established by human authority. Based on the thinking of Aristotle, St. Thomas Aquinas, and John Locke, the idea is that an act is morally wrong if it is incompatible with universal human nature. Thus, human nature provides the key how people ought to live their lives. This rules out acts which cause potential physical harm, such as drunkenness (leads to sickness, vile behavior, etc.) and "casual sex" (STD's are not a casual thing).

The political philosophy of the Greeks (and later of Aquinas) said that natural law can be discovered by reason, i.e., by observing the operations of nature and society and drawing logical deductions. One relevant application to business ethics is the concept of natural rights, i.e., certain basic rights that are believed to be self-evident; they stem from the nature of things. Such rights are based on the idea that there is an ideal standard of justice fixed by nature that is binding on all persons. This standard takes precedence over the particular laws and standards created by social convention, providing absolute standards against which the laws and policies of particular governments and institutions are to be measured.

Thus, natural rights are considered to be fundamental rights irrespective of merit, due to be respected because they are rooted in a knowledge of certain universal regularities in nature. They are not to be usurped by the sovereign power of kings (i.e., government).

For instance, the right to life is based on our status as rational beings, worthy of respect, and ends-in-ourselves. The natural right to property was discussed by the British philosopher John

Locke. In the Declaration of Independence the American Founding Fathers wrote about the natural rights of life, liberty, and pursuit of happiness in the context of the "laws of nature" and of "nature's God." Thus, their view of natural rights wasn't man-centered, it was God-centered. The idea was that all humans are endowed by God with certain rights and characteristics that no law or government can abridge, and that these natural rights exist apart from what laws or constitutions can give people.

Today it is more fashionable to speak of human rights than of natural rights It is supposed that human beings have essential properties of human nature that determines their fundamental rights that are to be respected by other people and social institutions. We shall look at these later when we discuss rights theory.

Divine revelation. Divine revelation (divine command theory) is the idea that God has revealed Himself, not only in nature, but also in other supernatural ways, e.g., through inspired writings in holy books (The Bible, Koran, etc.), prophets, etc. Theology, the study of the nature of God and religious truth, says that morality can be based on a "higher law," i.e., the revealed laws of our Creator. This higher law comes not from the minds of men, but from the word of God, i.e., divine revelation is God-centered, not man-centered. There is a standard above our own ideas of right and wrong (i.e., a transcendent standard). This approach postulates the universe to be an open system (vs. a self-contained universe) where morality is revealed from outside the human mind (say, of philosophers) and experience, i.e., it is given to us by our Maker. God is the moral Ruler of the universe. Ethics is founded not on situation ethics, but on what God reveals on the situation. Our duty is to obey God and His revealed will.

Most religions claim to provide an absolute set of moral guidelines and advocate living an ethical life. In the U.S., most believers rely on the Judeo-Christian value system derived from the teachings of the Bible (Orthodox Jews strictly adhering to the mandates of the Old Testament and Orthodox Christians adhering to the dictums of the New Testament, which claims that God has added to His self-revelation in Jesus Christ, as well as the Old Testament teachings which haven't been superseded by the New Testament). In other words, the answer to how we know there are moral values is found in the line from the simple children's hymn, "Jesus Loves Me," "For the Bible tells me so."

Traditionally in American culture it was felt by the majority that the Bible's moral revelation provides fixed permanent guidelines which humans can choose to accept or reject; these values provided a moral consensus or common morality.. The founding fathers believed in the Almighty and in the role of Divine guidance in human affairs. The Bible was considered to be a handbook of values, the best textbook ever penned on how to effectively and wisely live life. The basic truths of Western civilization were explicitly spelled out in the Old testament (e.g., the Ten Commandments) and the New Testament (e.g., the Sermon on the Mount) and implicitly in our great literature (e.g., A Christmas Carol teaches kindness and compassion, The Little Engine Who Could instructs on persistence in the face of adversity, and The Emperor's New Clothes warns of the danger of unreasoning conformity). There was a gradual turning away from this thinking in Western civilization in the seventeenth century with the advent of rationalism and the consequent secularization of culture.

However, there is now some evidence that in light of what many people see as a moral meltdown in society, they are either turning back to traditional religion or toward "New Age" spiritual beliefs, such as reincarnation. Most Americans still find strength and comfort in tradition and find that religion gives them "peace of mind" and "spiritual well-being." Bible-believing Christians believe that human nature is corrupt, and that when people lose something bigger than themselves to guide their behavior, society has no restraints to keep evil at bay. Some business executives are turning to prayer in seeking personal revelation and a form of guidance.

Not to be denied is that disagreements will ensue if morality is solely determined by theology or faith. If faith and reason overlap this is not problematic. For instance, the Golden Rule is perfectly consistent with Kant's categorical imperative (discussed below). However, if ethics is based purely on personal faith and individual interpretations of revelation, not reason, arguments can ensue. One person says, "God says do X" and another says, "God says do Y." The dispute is not reconcilable. Also, not all people grow up with access to religious training, but non religious people can nonetheless be ethical. And, within a given religious tradition people sometimes disagree on interpretation of the sacred writings. In any case, it cannot be denied that there is a body of moral values common to all religious traditions (common morality: don't lie, cheat, steal, etc.). Most conflicting truths among the various world's religions lie in the area of otherworldly concerns, such as the nature of God and the means of salvation (e.g., grace vs. works). Nevertheless, our common religious culture in the U. S. provides for us a basis of moral consensus which can be applied to modern-day circumstances. For instance, Exodus 23:8 speaks of the evil of bribery. Following biblical commandments, one would not permit misleading advertising ("Thou shalt not lie") nor corporate espionage ("Thou shalt not steal"). We learn from Scripture of Joseph's forgiveness of his brothers, David's cleverness and courage in facing Goliath, and the good Samaritan's kindness toward a stranger. In Dostoyovsky,s novel, The Brothers Karamazov, three brothers debate the source of evil in the world. Finally, one brother cries out, "If there is no God, then everything is permitted." Sin becomes whatever makes us feel uncomfortable. Being good is replaced by feeling good. We become a law unto ourselves. Who is to say for sure that Hitler was wrong in murdering six million Jews?

Other possible sources of absolute values include parental standards (often the first thing students will mention when you ask them where absolute values can come from), the educational system, and the workplace. However, these are all manmade sources and can be (and usually are) relativistic (changing) in nature.

<u>Analysis of relativism.</u> Relativism has some advantages to recommend it. It does presumably provide pragmatic, expedient solutions to moral problems, not idealistic, unworkable platitudes. Whatever works and gets the job done is acceptable. Convictions are not needed. Relativism leads to statements such as, "bribes are the only way to do business abroad." It works for

politicians who wish to perpetuate their incumbency sticking a wet finger in the wind and making decisions on the basis of public opinion polls. "Safe sex" is safer than casual, unprotected sex, but is it moral?

Another plus for relativism is its flexibility and ability to adapt to changing circumstances. After all, if you lived in the former USSR would you not lie if the KGB knocked on your door at midnight asking where your son was? And, in business the only constant is change. If it's best for our company or our situation, then all is well. This appeals to managers who wish to remain "state of the art" and move with the times. Morality becomes a moving target.

Also, this approach is considered "nonjudgmental," or tolerant. In our society, scorn is heaped upon those who are judgmental or intolerant; it is considered best to be broadminded or open-minded. However, where you draw the line on what you do or do not tolerate is not always clear. To say, "I'll tolerate what you believe if you'll tolerate what I believe is not logical if we disagree.

Situation ethics has some serious shortcomings. It can lead to inconsistencies since analysis is done on a case by case basis. Thus, it can result in perceptions of decisions being unfair or arbitrary. For instance, if a professor grades on a curve, the grade that a student receives is a function of that great academic lottery known as registration. She will do better in a less smart section of the course than in a smarter one. Grading standards become inconsistent from section to section and semester to semester in a given course.

Additionally, relativism often means no consensus; seldom will there be agreement among all concerned parties that you have made a morally correct decision (except in obvious cases of common morality issues). Because the different ethical perspectives (which we'll look at next) sometimes support different alternatives, the result can be moral anarchy. The absence of agreement or consensus establishes the absence of truth. You think puffery in advertising is okay; I do not. Who is to say which of us is correct? It is my opinion against yours. "You've got your morality, I've got mine. Where's the problem?" It's simply a matter of individual (or group or societal) preference. Being good has been replaced by feeling good. Wrongdoing is whatever makes you feel uncomfortable. The result could be a moral meltdown in society since almost anything goes.

Even if there is consensus, as determined by nose counting in which the Gallup Poll tells us what is moral, polls can be used to create public opinion rather than measure it; they become self-fulfilling prophecies. At best, morality is reduced to a show-of hands in which the majority, plurality, or those in positions of power determine what is right or wrong. However, just because something is average does not mean that it is normal. Average is the way most people are; normal is the way that people should be. (Lions ought to have manes. If a plague hits, maneless lions will be average, but they are not normal.)

The result when morals are in perpetual motion is uncertainty ("What's right?   Got Me."). Standards built on the shifting sands of personal subjectivity are no standards at all; relativistic principles are as fixed as water. We end up drifting in the shifting tides; without firm anchors our values are merely blowing in the wind without a moral rudder, and it is hard to steer clear of troubled waters. This makes us feel insecure in the correctness of our decisions since we have no anchors for those decisions.   Teaching in a vacuum of values teaches that no values are right. Psychologically, the notions that there are many kinds of ultimate reality, that truth is relative, and that no one possesses the whole truth are confusing. They cause a sense that life is meaningless, since meaning can only be built on certainties and convictions. In the business world, often the rules of the game change with the changing of the guard, as management turns over and a "new broom sweeps clean." Employees end up in a state of confusion and anxiety (codes of ethics and other techniques for institutionalizing ethics can help overcome this problem).

Finally, relativism is criticized as being morally impotent and corrupt. Clever formulas take the place of good old-fashioned morality. Due to our inherently corrupt nature, immorality will prevail by default. Relativism is considered by some to be the "yeah, but," "it depends" school of thought. "Doesn't that seem improper?" "Yeah, but, hey, this is 1993. Get with it, man," or "yeah, but my situation is different." These are often just rationalizations.

Analysis of absolutism. Absolutism offers much more certainty than relativism. It gives the most definitive answers to moral questions.   There are truths with a capital T which can be implemented with consistency over time and place (Yet relativists, like Pontius Pilate, rhetorically ask, "What is truth?" They don't think it can be answered). Things tend to be more black and white than murky gray. At least among absolutists there can be consensus.

Another advantage of absolutes lies in their simplicity. We don't need fancy jargon, esoteric theories, complex formulae, and the like. Any five-year-old can grasp the basic notions of honesty, kindness and compassion, generosity, forgiveness, individual responsibility, and other ethical norms. Also, it is easier to judge someone's actions than their motives, net gain to society, and other relativistic yardsticks we will be examining.

Furthermore, moral absolutes have been time tested and have proven to consistently work. History teaches that societies crumble when they jettison traditional values (e.g., ancient Greece and Rome, ancient Israel time and again, and perhaps the USA today).

Additionally, absolutes tend to be impartial and thus just. Everyone's behavior, whether prince or pauper, is judged by the same standards; in fact, discrimination is a violation of absolute norms.

Finally, moral idealism is not idealistic--it is rational (the name is "moral idealism," not "moral idealistic"). By its nature truth is absolute. When we arrive at truth we assume a conformity between mind and reality.

However, there are some perceived and real problems with an absolute approach to ethics. Perhaps the greatest difficulty is the fact that gray areas still abound; reasonable people can differ on how to interpret a given principle and at what point a person trips over the ethical line.

Thus, some would argue that what absolutes command is blind, unthinking adherence "Just following orders"). However, believing in moral absolutes isn't as simplistic as some believe; one still needs to make moral judgments. The trick is properly putting the principles into practice. For instance, if you believe in being "fair and just" in treating your suppliers and dealers, you must still interpret whether certain behaviors in given situations are "fair and just." Or, what, exactly, is "bad taste"? Even fundamentalist Christians disagree on the morality of such issues as dancing, playing card games, drinking alcoholic beverages, listening to rock music, attending R (or even PG)-rated movies, and the like, because while the Bible provides general guiding principles, it does not, for the most part, provide detailed standards of conduct. Should beer and wine be advertised to adults, so long as the pitch is moderation and drinking is not glamorized? Should we go shopping on Sunday, given that we are to "observe the Sabbath day, to keep it holy"? When faced with such less than clear-cut issues, the wise aphorism probably is "When in doubt, don't."

Another objection to absolutes is that they are perceived as being too rigid and inflexible. They do not adapt to nor bend for extenuating circumstances. Isn't it okay for the destitute widow to steal in order to provide food for her children? Admittedly implementation must still be done on a case by case basis.

Closely related is the charge that holding only to traditional values is "narrow-minded"; we need to "loosen up." The question is: how broad should broadminded people be? Where do you draw the ethical line?

Others do not like the fact that absolutes are intolerant. However, says the absolutist, what they do not put up with is wrongdoing, i.e. what they aren't tolerating are not just opinions but violations of true standards. A proper level of tolerance is a virtue, but one must draw the ethical line somewhere. For instance, the great faiths of the world pretty much expect the same virtues in their followers. Far from being narrow or intolerant, their moral values reflect the consensus of humanity about what makes for a good life and a good society.

People say that to rely on absolutes is to be judgmental. However, the judgment is based on a person's actions, not on what is thought to be in the heart. Every honorable individual has a responsibility to speak out against evil, to render moral judgmentsto say that this is right and that is wrong and that those who transgress are wrongdoers. The critics would subscribe to the ethics of noninvolvement: "I don't want to force my views on others; therefore I won't get involved." This is the person who would have said, "I do not believe it is right to murder innocent Jews, but I do not wish to impose my views on others; therefore I will remain silent." This is the politician who subscribes to the "personally opposed" view of morality: "I'm personally opposed to (such and such an action or policy), but who am I to impose my opinion on others?" Yet, you steal their wallet and they will find it absolutely wrong.

Then there is the argument that traditional values are obsolete or "Neanderthal" They belong back in the stone age; they are out of tune with the times; traditionalists are trying to "turn the clock back" on what relativists call "progress." As an extreme example, Nietze declared that God is dead and therefore religion cannot be used to determine values. Yet, some things in life are not to be manipulated or adjusted. This is understood in mathematics, science, and other intellectual disciplines, yet it is often denied regarding standards for human behavior. Common values live because they are invaluable.

Another perceived problem is that to teach absolutes is to indoctrinate. But, the dictionary defines a doctrine as something which is taught; hence we cannot teach without imparting doctrines.

Admittedly, to abide by moral ideals demands integrity--having the courage of one's convictions. It takes intestinal fortitude for a person to stand up for what they believe in the face of hostility and opposition. Biblical prophets such as Jeremiah, Ezekiel, et. al. were persecuted for speaking out against immorality. The unbelievers killed the messengers instead of dealing with the bad news. Usually, of course, it is not that bad; while there are some persons who ridicule a person with ideals and standards, most people admire persons who do what they believe is right and do not fear to speak out, rather than merely going along to get along. Integrity is sorely needed today when looking good, showing up well, and receiving favorable press coverage dominate. Integrity involves sacrifice, struggle, and perhaps non advantageous (in the short-run) decision making. For instance, when a conflict develops between an employee's ethics and his company's values, he basically has three choices. He can choose loyalty, ignoring his own values and staying with the company. He can vote with his feet, exiting with his values intact. Or, he can raise he voice, either to complain or dissent against what he believes is wrongdoing -- and that requires integrity. Economic security is not worth the psychological torment that normally follows a wrong choice.

To believe in absolutes is said to be arrogant: "How can you know for sure?" asks the relativist. Admittedly, answers will vary, depending upon which of the sources we examined you turn to for your value system.

Thus, a final and probably the most important sticking point with absolutes is disagreement on the source of the standards. Who is to judge what is ethical and what is not? Which religion? Which law? Which society's norms? Who is the ultimate authority? (Students should be challenged to think through what their world view is and the source of authority for the moral principles they hold.)

Five Ethical Theories

Work in the field of normative ethics in this century has evolved from three basic kinds of moral theories. Each approach uses different kinds of criteria to evaluate the ethics of human behavior, and hence the different perspectives often provide entirely different conclusions on what ought to be done. They are utilitarian theory, the theory of rights, and the theory of justice or fairness. We will also discuss the more simplistic approaches of intuitionism, ethical egoism, and Christian consequentialism.

By and large these approaches are all relativistic in nature (except when rights and justice approaches adhere to absolute standards of rights and justice). They are more abstract and don't yield as indisputable results as absolutism. Utilitarianism, egoism, and Christian consequentialism all use teleological frameworks, i.e., they look at the consequences of a particular act. Rights and justice theories use deontological frameworks, i.e., they focus on duties to respect rights and promote justice.

Intuitionism. The intuitionist judges the actor's motives or intentions. The answer to whether the behavior is ethical is relative to the individual. Thus, this approach is also known as naive relativism, which is the idea that all human beings are themselves the standard by which their actions should be judged. The decision is correct if the individual's conscience tells him that it is right. As Jiminy Cricket told Pinnocio, "Let your conscience be your guide." If the person can "feel in her bones" and knows in her "heart of hearts" that it is proper, then for her it is. As long she feels that her motives are good (i.e., she is "sincere"), she does not intend to harm anyone, and she feels comfortable doing it ("If it feels good, do it") then all is well. It is the "what's right for me" value system. The only authority is the self, i.e., your common sense. What appears right to you is, indeed, right. "I'm okay, you're okay."

This method has several things going for it. First, it is easy to justify ("I made a good faith effort"). Second, it is simple to implement; no hard thinking or heavy lifting are required. Hence, by default it is probably the most widely-used approach to ethics. Third, it is often experience-based, and as the old saw says, "Experience is the best teacher." The well-seasoned manager knows best.

Fourth, for independent types, there is no authority to answer to but yourself. Fifth, presumably an intuitive approach allows one to sleep at night. It is guilt-free; one fells good about themselves if they can say "I wrestled with my conscience, and my conscience won." No cognitive dissonance creeps in.

But, there are some things going against intuitionism too. A person can be well-meaning but misguided, sincere but sincerely wrong. There is a lot to truth to the old adage, "The road to hell is paved with good intentions." "There is a way that seems right to a man, but its end is the way of death." says a biblical proverb. Frequently, feelings deviate from what is ethical. There is no objective guideline.

This approach is the least likely to yield consensus. Whose intuition can we trust? Ours? Certainly. Our co-workers'? Maybe. Our boss's? Possibly. At the extreme, each person becomes a law unto themselves. And yet, humans are imperfect (an understatement). The great Russian author Aleksandar Solzhenitsyn said that if people believe all that matters is what feels right, they have no means to disarm the evil within them and do good.

Also, a person's feelings can be changing and contradictory. Think of a youngster faced with the temptations of adolescence, a frustrated couple considering divorce, or a businessperson struggling with a difficult decision. How do they know which impulse is right? Feelings can go astray. Did you ever get the impulse to bump off a lousy driver who cut you off?

This is a shortsighted perspective; it does not incorporate others' views. Yet, another proverb says, "In many counselors there is wisdom.

Also, in another sense, it is difficult to justify intuitive decisions. Especially in business, scientific, analytical decision making is preferred to relying on slippery, squishy feelings. At best, decisions are made on a rational basis and then rationalized after the fact.

Finally, there is the delicate issue of judging another person's motives. Since we can't read minds, this is difficult to do. And actually, we are not permitted to, for each person knows best (a logical contradiction if we disagree).

<u>Teleological moral theories.</u> Theology (from the Greek word "telos" which means "end" or "result") refers to moral theories which consider an act morally right if it produces desirable end results or consequences, be it pleasure, fame, fortune, career growth, or whatever. The following moral theories are also referred to as consequentialism.

<u>Utilitarianism.</u> The utilitarian model is a direct descendent of Adam Smith's work and was more precisely formulated by Jeremy Bentham and John Stuart Mill in the eighteenth century. It has an economic basis and is therefore widely accepted in business (research shows that it is the most widely used ethical perspective in business). Adam Smith believed that when each individual pursues their own self-interest, the invisible hand will assure that the good of the whole society is met. The focus was on aggregate economic welfare: the market works by itself to ascertain that individual needs are satisfied, according to classical economic theory. Corporations are accountable to the marketplace where consumers are deemed sovereign and government policy should be laissez faire. Perfect competition leads to use of resources and prices which enable consumers to maximize the utility (satisfaction) per dollar spent.

In its modern formulation, utilitarianism looks at the societal (not just economic) consequences or end results of an act to determine its moral worth; "the proof is in the pudding." The underlying idea is to act so as to produce the greatest good for the greatest number (rather than just the good of the individual or of the firm). If the consequences of an action result in a net increase in society's well being or welfare (or at least not a decrease), then that act is considered to be morally right. Thus, two types of acts are considered unethical: (1) those that do not produce the greatest good for the greatest number and (2) those that represent inefficient means to accomplish such ends (i.e. one should consume as few inputs as possible and minimize external or social costs (externalities) of organizational activities on stakeholders.)

Restated, the goal is to increase benefits and decrease harms for all stakeholders. Thus, an action is morally appropriate if it maximizes net benefits and minimizes overall harms for all stakeholders, i.e., if it maximizes the societal good. For instance, at the systemic level, squandering of societal resources would be considered bad, since it is an inefficient means. Capitalism is often considered ethical since it tends to produce the greatest good for the greatest number. Monopolies or large conglomerates might be most efficient, resulting in an optimal allocation of society's resources. If a company is polluting the air or water, it should invest in pollution control devices to the point where its costs equal the benefits society derives from pollution control (it internalizes the externalities, i.e., social costs). Job discrimination against minorities and women is wrong because society's productivity is optimal only if jobs, promotions, and pay raises are awarded on the basis of competency and merit, rather than on the basis of race or gender. At the corporate level, it would be unethical to sell product A to a customer if product B gives greater utility per dollar spent (bang per buck).

Measurement of the "greatest good" is done using a formal ethical calculus variously in terms of pleasure and pain, satisfaction of individual revealed preferences, and overall economic well-being (welfare economics) using societal cost/benefit analysis to arrive at a utilitarian coefficient. Alternatively, the calculations can be done intuitively, considering the advantages and disadvantages of a given course of action.

The procedure utilitarian decision makers are required to use is:
   (1) Identify relevant stakeholders.
   (2) Identify alternative strategies.
   (3) Estimate costs and benefits of each alternative for each stakeholder.
   (4) Select the best option, i.e., the one that produces the greatest good for the greatest number.
For instance, a firm could establish cost-benefit tradeoffs for decisions involving potential employee risk of occupational accidents, illnesses, and/or deaths. Or, a firm could justify a minor deception in conducting marketing research (such as concerning the sponsor of or purpose of the research) if the resulting lack of bias on the part of respondents leads to more valid research, which, in turn, results in better products and services.

Utilitarian moral philosophers are conventionally divided into two groups, act utilitarians and rule utilitarians. Act utilitarians hold that each individual act should be subjected to the utilitarian test. Although we can have general rules of thumb which work in most cases to maximize utility, such as, "Don't break contracts," these are just generalizations about past instances, and some particular future instance might prove to be an exception to the rule. Rather than being categorically wrong, an act might be contingently wrong. In a particular case, breaking the contract could be morally permissible if it leads to the greatest good for the greatest number. The justification for this approach is that it considers the merits and demerits of each individual action. The criticism of this approach is that we can't always know all the consequences and it leads to a bias toward breaking moral rules.

Rule utilitarians, on the other hand, hold that there are general moral rules (e.g., "Bribery is wrong.") as to what we should do to maximize utility which cannot be compromised by the demand of particular situations. Such compromise would threaten the general effectiveness of the rules. Rules are not subject to change by demands of individual circumstances. The correct moral rules are those that would produce the greatest good for the greatest number if everyone were to follow them all the time. Thus, by looking at general consequences of breaking contracts in the past, we conclude that it is never right to break contracts, no matter what. Likewise, we should never lie, steal, murder, etc. The justification for this approach is that it considers general norms and values. The criticism is that it neglects that each case might be unique; exceptions to the rule might sometimes maximize utility.

There are several advantages to the utilitarian approach. First, it results in "optimal" solutions (Pareto optimality in the language of the welfare economist). Most people end up satisfied and better off.

Second, presumably it uses rational, objective analysis (vs. intuition) and yields quantifiable results. And, the most fundamental lesson in business is that in making decisions you should compare benefits to costs.

Third, it is goal oriented (teleological); therefore managers feel comfortable using it and it is easy to justify to others. For instance, it is often argued that if business decisions increase profits, market mechanisms ensure that most customers are better off; otherwise they would buy from someone else (this ignores stakeholders other than customers).

Fourth, it considers all stakeholders, including animals (e.g., in animal research by cosmetics and pharmaceutical companies). Fifth, pleasure and pain are important considerations. Sixth, it encourages efficiency and productivity. Finally, utilitarianism impartially takes everyone and all interests into account.

On the downside, there are some serious shortcomings to the utilitarian model. First, due to convenience and the fact that hindsight is 20-20, there is a tendency to neglect long-run outcomes and only measure short-term consequences. Thus, unintended, unanticipated long-run consequences are not accounted for. For instance, "free sex" might be pleasurable, but in the end the result could be a communicable disease or an unwanted child. Marketing flavored cigarettes or junk food can make customers happy but yield ultimate negative results.

Second, minorities often suffer the "tyranny of the majority," i.e., someone or some group gets burned when the majority rules, resulting in an unjust allocation of resources and/or individuals being deprived of their rights. That is, utilitarianism ignores the important concepts of rights and justice. For example, in the "bad old days" many marketing efforts were targeted toward WASPs while largely ignoring ethnic minorities. As another example, state lotteries are generally favored by taxpayers (the majority) since their taxes can be slightly reduced. But those who suffer are the heavy users, i.e., the poor who cannot afford to throw away their hard-earned dollars and gambling addicts whose addictions are further fed. In the difficult issue of abortion for poor single mothers, welfare costs and inconvenience to the mother are minimized, but what about the rights of the unborn child? Or, an automobile manufacturer could build a lower level of safety into each car, saving each consumer, say, $150, but the results would be death or serious injury to one out of each 115,000 consumers. Can we balance lives against cost savings? Utilitarian analysis forces us to make such cold calculations, placing a value on human life.. (The Ford Pinto's cost/benefit analysis showed that it was more profitable to settle out of court any claims from life-threatening fuel system problems rather than recall the product.)

Thus, a third difficulty is that using utilitarianism can be a calculative nightmare. It can take much time and effort to make calculations and forecasts for many different stakeholders. Although it is usually pretty straightforward to measure costs since these are tangible items, intangible benefits are more problematic to quantify and measure. How do you measure the worth of a human life? In fact, interpersonal comparisons of utility are impossible; there is no scientific way to measure the increase in welfare to the majority against the decrease in well-being to the minority. For instance, no smoking on continental airline flights is now federal policy. Does the satisfaction to the 80% of nonsmokers outweigh the frustrating pain visited on the 20% of smokers? Many benefits, and sometimes even costs, are difficult to forecast in advance. To partially alleviate calculative problems, boundaries can be placed on the utilitarian measurements. For instance, often calculations are confined to the economic realm or else only the interests of those directly affected are considered. Anyway, the objectivity of the measurements is open to serious question.

A fourth problem is that utilitarianism encourages individualistic, selfish behavior since it ignores and can result in an abridgment of others' rights. It could be used to rationalize almost any behavior, including emotional acts. For example, the parties to an adulterous act might be happy, but what about the spouse and the underlying moral issues which remain unaddressed?

Fifth, a desirable end might be caused by an unjust means or a bad motive. For instance, Robin Hood, with a "soak-the-rich" mentality, stole from the rich to assist the poor. The American Heart Association could justify running false and misleading advertising if the result is to discourage many young people from smoking. In effect, utilitarianism is analogous to the Marxian notion that "the ends justify the means." If the student's end is to get good grades so as to land a good job and the means is to cheat, fine. Using this line of reasoning some have advocated fetal harvesting as long as the fetal tissue is used for "humane" purposes such as transplants or medical research. We could presumably even justify having prostitutes work out of church basements if we will use the money for feeding the poor and missionary work. In fact, some studies suggest that most unethical acts in business are committed by basically honest people under pressure to achieve bottom-line results, which are believed to be all that really matters. In effect, sometimes we are saying, "Let us do evil, that good may come."

Sixth, despite supposedly hard and fast calculations, there is still some uncertainty since the definition of "the greatest good" is left open to dispute.   For instance, which stakeholders should get more happiness? (Different groups can be weighted, but this involves subjective judgments and biases.) There is also uncertainty in the sense that, at least with act utilitarianism, no actions are always right or wrong. For instance, dishonesty or theft might be justifiable if it increases net benefits.

Ethical egoism. This approach defines acceptable behavior in terms of consequences for the individual decision maker. Ethical egoism says that one should promote their own self interest, seeking the most good (consequences) for themselves above that of all others ("You've got to look out for number one"). Maximization of self interest is defined differently by each person. Depending on the egoist, an act could be considered right if it gives one more pleasure than pain, gives one the most power, results in fame, promotes a satisfying career, etc. In short, "Do the act that promotes the greatest good for the self."

An enlightened form of egoism, postulated indirectly by the philosopher Thomas Hobbes, takes a long-term perspective and allows for consideration of the well-being of others, although this is a secondary consideration to one's personal well-being. In other words, one should consider the interests of others when it suits their own interests. One should accept moral rules and assume certain obligations only when doing so promotes one's own welfare. One should back down on an obligation (e.g., to tell the truth, fulfill an obligation) whenever it is not in one's best interests. Thus, an enlightened egoist might call management's attention to a colleague who is cheating customers, but only to safeguard the firm's image and hence the egoist's own job security. A lot of philanthropic and "socially responsible" actions appear to be motivated by enlightened ethical egoism rather than by pure altruism. By being a good "corporate citizen," the firm receives good public relations.

The major advantage to egoism is that it benefits the individual. This is seen by some thinkers as being reasonable; in fact, acting against one's own interest is viewed as contrary to reason - conventional moral standards are fraught with irrational sentiment and unreasonable constraints on the individual. If enlightened egoism is practiced, some feel that this leads to utilitarian outcomes (e.g., Adam Smith's invisible hand, discussed shortly).

Problems are that it is hedonistic and selfish (and therefore morally unacceptable); ethical egoism ignores other stakeholders (possibly even stepping on their toes), and therefore invites regulation; and this perspective can lead to conflicting directives in situations of moral conflict (e.g., a consumer activist fights to halt production of an unsafe car while the manufacturer fights against the activist's initiatives). However, Adam Smith argued that the public good evolves out of a suitably restrained clash of competing interests (the guiding "invisible hand" ensures that public good is served when each person pursues their own agenda). Thomas Hobbes, on the other hand, proposed the need for the all-powerful sovereign state (in modern terms, government regulation) to ensure the public good (although Hobbes believed government's powers should be fairly limited). Many modern business people recognize that when their interests do clash with those of others within the established rules of the competitive game, they should pursue their own interests. However, business practices are thus restrained because self-interest is subservient to the rules of business practice.

Christian consequentialism.   Although Judeo-Christian morality is founded on absolute moral rules, some Christians have tried using a relativistic approach, in the form of Christian consequentialism. This says that an act is right if it causes one to love his neighbor or to further the Kingdom of God. Aquinas labeled this the "perfect good" and Augustine called it "happiness."

Cited advantages are that it focuses on positive end results, is flexible, follows the spirit rather than the letter of the law, and avoids legalism and rules. However, on the negative side of the ledger, it tends to be vague, Jesus did not come "to abolish the law but to fulfill it," (Matthew 5:17) and we presently "see through a glass darkly," i.e., we don't know for sure if our actions further the Kingdom of Heaven. Scriptural support for this approach seems to be lacking. The Bible denounces the days when "everyone did what was right in his own eyes." (Judges 21:25).

Deontological moral theories.   Deontology refers to moral philosophies that focus on duties (deontology is derived from the Greek for "duty"), on the rights of individuals, and on the intentions or motives of the moral agent. Being duty-based, deontological moral theories deny what teleological moral theories assert - that only the consequences of actions and rules count. Deontological theories consider the means of actions, whereas teleological theories consider the ends. Thus, there are some things we should not do, even to maximize utility. For instance, the fact that one has made a promise obligates one to keep the promise, even if it becomes clear that keeping the promise will not lead to the greatest good.

Thus, we have duties such as being fair, keeping promises, fulfilling debts to others, or abiding by a contractual relationship, regardless of consequences. Corporations have special moral obligations to their customers employees, independent of the general good.

As was true of utilitarians, deontologists can be divided into two groups: those who focus on moral rules and those who focus on the nature of the acts themselves. Rule deontologists believe that conformity to general moral principles determines ethicalness. For example, the traditional Judeo-Christian approach to morality is rule deontological (e.g., the Golden Rule). These rule deontologists also hold that individuals have certain absolute rights which should not be violated, such as freedom of conscience, freedom of consent, privacy rights, and free speech rights, among others. Rule deontologists regard the nature of moral principles as permanent and stable, and they believe that ethical people act in accordance with these principles.

Act deontologists hold that actions are the proper basis on which to judge morality. Act deontology requires that one use equity, fairness, and impartiality in decision making, and that rules serve only as general guidelines.

One perspective on deontology, prima facie duties, says that there are certain duties that are to always be acted upon, except if in a particular situation a given duty conflicts with a given or stronger duty. Thus, prima facie duties are not absolute; they can be overridden under some conditions. Prima facie duties "tend to be our duty." For instance, if the prima facie duty to keep promises were to conflict with the duty to protect innocent persons from harm, then the actual duty would be to protect innocent persons, overriding the prima facie duty to keep promises.

Deontologists also insist on the importance of motives. The same action could be due to different intentions. For instance, the person who keeps a promise simply because she knows she'd look bad by breaking that promise is less ethical than the person who keeps the promise because she really cares about the other party's welfare.

There are two major deontological theories: the theory of rights and the theory of justice. The theory of rights, a type of rule deontology, focuses on individuals' rights and the corresponding duties of moral agents to respect those rights. The theory of justice, a type of act deontology, focuses on equity, fairness, and impartiality in decision making. These theories can be relative or absolute in nature, depending on how they are interpreted.

Theory of rights. The theory of rights (or moral entitlements or duty), with its roots in the seventeenth century work of Thomas Hobbes, John Locke, and Immanuel Kant, recognizes moral entitlements of individuals. Moral rights are fundamental personal rights based on moral norms and principles, like the right to life, freedom, health, safety, and property. They are universal and therefore exist prior to and independent of social conventions and laws; they cannot be abolished by political powers. These rights exist irrespective of merit, just because we are human. Thus, these fundamental human/personal rights are given as birthrights (rather than as a privilege for being a Ph.D., member of a certain institution, etc.). Our humanity is said to confer rights to impartial treatment in matters of justice, freedom, equality of opportunity, and the like. The theory of rights mandates that any individual has the right to be treated in ways that ensure the dignity, respect, and autonomy of that individual.

Such rights as free/informed consent, privacy, freedom of conscience, free speech, and due process have been codified in the U.S. Bill of Rights, in the Declaration of Independence, and in the U.N. Universal Declaration of Human Rights. The Declaration of Independence asserted that these rights come from God (..."We are endowed by our Creator with certain inalienable rights...life, liberty, and the pursuit of happiness.").

It is respect for these rights which should guide decision making. Most rights theorists believe that the rights of individuals take precedence over the rights of organizations and institutions. Rights theory is duty based; we judge the actor's fulfillment of her duties/obligations to other individuals in the exchange process. Focus is on the means rather than the consequences of the actor's behavior. The arguments for rights are twofold: (1) It is necessary for individuals to have self-respect and (2) rights support freedom and well-being. Thus, rights boil down to: (1) the need for self-respect and (2) the need for freedom and well-being. Rights, in effect, show respect for humanity. Our obligation is to respect others' moral rights.

Business, then, should be viewed not simply as an economic institution but also as a moral institution. Consequently, various stakeholders should be treated with respect for their rights.

In the workplace, some commonly accepted rights include employees' right to equal pay for equal work and consumers' right to know (and JFK's other three consumer rights). Managers sometimes complain that unions violate their right to manage, and investors grouse that taxation violates their property rights.

One variation on rights theory is the Golden Rule model, with its foundation in the Bible. This states that one should choose the action which treats others with the same dignity and respect that he would expect (costs or consequences are only of secondary importance). Thus, an action is morally appropriate if it treats all stakeholders with the same respect and dignity one would expect from others.

Another variation on rights theory is the Kantian model, which holds that each person has a basic right to respect and to be treated as a free person equal to everyone else, and everyone has a duty to treat people this way. An action is morally correct if it minimizes the violation of the rights of all stakeholders. Kant emphasizes performing one's duty for the sake of duty and not for any other reason (such as utility or self-interest). The person's motive for acting must be fulfillment of one's moral duty. Moral law states an imperative - something that must be done. We must do our duty categorically, i.e., unconditionally, no matter what, no exceptions.

Kant's categorical imperative is something that must be done and is applicable to all and binding on all unconditionally. Everyone has a right to be treated as a free person equal to everyone else, and everyone has a duty to treat people this way.

Kant gave three formulations of the categorical imperative. A moral action must: (1) be universally applicable, (2) respect human beings as ends in themselves, and (3) stem from stem from and respect the autonomy of rational beings. These three formal conditions all derive from reason and what it means to be a rational being. They suggest that self-interested (non cooperative, self-seeking) behavior is not always in each person's best interests.

Kant's first principle is universalization (or universalizability): what is morally right for you must be morally right for everyone else. Kant said that reasonable, thinking people would arrive at that judgment that, if universally applied, would be best for everyone. As Kant said it, "I ought never to act except in such a way that I can also will that my maxim should become a universal law." In other words, ask the following question regarding the action in question: "What if everyone did that?" That is, if everyone were to behave as you do (to act on your principle) and the result were chaos, then your principle is immoral. For instance, cheating on an examination only succeeds if others do not cheat; everyone cannot receive an "A." Cheaters must free ride off of honest people. Or, consider that if everyone lied, there would be no social order; language would lose its meaning. Liers must free ride off of truth tellers. Lies increase what in economics-speak are known as transactions costs, making exchange (the essence of marketing) less efficient. Or, think about queuing and the character that drives in the right-hand lane while all others merge left, and then cuts into the left-hand lane at the last possible moment. If there were universalized cutting in line the result would be social chaos. If the majority of business people became dishonest or unethical, the result would be destruction of the economic system as it operates today.

Another criterion for Kant's first formulation of the categorical imperative is reversibility: your reasons for acting must be reasons you'd be willing to have all others use, even as a basis for how they treat you. In other words, "How would you like it if he did it to you?" or "How would you like it if you were in her place?"

The second formulation of Kant's categorical imperative says to respect people as ends (a rational person) in themselves, not as means. Always act with recognition of every person's right, including self, to be treated with respect and dignity. Each person has intrinsic value; therefore one should not use other people as a means for her own ends (advancing her own self-interest). Thus, in the immortal words of Immanuel Kant, "Act so that you treat humanity, whether in your own person or in that of another, always as an end and never as a means." For instance, to subject employees to health risks without their knowledge would be to violate this principle. Deception and coercion are immoral because they fail to respect peoples' freedom to choose for themselves. Job discrimination and sexual harassment are immoral because they treat certain people as less than fully human, i.e., as less than free persons equal to all others. Likewise, lying, theft, and murder fail to show respect, treating people as means. The kind of treatment that people deserve as rational beings, as ends in themselves, is sometimes put in terms of the rights we are discussing here.

The third formulation of the categorical imperative is that moral law must stem from and respect the autonomy of human beings. We have the freedom to choose to accept the moral law and to act morally or immorally (vs. animals, who act on instincts), and we should live as members of the moral community in accordance with the moral law.

Many different human rights have been proposed. Some rights are controversial i.e., some people consider them wrongs (e.g., childrens' rights, animal rights, gay rights, rights of various special interest groups), while the limit on the scope of many rights is not clear; most rights are not absolute. For instance, in 2000 years of Western civilization, there has never been a recognized right to absolute control over one's body, such as taking heroin or committing suicide. Even though we have free speech rights, you don't have the right to yell "fire' in a crowded theater, nor do you have the right to perjury, libel, incite violence, or fraudulently advertise. My right to swing my fist ends where your face begins. And, rights are certainly not the same concept as virtues. For instance, is there a right to sexual gratification outside of marriage?

Two basic categories of rights can be identified: rights to liberty and rights to welfare. Liberty rights (AKA negative rights), recognized by all philosophers who are rights theorists, suggest that people should be free from restriction or control. An individual should have the right to act, believe, or express herself as she wishes. Basic liberty rights include privacy, free speech, freedom of conscience, and free consent. These traditional rights mean that people have the right to be left alone and suggest limits on state power. Free markets protect two natural rights: the right to freedom (voluntary exchange) and the right to private property. An example of a controversial liberty right is the freedom of association (many men's clubs have been forced to admit women in recent years; some country clubs still exclude blacks).

Second, are welfare rights (AKA positive rights or entitlements), which are not recognized by libertarians. Generally, these boil down to health, happiness, and general well-being, and they assert a right to a minimum standard of living where a person can't provide for themselves but these are available. Specifically, welfare rights include employment, food, housing, and education.

Traditionally, such rights were felt to be a government responsibility (and they enhance the state's power), not a business responsibility. Today, more businesses, acting as "good corporate citizens," are paying more attention to these and are helping to meet some community needs (e.g., McDonald's Ronald McDonald houses). Another example of a welfare right would be an employees' right to an enhanced quality of life, which could be infringed by an organization that promotes or grants raises only to those who spend large amounts of time in the working environment at the expense of family, church, and community.

The concept of duties or obligations means that for every right that someone has, there is a duty of someone else to respect that right, either by refraining from taking certain actions (liberty rights)or by taking certain actions (welfare rights).

Regarding liberty rights, the duty is simply not to interfere with another person's intended course in life., i.e., one need not really do anything to fulfill his duty. For instance, my right to life negates your "right" to kill me. One could argue that one should not prevent another from going to the grocery store, going to a porno theater, or even from having an abortion (the latter perhaps ignores the baby's right to life). The Bill of Rights in the U.S. Constitution says that the duty of government is to not interfere in certain areas of citizens' lives (civil liberties). For instance, people have the right to worship as they choose (although the line is drawn in places like animal sacrifice and drug use). An advertiser has the right to honest free commercial speech. A businessperson has the right to use, sell, or destroy personal business assets.

With respect to welfare rights, the duty is to provide people with what is needed (an education, food, shelter, employment, adequate health care, etc.). These are called positive rights because others have a positive duty to provide a person with whatever she needs to pursue her interests. Thus, homelessness could be viewed as a failure to provide one's right to shelter. Inner-city dwellers could be viewed as having a right to be served efficiently by retailers. Roles or positions within social institutions and organizations create positive rights. For instance, a married couple has the duty to care for their children, doctors have a duty to care for their patients' health, and business managers have a duty to care for the organization they manage (the law of agency).

Welfare rights can clash with liberty rights; tradeoffs are sometimes necessary. Some people could feel that their liberty rights (e.g., right to use their private property as they see fit) are infringed by those telling them they have a duty to provide. For example, lawyers sometimes are expected to do pro bono work to aid the poor. The lawyers challenge the fairness of being asked to work for no pay, while proponents of this policy say that it is only fair that poor defendants have legal counsel. This gets back to the debate - do business organizations exist solely to make money for their stockholders, or do they have responsibilities to other constituencies as well?

Some people view contractual rights and duties as a third set of rights. These arise when someone enters into an agreement with someone else in a specific transaction. Each party has the right to receive what they were promised in the contract and the right to be left free and fully informed when contracts are made.

Here are some examples of generally agreed upon rights (although interpretations vary in certain situations, e.g., does a woman's right privacy permit her to get an abortion?), along with marketing applications

1. The right to free/informed consent. Individuals have the right to be treated only as they knowingly and freely consent to be treated. This suggests that marketing research data collected secretly against an individual's agreement (some kinds of observational studies) might be immoral.

2. The right to privacy. People have the right to do whatever they choose to do outside of working hours and to control information about their private life, including information not intended to be made public. This suggests that retailers who enter customers' names and addresses into computer files and later sell the data bases to other marketers are violating customers' privacy rights.

3. The right to freedom of conscience. Individuals have the right to refrain from carrying out any order that violates moral or religious norms to which they adhere, as long as these are commonly accepted norms. Thus it would probably be immoral for an ad agency principal to force an ad executive to work on a cigarette or beer account if they object to the morality of those products.

4. The right of free speech.   This includes individuals' right to criticize conscientiously and truthfully the ethics or legality of the actions of others or of an organization, so long as the criticism doesn't violate others' right.   This argues in favor of whistle blowing; some say that an employee has a duty to whistle blow to honor the employer's right to know about unethical business conduct.   It argues against false criticism of another company's salespeople.

5. The right to life and safety.   This suggests that products that pose needless safety hazards shouldn't be marketed.

The procedure rights theorists are required to use is:
1. Identify all relevant stakeholders.
2. Determine all of each stakeholder's rights.
3. Figure out management's duties to the various stakeholders.
4. Prioritize the duties.

Rights theory has certain advantages to recommend it.   One is its relative simplicity.   One should (at least regarding negative rights) just avoid interfering with others' rights.   Acts are rejected when they victimize just one person, even if societal welfare could be increased.   Rights theory takes an individual perspective (vs. making utilitarian calculations involving many people and society).   Second, rights theory assures minimal levels of satisfaction for all individuals (vs. some suffering the tyranny of the majority).   Third, it can lead to certainty if absolute rules/principles are followed in determining rights.   For instance, natural rights are absolutes, although legal, positive rights can be relativistic since they are manmade.

On the negative side of the ledger, there is often disagreement on which rights are right and which rights are wrongs.   Do children have certain rights which can be asserted against their parents? Do employees have the right to advance notification of termination of employment for just cause? Do teenagers have the right to have sex and to have it with whomever they want?   The Declaration of Independence suggests that rights come from the Creator, and so some major religions proscribe the latter "right."   If rights are relativisticly derived, of which human rights can we be certain and how? Where do rights come from?

Second, as already noted, the limits of rights aren't always clear.   Does the right to free speech allow flag burning or nude dancing? Should we suppress speech which is distasteful, offensive, or disturbing to a few? To many? How much advance notification should be given employees prior to a plant closing?

A third, and very difficult problem, arises when there are conflicts among rights of competing individuals or groups (there almost always are).   Positive rights often conflict with negative rights (e.g., welfare rights vs. liberty rights).   For instance, affirmative action quotas embody the liberal view that group rights should take precedence over individual rights.   One person's exercise of their rights might infringe on another's rights. In the abortion issue, we have the woman's right to control her body vs. the rights of the father and of the unborn child. Consider the issue of drug testing in the workplace. On the one hand, the employee has the right to privacy, but on the other hand employers and other employees have the right to know whether certain employees are likely to pose a threat to a safe work environment. Or, how do we balance the rights of smokers to enjoy a drag against the rights of nonsmokers to breathe clean air? How about privacy rights of AIDS victims vs. the right of the general public to health and safety? Environmentalists argue that people have a right to a clean environment, that businesses have a duty not to foul our natural resources no matter what the cost, while some business people hold that this could interfere with their private property rights. Employees claim the freedom to unionize while employers claim the right to hire nonunion labor. Property rights sometimes conflict with zoning restrictions on use of private property. Consequently, there is sometimes the difficult task of prioritizing duties. This necessitates examining the relative importance of the interests that each right protects, an admittedly subjective process.

Another problem is that rights theory can encourage individualistic, selfish behavior when people scream about "my rights." If taken to an extreme, this could lead to anarchy.

Finally, rights theory, as opposed to utilitarianism, can lead to sub optimal consequences since consequences are inconsequential. Personal prerogatives might set an obstacle to productivity and efficiency, as in the case of drug-impaired employees.

Theory of Justice.   The theory of justice or fairness, with its origin in the fifth century B.C. writings of Aristotle and Plato, holds that equity, fairness, and impartiality should guide decision making. This means that a person receives "what they deserve." A person has been treated justly when she has been given what is due or owed, what she deserves or can legitimately claim. What might be deserved can be either a benefit or a burden. Any denial of something to which someone has a right or claim is an injustice. Thus, in the abortion issue, some would say that taking the life of an unborn child is unjust while others would argue that denying a woman the right to control her body is unjust. There are three types of justice, each defining differently the concept "what they deserve": distributive justice, retributive justice, and compensatory justice.

The concept of distributive justice focuses on distribution effects of actions or policies. Distributive justice refers to the proper distribution of social benefits and burdens, including economic goods and political rights. Justice arises from fairness in the distribution of benefits and burdens in society. For instance, should the special needs of certain geographic, ethnic, age, or religious segments receive special or unequal treatment? Canons of justice include distributive rules and principles for administering rules.

Distributive rules put an emphasis on equal treatment, i.e., fair treatment: equals ought to be treated equally and unequals unequally. Programs or services designed to assist people of a certain class must be made available to all members of that class.

First, differentiated treatment of individuals should not be based on arbitrary characteristics: individuals who are similar in the relevant respects should be treated similarly, and persons who differ in relevant respects should be treated differently in proportion to the differences between them. Thus, financial rewards, promotions, and opportunities to have additional authority and responsibility should be commensurate with the quality and quantity of work performed (rather than being based on political considerations). For instance, job discrimination in terms of distributing benefits such as salaries and promotions is wrong. If Jack and Jill each hold the same job, have the same skills sets, equal experience, etc., and Jack is paid twice as much as Jill, this is an unjust situation if gender is an irrelevant characteristic. Bribery can be considered unjust in that it unfairly favors the bribe payer. Executive compensation has become a disputed issue; some believe many CEOs are receiving a greater share of corporate profits than they deserve. Some people see affirmative action programs as unjust in that they give preference to women and minorities, resulting in "reverse discrimination." However, some people would also justify differential treatment based on differing degrees of need.

A second distributive rule says that relevant attributes and characteristics on which differential treatment is based must have a clear relationship to goals and tasks. Price discrimination is illegal except where price differences to different buyers are cost justified. Large industrial accounts receive quantity discounts which small firms do not get. In some circumstances on the job, age discrimination might be justifiable if older people tend to perform more poorly due to physical restrictions.

Thus, an action is morally correct if it treats all stakeholders the same except where there are sound reasons for giving different treatment to different individuals. An unfair/unjust/discriminatory action awards benefits or imposes burdens on a basis not related to relevant characteristics or needs.

However, there is disagreement on what are valid rules for distributive justice. The following is a sample list of major candidates of valid principles of economic distributive justice:

1. To each person an equal share.
2. To each person according to individual need.
3. To each person according to that person's rights (e.g., economic and social liberty).
4. To each person according to individual effort.
5. To each person according to societal or group contribution.
6. To each person according to merit.

Different rules are considered to be appropriate in different situations.

The different views on relevant characteristics for equal/unequal treatment have led to rival theories of social justice at the systemic level (a full discussion of each of these is beyond the scope of this lecture):

1. Egalitarianism. To each person an equal share of society's benefits and burdens (e.g., free public education). There are no relevant differences among people that can justify unequal treatment.

2. Capitalism (capitalist justice). To each person according to societal or group (e.g., the firm) contribution. This could be measured in terms of work effort (input) or productivity (output, the usual measure in business).

3. Socialism/Marxism. "From each according to ability, to each according to need." Work burdens should be distributed according to peoples' abilities and benefits should be distributed according to peoples' needs.

4. Libertarianism. To each person according to her rights to social and economic liberty. Any distribution of benefits and burdens is just if it is the result of individuals freely choosing to exchange with each other the goods the person already owns. "From each as they choose, to each as they are chosen." Libertarians see excessive taxation as robbing Peter to pay Paul, i.e., as coercive and confiscatory.

There are two major principles for administering rules and policies. First, rules are clearly expressed, administered fairly, and enforced consistently and impartially. If someone feels that they have been unfairly treated, they should have a right to an impartial hearing. Fair administration of rules and policies should occur both within the organization (e.g., a bonus plan for the sales force should be available to all salespeople) and outside of the organization (e.g., performance-based discounts should be equally available to all distributors). Second, those who act in ignorance, under duress, or involuntarily are excused.

One particular theory of distributive justice concerns itself with justice of process vs. justice of results. The term "distribution" may refer to the procedure of distributing, or it may refer to the results of the distribution process.

The first concern is for a just procedure ("fair play" or "due process"); focus is on the means. If the process is fair in that the system operates fairly and procedures are in place to safeguard individual rights, the outcome is irrelevant. For instance, if a fair trial was held but the wrong party was judged guilty, this would be okay if the concern were only just procedure. Sexual harassment certainly does not involve fair play. A superior who takes credit for subordinates' successes but lets them take all the blame for their mistakes is operating unfairly. Economic and social conservatives tend to favor just procedure.

A second concern is for just results; focus is on the ends. The act is just only if the outcome is fair, regardless of procedures used to arrive at the outcome. For instance, advocates of comparable worth wish to rectify the 60% wage gap between males and females, not by relying on the free forces of supply and demand which determine labor market rates, but by trying to determine the relative value of various jobs to an organization. Underlying the welfare state is the concept of "social justice" in which material equality is the goal. Liberals tend to prefer just results.

Business people like to point out that the competitive free enterprise system leads to a fair distribution of wealth because it offers (at least in theory) equal opportunity to all. Unfortunately, it does not guarantee and does not result in equal results for all. Ideally it is desirable to have both just procedure and just results, but in practice there is often a tradeoff between the two.

The advantages of relying on just procedure are that it focuses on equal opportunity and rewards merit. On the downside, it ignores needs and is harsh on the less fortunate or less naturally endowed (as a result capitalistic economies usually have some sort of welfare system built in).

The positives for using just results are that they focus on consequences, consider need, and result in an egalitarian distribution of wealth. The negatives are that incentives might be stifled and needs are rewarded over merit (for instance the socialist catch phrase "From each according to his ability, to each according to his need").

A second type of justice is known as retributive justice. This is concerned with the justice deserved by the person who did wrong. It focuses on distribution or imposition of penalties and punishments on those who do wrong. For example, a firm polluting the air should internalize the external costs by either paying those harmed or paying the cost of pollution control equipment. However, if a person was either ignorant or unable to freely choose to do right or wrong, then they can't be justly punished or blamed. Thus, if the owner of a cotton mill whose conditions created brown lung disease didn't know about the hazardous condition, he would be blameless. The insanity plea is used to excuse murderers since they were supposedly unable to choose to do right. Also, a due process system should be used to ascertain whether the person really did wrong (e.g., circumstantial or flimsy evidence isn't good enough). And, punishments must be consistent over time and place and proportional to the wrong; the penalty should be no greater than the harm done (this argues against treble damages and punitive damages awards). This is because the punishment's purpose is to deter others from committing the same wrong or to prevent the wrongdoer from becoming a repeat offender.

The third type of justice is known as compensatory justice. The idea here is to provide a just way of compensating people for what they lost when wronged by others. A just compensation is one that is proportional to the loss. Norms of compensation/restitution exist for injuries or harm, both economic and psychological. First, individuals are not held responsible for matters over which they have no control. Second, individuals should be compensated for their losses by the party responsible for those losses. Examples include monetary compensation for damage done and media make goods for advertisements which do not run as scheduled.

A controversial concept of compensatory justice in the business world is that of "preferential treatment" or affirmative action.   This involves programs that attempt to remedy past injustices against groups (especially minorities).   Does justice mandate that members of a group formerly discriminated against be compensated by being given preferential treatment in hiring, training, and promotion procedures? Or is such treatment itself a violation of justice by violating the principle of equal treatment? Does justice require quotas of minority members even if this necessitates turning down more highly qualified non minorities?

In general, the advantages of justice approaches to ethics include the fact that it ensures a "fair" allocation of resources (however one defines "fair"), is democratic in that it does not allow a society to become status- or class-conscious, it protects interests of minorities, and can result in certainty when absolute standards of justice are applied.

However, it is difficult to apply justice criteria (e.g., determining the criteria upon which differential treatment is based), justice can encourage a sense of entitlement that reduces risk/innovation/productivity as well as diminished incentives to produce goods and services (especially true for just results), it can result in curtailing some peoples' rights to achieve canons of justice (affirmative action, for instance, has been labeled by some as "reverse discrimination"), and there often arise conflicts among different claims of justice, especially where fixed standards aren't in place.

Regarding clashing claims of justice, there is a conflict between just procedure vs. just results; different economic systems for ensuring economic justice (capitalism vs. socialism, etc.); seniority vs. merit; and market values vs. other criteria in determining compensation.   Affirmative action opponents say that quotas violate our culture's principle of equal treatment for equal skills; supporters say that justice demands compensation for the horrors of past discrimination. Some view attempts to redistribute wealth as unfair since policy makers take money away from one section of the community to give it to another. Looters in the 1992 Los Angeles riots following the Rodney King verdict claimed they were just getting "justice." Is "vigilante justice" really justice?

Conclusion on ethical theories. Work in the field of normative ethics in the twentieth century has evolved from two basic approaches: teleological theory (focus on consequences) and deontological theory (focus on duties). The major teleological theory is utilitarianism, and the major deontological theories are rights theory and justice theory.

One might ask: why do we need moral theories? Why not just rely on generally accepted moral rules (conventional morality) such as "Do no harm," "Do not kill, and "Tell the truth"? First, although these rules are generally sufficient in black and white cases they are not always so in gray areas. The theories are especially useful for resolving difficult moral issues, i.e., ethical dilemmas. Second, using these ethical theories for moral reasoning makes it possible for an individual who makes a moral decision to explain and justify it to others. For instance, the manager who hires and fires employees must be able to explain the fairness of her decisions to others.

Each of the different moral theories uses different kinds of criteria to evaluate ethical behavior, and each looks at ethical dilemmas from a different moral point of view. None of the theories captures all of the factors that must be considered when rendering moral judgments (e.g., utilitarianism considers societal welfare, rights theory considers individual moral rights, and justice theory considers the distribution of benefits and burdens among individuals). Therefore all three theories should be given consideration, although only one might be most relevant in a particular situation. These are not moral decision rules per se but, rather, constitute moral perspectives to be used in analyzing cases and scenarios. They enable use of critical reasoning skills in reaching a post conventional level of analysis.

Different ethical theories sometimes promote rival answers to moral dilemmas, which present obvious problems for corporate executives, employees, or others who are called to make ethical decisions. When there is a conflict among the results yielded by the different approaches judgment should be used in weighting the different theories. Some ethicists feel that rights take precedence over justice, which take precedence over utilitarian consequences. Where there is conflict among criteria within a given approach (e.g., between utilitarian consequences, between the rights of competing individuals, or between different canons of justice), again a weighting procedure is recommended. also, the ethical theories can be combined with application of moral rules. In any case, ethical theories force critical and constructive reflection on moral problems.

Areas of Difficulty--Obstacles that Detract from Building Moral Corporate Cultures
The state of perceived and perhaps actual ethical business conduct is at a low level. Business has been weighed in the moral balance and found wanting. Why is this so? Perceptual reasons could include the fact that our society is increasingly pluralistic regarding beliefs and values (e.g., environmentalism vs. unbridled free enterprise and growth), business decisions are increasingly being judged publicly by groups with diverse values and interests (e.g., R.J. Reynolds' decision to market Uptown cigarettes to blacks was applauded by some marketers and booed by black community leaders and anti smoking groups), and the public's expectations for ethical business conduct have increased. There are also some real reasons why business ethics might actually be in a freefall.

First, there is the pressure for performance. An overemphasis on economic values (vs. moral values), on beating the competition, and a constant eye on the bottom line can create an atmosphere where it is easy to give in to the short-term pressures. The bad barrel argument says that corporate cultures become unethical, not because individuals are rotten (the bad apple argument) but because pressures create such a state. Most ethical lapses are probably unpremeditated acts committed by basically honest, hard-working people with moral fiber who are thrust into situations where they are pressured to wrestle with their conscience and win (vs. white collar career criminals who engage in such outright crooked goings on as selling bogus securities or embezzle funds from the corporate coffers).   Thus people give in to temptation and end up doing questionable things like accepting gifts shipped to their home by suppliers and approving advertising which stretches the truth a bit to make the cash registers ring. Many people become involved in white collar crime not out of greed or malevolence, but out of weakness or due to blunders which lead them to step over the ethical line rather than crossing it purposively. The pressure on corporate executives for favorable quarterly earnings increases creates a dog-eat-dog environment whereby everybody looks out for themselves.

Second, decisions in the workplace are sometimes invisible. Many decisions are made in groups or pass through multiple approval points. Thus, it becomes easy to hide behind the corporate shield.

Third, ties are less personal at work, especially in large corporations. In such environments, it becomes easier to, for instance, be loyal to the boss, no matter what it takes.

Fourth, too many top corporate managers are hypocrites who only pay lip service to ethics or talk out of both sides of their mouth. They are competent administrators but leaders in terms of moral guidance when they informally set different standards for different levels in the corporate hierarchy. In effect, they say, "Do as I say, not as I do." And yet, as the saying goes, "The fish rots from the head down."

Fifth, is the dehumanization of employees and customers. Too many organizations are only concerned with efficiency and productivity, not with employees' quality of life. Instead of treating employees with respect and dignity (as Kant would suggest), managers treat them as cogs in a machine, depriving them of meaningful work lives. And, if employees see that top management views customers as gullible, unenlightened, and an easy prey for deception, they might fear that management will treat them similarly.

Sixth, is the overemphasis on image. Too many activities done in the name of social responsibility and alleged concern for ethics are merely public relations ploys (ethical egoism in practice).

Seventh, is nonparticipative management, top down dictation of rules and procedures. A more ethical climate evolves where, instead, employees are encouraged to freely express ideas, concerns, and personal values. Corporate power, responsibility, and wealth are shared, which helps build the trust which allows employees to work more collaboratively and selflessly.

Finally, some would say that a major barrier is the omnipresence of immorality in society overall, due to decline in the family structure and in religious institutions in preaching good old-fashioned morality.   The highest values in a society lie in the integrity and quality of relationships among people. These values are cultivated primarily in family institutions(via direct teaching using rewards and punishments) and religious institutions(via instilling the importance of knowledge of and obedience to God's will).

With the decline of the family and formal religion, the burden of instilling ethics is increasingly being left to educational and workplace institutions. Yet it is curious that, despite all the efforts of the last 15 to 20 years, standards of business conduct have not been raised and might still be falling. Some have speculated that this demonstrates the pitiful failure of the predominant relativistic approach in ethics education. Ethics should, they say, be moved from being merely an intellectual exercise to one in which sound values are internalized.

Practical Difficulties in Using Moral Philosophies

Two problems arise in trying to apply the theoretical moral philosophies in order to do the right thing. If either or both of these conditions is present, the individual isn't morally responsible or culpable and can be excused for her immoral decision. One is lack of information by the decision maker on either the moral standards or factual information needed to render a moral judgment (e.g., intangible consequences for utilitarian decision making). For example, asbestos manufacturers claimed they didn't know that conditions in their plants would cause lung cancer. However, the person isn't excused if she deliberately kept herself ignorant or if she negligently failed to take adequate steps to keep herself informed.

The second problem is the decision maker's lack of ability to employ the criteria in the moral theories (e.g., if she is not permitted to or she is pressured by her supervisors). This is usually due to lack of power, skill, opportunity, or resources to act. If a person is under great pressure or duress, their responsibility for immoral actions is correspondingly reduced.

These two problems can occur at all three levels of analysis.

At the systemic level, for example, there is the impact of the law, which, although usually an ally of ethics, can also be an enemy. For instance, an employer can be sued for telling an ex-employee's prospective employer negative things about the fired employee. Thus, he withholds potentially valuable information, which seems to be morally problematic since it violates the prospective employer's right to know. Or, as liability laws get stricter, we will see more drug testing, which violates the employee's right to privacy. Another systemic level difficulty can be the impact of unfair competition, which makes operating above board and earning a profit difficult. Cultural differences, i.e., the fact that different societies play by different rules (such as bribery) poses another problem, as we have seen. industry practices can also be constraining factors.

At the corporate level, corporate cultures or corporate policies which encourage immorality can make moral behavior challenging. Incentive systems sometimes encourage short-run opportunistic behavior such as pressure selling. A dishonest superior can make moral turpitude tempting. Constrained corporate resources might make unethical behavior the easy way out.

Finally, at the individual level, the clash of values between an individual and his peers, an inability to act, pressure from superiors, personal hardships and risks, personal financial constraints, and conflict between family/church/community organizations and the business organization can lead to difficulties. For instance, although a professor could spend all of her spare time doing scholarly research, this would be fair neither to her family nor to her students.

Solving Ethical Cases

A seven-step model has been developed by Manuel Velasquez and has been used by ethicists working in conjunction with Arthur Andersen & Co., SC. (this author is developing it a bit more fully here). The model can be used by a person confronted with an ethical dilemma and in using the case method. The approach is similar to the traditional case analysis approach used in most business courses, and it is an attempt to apply general rules to the full complexity of specific circumstances. It consists of seven questions to be asked in a class discussion where various viewpoints can be brought out and assertions can be probed and challenged:

1. What are the relevant facts? Recall that the second element in the moral reasoning model was factual information concerning the policy, institution, or behavior in question. The decision maker should separate out facts that are needed to identify the ethical issues. The decision maker must also be able to clarify/distinguish facts from her assumptions and interpretations in the situation. And, decision makers should be critical of information sources (watch for possible biases).

2. What are the ethical issues? An ethical issue is a problem, situation, or opportunity requiring an individual or organization to choose among several actions that must be evaluated as right or wrong, ethical or unethical (e.g., conflicts of interest, unfairness, discrimination, bribery). Critical ethical issues, i.e., possible violations of moral standards or common morality, need to be defined at all three levels of analysis. Ethical values can be classified as either bad (e.g., violence, threats, property damage, violation of rights, deception, unequal distribution of wealth) or good (e.g., freedom, equality, respect for individuals, justice, integrity, honesty, courage). One must identify the moral agent(s) (individuals, organizations, government policy makers, etc.) and whether they know the ethical value of the act or policy in question.

3. Who are the primary stakeholders? Rather than coming up with an exhaustive list of individuals or groups which might be affected by a decision (which is usually impossible), key persons and groups should be identified.

4. What are the possible alternatives? The possible courses of action should be creatively identified without regard to their ethical impact.

5. What are the ethics of the alternatives? Moral standards (the first component of the moral reasoning model) are applied to the situation. The three ethical theories (utilitarianism, rights, justice) should be used to determine how each alternative affects all stakeholders and which

alternatives offer an acceptable moral solution. Moral rules/norms/values can also be applied, especially where the ethical theories give conflicting answers.

6. What are the practical constraints? Factors which might limit the decision maker's ability to implement an alternative, such as ignorance (e.g., where one couldn't foresee consequences of an action) or lack of ability (e.g., an involuntary choice) should be identified.

7. What actions should be taken? A moral judgment (the third component in the moral reasoning model) is made on the rightness or wrongness of the behavior in question. This includes selection and implementation of an alternative, along with justification why this was chosen over alternative courses of action. Key considerations are the ethical evaluation and the practical constraints.

Appendix: Methods for Leading Discussions of Ethics

The following is non-lecture but, it is hoped, provides useful background information on teaching ethics and integrating ethics into the marketing curriculum. Most of the ideas offered here come from materials supplied by Arthur Anderson & Co, SC, although other sources and the author's own experiences are also drawn upon.

The Place of Ethics in the Curriculum

There are three possible ways to integrate ethics into the business curriculum. First, it can be offered as a stand-alone course, taught by either a philosopher, theologian, or business professor well-versed in ethics, or by a combination of these. The advantages are that this offers a concentrated, systematic look at the subject, and it is usually taught by professors formally trained in ethics. The downside is that the professor is often not very familiar with business issues.

A second possibility is to use the integrative approach whereby ethics is treated as an intrinsic part of various functional area business courses. The ethical dimensions of marketing subject matter can be discussed throughout the course. This does not mean that you merely have an "ethics day" or "ethics week," which leaves the perception that ethics is merely an add-on, afterthought, or separate area of business. Rather ethics is taught and ethical issues are discussed at several points during the course. The advantages are: if students keep hearing about ethics, they begin to realize what an important component of business decision making ethics is; the professor has expertise in business and her functional area; and there is no burning need to add an additional business ethics course into an already overly crowded business curriculum (such additions are, of course, always thorny political issues). The downside is that the professor might feel uncomfortable in teaching this material and might lack effectiveness since she isn't formally trained in ethics (more on this next).

A third possibility, which is ideal if there is room in the curriculum, is to use a combination approach: include both a stand-alone course and integrate ethics into the various business and marketing courses, thereby obtaining the advantages of both of the above approaches. The business ethics course need not be a full-semester course; it could be a workshop during freshman orientation, a half-semester course or minicourse, a significant component of an Introduction to Business course, etc. You need not be an expert.

You don't need a Ph.D. in ethics or to be an accomplished ethicist to teach the basics of ethics and to lead ethical discussions. The material in this lecture should be more than ample to equip you with the basic ethics concepts and models. If you plan to devote one 75-minute lecture to this material, you will find what you need to be selective in what you present. However, the additional material you don't have time to present will give you additional background information to help you feel more confident and be able to answer student questions. You will need to communicate the foundation ethical reasoning models and guide your students through the ethical decision-making process.

Your Task
This is the controversial issue. The prevailing opinion is that your task is not to change the moral character of your students but rather to sensitize them to the moral dimensions of business. Your job is to provide them with the intellectual foundation for moral reasoning.

The problem here is that being ethical involves more than just going through an intellectual exercise. We need to touch the conscience. This can only come through a strong emphasis on the idea that there is right and wrong, good and evil. An emphasis on moral values is sadly lacking in most ethics curricula.

The related advice given by the "experts is to avoid introducing value judgments. This would be to "indoctrinate" students.

However, the question is: "What's wrong with indoctrination?" The word indoctrinate simply means to impart doctrines. Isn't that what teaching is all about? It is amazing how we are able to teach basic rules and truths in math, science, and other disciplines, including business, but not in ethics. Thus, while the ethicists solemnly warn us not to tell our students what is right or wrong, this author suggests that this is nihilistic; it teaches that right and wrong are just matters of personal preference. What we suggest is to defer revealing moral standards until near the end of a discussion. This allows for freer and more open airing of student opinions. If students are encouraged to voice and analyze their positions in an organized fashion and if the instructor carefully respects these various opinions, then disagreement can be tolerated and the discussion can move forward. If there is disagreement in the classroom following an ethics discussion, try to achieve closure by reconciling the results of the ethical theories with the moral values. Students must be challenged to think through what their world view is (e.g., absolutism vs. relativism) and the source of authority for the moral principles they hold (culture, religion, etc.). They must then search out what moral principles are relevant in a particular ethical scenario.

Use Lecture
The most critical things to emphasize in the lecture is the foundation concepts about world views, moral theories, and how to systematically conduct an ethical analysis. Present other material as it suits your students' needs and interests.

Use an Ethical Reasoning Model to Facilitate an Analytical Perspective of Business Ethics
The Arthur Andersen & Co, SC seven-step model is not the only moral reasoning model available for analyzing and resolving ethical dilemmas. However, it ties in nicely with the Moral Reasoning Model it is becoming widely used by the many business and marketing professors who have been through Arthur Andersen & Co.'s business ethics conferences, and it is well-suited to case discussions since it is similar to the case analysis process.

This case method teaches by discussion instead of by lecture, and it focuses on a concrete event instead of on theoretical concepts. Students are expected to take a stand on the ethical issues in the case and to provide reasoned arguments for their position. They are to put themselves in the shoes of the moral agent (ethical decision maker) and not merely be a passive observer. The instructor leads the discussion through Socratic questioning, keeping it moving and on track. The case method trains students in analytical thinking and sharpens their decision-making skills. The seven-step model helps here by leading students through a logical decision-making process. However, the model shouldn't be viewed as a rigid set of steps which must be followed in lock-step fashion. Rather, it provides a general logical procedure to use in ethical reasoning; generally, the later steps build on the earlier steps. However, sometimes steps can be skipped and returned to later if this makes more sense. Thus, the model is both flexible as well as systematic.

The following are a few additional pointers, most from Manuel Velasquez, for each step in the seven-step model:

1. Identify the relevant facts. Students must determine which facts are critical to understand the ethical issues. Often they will say that they need additional information in order to render a moral judgment. If so, one possibility is for you to remind them that in the "real world" decisions are often made with inadequate information. Or, in some cases it might be more fruitful to have them (or you) make reasonable assumptions. Alternatively you can direct them to the library to gather additional background information.

2. Identify the ethical issues. This is where moral standards can be emphasized, since an ethical issue is generally a question about whether a behavior, policy, or institution is consistent with personal or societal moral standards.

3. Identify stakeholders. Your goal here is to get students to see things from different perspectives and to learn to empathize and identify with others.

4. Develop alternatives for resolving the ethical issue. This is where students can put on their creative thinking caps. The instructor's job will be to help students winnow down a potentially long list of viable alternatives to the best few for further analysis.

5. Evaluate the ethics of each alternative. This is the heart of the ethical analysis, and it will require a good portion of the discussion time to apply the three major ethical theories. Here are some suggestions for guiding the discussion using each ethical theory:

a. The utilitarian perspective. For each alternative, ask students to spell out the costs and benefits each stakeholder incurs. Then students must estimate which alternative seems to provide the greatest net benefits (or least net harms), considering the interests of all stakeholders. This alternative is "ethically best" from the perspective of utilitarianism. Since students will differ in their estimates of benefits and harms, these differences should be discussed and resolved where possible.

b. The rights and duties perspective. Students should be asked what moral rights they believe each stakeholder has and what moral duty each owes other stakeholders. Then, students must weight or prioritize the various rights and duties. Finally, students must identify the alternative which promises to respect the most important rights and duties of the stakeholders. This alternative is "ethically best" from the perspective of rights theory. Since students will differ in their views of what constitute rights and duties, they should be asked to defend their ideas.

c. The perspective of fairness or justice. For each alternative, students should be asked which stakeholders win and which ones lose in the distribution of benefits and burdens. They should then be asked which of these distributions is the fairest (the "ethically best" alternative) and why. Since students will differ in their answers, they should be asked to support their reasoning by describing the criteria they used for defining fairness.

While these three perspectives will tend to rule out those alternatives that are unequivocally unethical, often more than one alternative will be recommended by the analysis. In this case, ask students which of the three ethical theories makes the most sense to use in the particular situation. Also, analyze the alternatives in terms of the moral norms.

6. Consider the practical constraints. This encourages students to think pragmatically as well as theoretically.

7. Choose and implement an alternative. A decision is made, based on the ethical evaluation and possible constraints. Use Minicases

Use minicases from textbooks, casebooks, and the Arthur Andersen collection as a basis for group discussion (either the entire class or breakout groups). The advantage of short cases is that they are quicker for students to grasp and hence provide a more efficient way to apply ethical principles.

Another option is for you or even your students to create your own minicases. Her are a few guidelines for doing so:
    . Be sure that the situation is suitably ambiguous.
    . Select realistic business situations.
    . Center the vignette around situations that entry-level business people would face.
    . Make sure that only one person faces a dilemma, so that students can put themselves in that person's shoes. When students develop their own vignettes, they can draw upon personal ethical dilemmas they have faced in their academic or professional careers.

Use Role Plays
You can set up a role-playing session where students volunteer to assume the roles of various characters in an ethics case or minicase, and have them act out the situation.

Use Videos
More and more textbook publishers are offering videos free to adopters of their texts. Some of these either focus on or (more often) have integrated into them ethical issues. The Arthur Andersen videos are also very useful (see the Resources section for a description). One of the strengths of vignette videotapes is that your students can start thinking about what it will be like to encounter ethical dilemmas in their first full-time job out of college.

Use Articles
Articles in national newspapers (Wall Street Journal, USA Today, Marketing News, etc.) and in local papers and magazines report current ethical issues and ethical lapses. These can be described and discussed in class.

Use Guest Speakers
Local business leaders, faculty experts, or former students/alumni can be invited to speak on the importance of ethics and issues they have grappled with.

Key References:

Arthur Andersen & Co., SC. Business Ethics Program Reference Guide. St. Charles, Illinois, 1990.

Robert A. Cooke. "Ethics in Business: A Perspective." Arthur Andersen & Co, SC, 1991.

Geoffrey P. Lantos. "Arthur Anderson Business Ethics Overview," in Christianity and Business: A Collection of Essays on Pedagogy and Practice, ed. Edward S. Trunfio. Christian Business Faculty Association, 1991. pp. 3-28.

Manuel G. Valasquez. Business Ethics: Concepts and Cases. Englewood Cliffs, N.J., 1982.

Table of Transparencies

Types of Ethical Dilemmas

I. Individual Values and the Business Organization
    A. Employee Conflicts of Interest
    B. Inappropriate Gifts
    C. Security of Company Records
    D. Personal Honesty
    E. Government Contract Issues

II. Individual Rights and the Business Organization
    A. Corporate Due Process
    B. Employee Screening
    C. Employee Privacy
    D. Sexual Harassment
    E. Affirmative Action/Equal Employment Opportunity
    F. Employment at Will
    G. Whistle-Blowing
    H. Employee Rights
    I. Comparable Worth

III. Business Operations
    A. Financial and Cash Management Procedures
    B. Conflicts Between the Corporation's Ethical Code and Accepted Business Practices in Foreign Countries
    C. Unauthorized Payments to Foreign Officials
    D. Workplace Safety
    E. Plant Closures and Downsizing

F. Environmental Issues
G. Purchasing: Conflicts and Bribery

IV. Business and Its Competition
    A. Advertising Content
    B. Appropriation of Others' Ideas
    C. Product Pricing

V. Business and Its Product
    A. Contract Relations
    B. Product Safety
    C. Product Quality
    D. Customer Privacy

VI. Business and Its Stakeholders
    A. Shareholders' Interests
    B. Executive Salaries
    C. Corporate Contributions
    D. Social Issues

Language to Watch For:
Rationalizations for Ethical Breaches

1. "Everybody else does it"

2. "If we don't do it, someone else will"

3. "That's the way it's always been done"

4. "We'll wait until the lawyers tell us it's wrong"

5. "It doesn't really hurt anyone"

6. "The system is unfair"

Categories of Unethical Behavior

1. Taking things that don't belong to you

2. Saying things you know are not true

3. Giving or allowing false impressions

4. Buying influence or engaging in a conflict of interest

5. Hiding or divulging information

6. Taking unfair advantage

7. Committing personal decadence

8. Perpetrating interpersonal abuse

9. Permitting organizational abuse

10. Violating rules

11. Condoning unethical actions

12. Balancing ethical dilemmas

Resolving Ethical Dilemmas:

Blanchard/Peale

1. Is it legal?

2. Is it balanced?

3. How does it make me feel?

Front Page of the Newspaper Test

"Contemplating any business act, an employee should ask himself whether he would be willing to see it immediately described by an informed and critical reporter on the front page of his local paper, there to be read by his spouse, children and friends. At Salomon we simply want no part of any activities that pass legal tests but that we, as citizens, would find offensive."

Warren E. Buffet
Chairman, Salomon, Inc.

"If we were making that decision now in light of the press scrutiny we have been receiving, we probably would not have taken that risk."

Robert C. Winters
Chairman, Prudential Insurance

Resolving Ethical Dilemmas:

Laura Nash Model

1. Have you defined the problem accurately?
2. How would you define the problem if you stood on the other side of the fence?
3. How did this situation occur in the first place?
4. To whom and to what do you give your loyalty as a person and as a member of the corporation?
5. What is your intention in making this decision?
6. How does the intention compare with the likely results?
7. Whom could your decision or action injure?
8. Can you discuss your decision with the affected parties?
9. Are you confident that your position will be as valid over a long period of time as it seems now?
10. Could you discuss your decision with your CEO, board, friends, boss, family?
11. What is the symbolic potential of your action if understood? If misunderstood?
12. Under what circumstances would you make exceptions to your position?

Case 1.1: Commodities, Conflicts, and Clintons

Case 1.2: The Realty with the Disguised Ownership

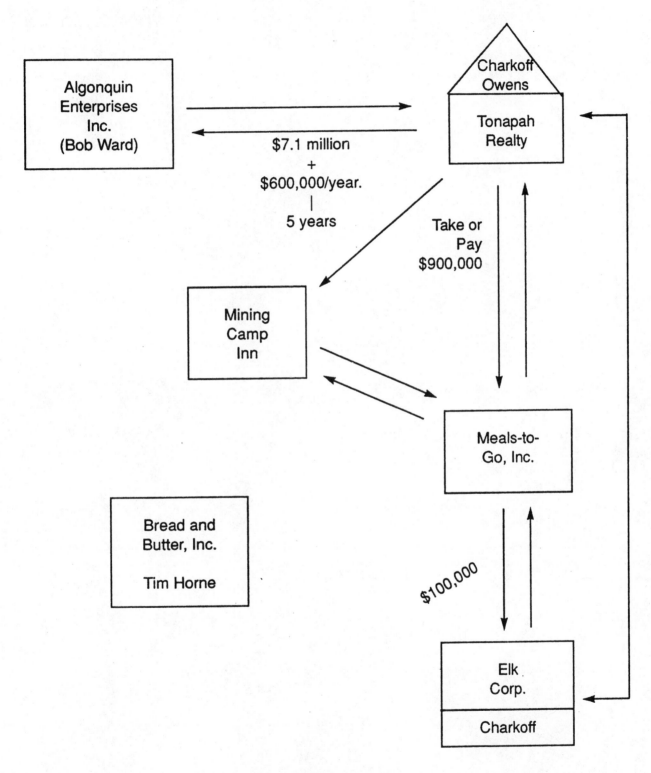

© 1995 West Publishing Company

Case 1.5: The Chain of Command and Purchasing

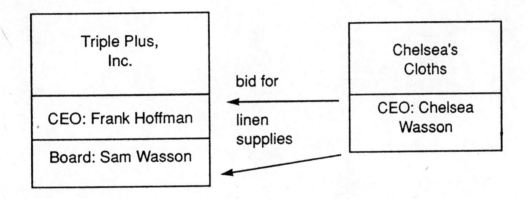

Case 1.10: Incidental Beneficiaries of the Philanthropist's Estate

Elaine Wynn $\longrightarrow$ Chair, UNLV Foundation
Executive, El Mirage
Spouse – Steve Wynn,
Owner of El Mirage

Lyle Rivera $\longrightarrow$ Director, UNLV
Foundation

Arthur
Nathan $\longrightarrow$ Human Resources
Director, El Mirage

Madison Graves $\longrightarrow$ Real Estate Agent, Lyle
Rivera's friend

Shelli Lowe $\longrightarrow$ Appraisal and Purchase
of
Property

Case 1.10: Incidental Beneficiaries of the Philanthropist's Estate

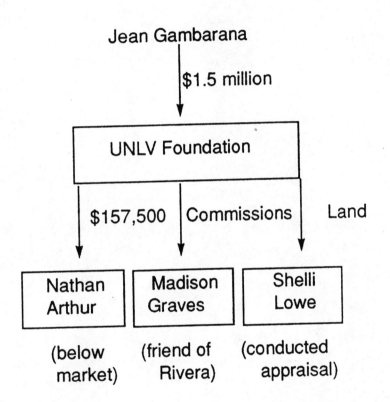

Jean Gambarana

$1.5 million

UNLV Foundation

$157,500   Commissions   Land

Nathan Arthur
(below market)

Madison Graves
(friend of Rivera)

Shelli Lowe
(conducted appraisal)

Case 1.11: The Secretary of Agriculture, Chicken Processors, and Football Sky-Box Seats

Secretary of Agriculture's Gifts While in Office:

Gift	Donor
Lodging for Arkansas Poultry Association	Tyson Foods
Flight to Russellville, Arkansas from Washington, D.C. and Back	Tyson Foods
Ticket to Chicago Bulls Playoff Game	Quaker Oats CEO, Smithburg
$1,200 Scholarship to Mr. Espy's Girlfriend, Ms. Dempsey	Tyson Foundation
Birthday Party for Espy	Sun Diamond
Tyson Sky-Box Seats at Dallas Cowboys/New York Giants Playoff Game	Tyson Foods

Case 1.13: Pharmaceutical Honorariums to Researchers: Graying of the Line between Industry and Academic Research

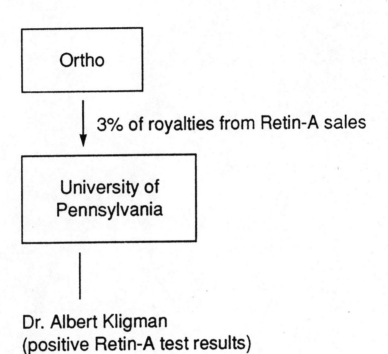

Ortho

3% of royalties from Retin-A sales

University of Pennsylvania

Dr. Albert Kligman
(positive Retin-A test results)

Case 2.1: Ann Hopkins, Price Waterhouse and the Partnership

The Differing Descriptions

"Deft touch"

"Outstanding professional"

"strong character, independence, integrity"

"extremely competent, intelligent"

"strong and forthright"

"very productive, energetic, creative"

"intellectual clarity"

"stimulating conversationalist"

"highly competent"

"overly aggressive"

"unduly harsh"

"difficult to work with"

"impatient with staff"

"macho"

"overcompensated for being a woman"

"needs to take a course at charm school"

"lady using foul language"

"appealing lady partner candidate"

"walk more femininely, talk more femininely, dress more femininely, wear make-up, have her hair styled, and wear jewelry"

Case 2.2: Handwriting Analysis and Employment

HANDWRITING ANALYSIS

More than 100 personality traits are scored in handwriting analysis, and the results may be used to determine whether an applicant is right for a job. The samples below illustrate how a handwriting trait may be isolated to define a personality trait in an individual.

The sales job
Two applicants trying to land a job in sales.

A *[handwriting sample]*

B *[handwriting sample]*

Trait highlight
A more rhythmic pattern of writing and dotting the i's to the right is believed to indicate a persuasive personality.

would *[highlighted sample]*

Trait highlight
Extra humps on n's and m's, and an erratic writing pattern, are said to show less persuasiveness.

next to myself *[highlighted sample]*

Overall analysis
Applicant A scored higher than Applicant B in several traits pertinent to a sales job, including "persuasive," "energetic," "shrewd" and "self-motivated."

The management position
Two applicants for a management job.

C *[handwriting sample]*

D *[handwriting sample]*

Trait highlight
Simplified letters and angular shapes in writing are believed to show ability to handle pressure.

[highlighted sample]

Trait highlight
Elaborate letters and a tendency to overlap descenders are said to show less ability to handle pressure.

[highlighted sample]

Overall analysis
Applicant C appears to have a personality that better fits the job than does Applicant D. Applicant C scored higher in the "analytical," "organized," "decisive" and "handles pressure well" categories.

Source: Handwriting Research Corp.

The Arizona Republic

Case 2.16: Wards Cove: Salmon Cannery Jobs

Cannery Jobs

Unskilled labor

Nonwhites

Filipinos

Alaska natives

Separate dormitories

Separate mess halls

Noncannery Jobs

Machinists

Engineers

White workers

Higher wages

Separate dormitories

Separate mess halls

Quality control

Office jobs

15% of new hires are nonwhite

Case 2.19: Catherine Wagenseller: The Fired Killjoy

Chronology of Events

March 1975	Wagenseller hired as staff nurse (recruited by Kay Smith)
1978	Wagenseller promoted to ambulance charge nurse
1979	Wagenseller promoted to management: Paramedic Coordinator
March 1979	Wagenseller's Annual Evaluation; Smith rates as "Exceeding results expected"
May 1979	"Moon River" personal raft trip
August 1979 October 1979	Smith says Wagenseller has attitude problem
November 1979	Wagenseller terminated after refusal to resign

Case 2.20: Beech-Nut and the No-Apple-Juice Apple Juice

1977	Beech-Nut and Interjuice contract for apple concentrate
1978	LiCari sends Beech-Nut employees to Interjuice plant; access to tanks denied
1979	Nestlé buys Beech-Nut
Early 1981	LiCari goes to plant manager Lavery with suspicions and circumstantial evidence; "Chicken Little" meeting
August 1981	LiCari takes chemical tests to Lavery; "Team Player" meeting
August 1981	LiCari takes evidence and tests to Hoyvald; "Naivete and Impractical Ideals"
November 1981	LiCari leaves Beech-Nut
1982	Processed Apples Institute lawsuit against Interjuice; Beech-Nut cancels Interjuice contracts
March 1983	Bogus juice sales stopped
1986	Lavery and Hoyvald trials (conspiracy, fraud, food and drug law violations)

Case 2.22: Dow Corning and the Silicone Implants: Questions of Safety and Disclosure

History and Ownership of Silicone Implant Manufacturers

Case 2.22: Dow Corning and the Silicone Implants: Questions of Safety and Disclosure

Dow Corning Chronology

1960s	Implants first developed
1976	Thomas Talcott, Dow engineer raises safety questions
1976	Heyer-Schulte "Dear Doctor" safety letter
1980	Salesman questions sale of implants
1984	Bill Boley, Dow Corning scientist, says no safety data established
1984	Stern case in Nevada; $1.5 million in punitive damages against Dow Corning
1987	Dow Corning does not dispute leaks; only connection with harms
1987-1991	Increasing litigation; medical documentation of immune system problems
1991	New York $4.5 million verdict
Oct. 1991	FDA Hearings
Dec. 1991	Hopkins' $7.3 million verdict against Dow
January 1992	FDA requests ban on sales of implants
Mid-Jan. 1992	Dow Corning's stock falls $10
March 1992	Dow Corning withdraws from implant market

Case 2.28: Seattle's Comparable Worth

Low Percentage of the Labor Force Are Women	
Engineers	5.8%
Precision production, craft, and repair	8.1
Architects	12.7
Lawyers and judges	15.8
Farming, forestry, and fishing	16.0
Operators, fabricators, and laborers	26.6
High Percentage of the Labor Force Are Women	
Service occupations	60.1%
Teachers (except college and university)	70.9
Administrative support (including clerical)	79.9
Health assessment and treating occupation	85.8
Financial records processing	89.4

Percentage Comparison of Women in the Labor Force

Source: U.S. Bureau of the Census, *Statistical Abstract of the United States*, 1992, 392-94.

Case 2.28: Seattle's Comparable Worth

Factor Point Method

Factors	Degrees					Weight of this factor
Skills required	1	2	3	4	5	40%
Effort required	1	2	3	4	5	30
Responsibility	1	2	3	4	5	20
Working conditions	1	2	3	4	5	10

Example: Job X

	Degree	× Weight	= Points
Skills required	2	40%	80
Effort required	3	30	90
Responsibility	3	20	60
Working Conditions	1	10	10
Total points for Job X = 240			

Source: Milkovich, George T., and Jerry Newman, *Compensation*, Boston: Richard D. Irwin, Inc., 1993.

Case 3.1: BCCI and the Role of Internal Auditors

Case 3.2: Check Kiting or Aggressive Cash Management and E.F. Hutton

1. Two E. F. Hutton branch offices deposit $10,000 each in customer checks at two different banks. Total balance: $20,000

2. In a process called "chaining," one Hutton office writes a check for $5,000 on its account in Bank A and sends it to another branch office for deposit in that office's account in Bank B. The Bank B account then shows a $15,000 balance.

3. The account in Bank A remains at $10,000 because it will take a few days for the $5,000 check to be processed by the Federal Reserve and sent back to be subtracted from the account. Until then, the two accounts total $25,000.

4. Taking advantage of a similar lag, the branch offices arbitrarily multiply the balances in their accounts by two and report that amount to E. F. Hutton's regional office.

5. The regional office then writes checks totaling $50,000 on the two banks and deposits the two checks in the regional office's account in Bank C.

6. Next, Bank C sends a single check for $50,000 to Hutton's primary bank, Manufacturers Hanover Trust Co. in New York. Hutton now can write checks on the "deposit" in its Manufacturers Hanover account to pay the firm's bills, Hutton must cover the checks, of course.

7. In the few days it takes for the various checks to be subtracted from the accounts on owhich they were drawn, Hutton has had the equivalent of a $30,000 interest-free loan — the excess over the original $20,000 in the branch accounts.

Because the process was repeated over and over, the Justice Dept. says Hutton had the use of "well in excess of $1 billion" during the year and a half the scheme was in operation.

Anthony Bianco, et al., "What Did Hutton's Managers Know – And When Did They Know It? *Business Week* (May 20, 1985): 111. Reprinted by special permission. © 1985 by McGraw-Hill, Inc.

Case 3.3: Medical Billing Errors and Practices Terminology

Upcoding   code as different procedure to bring more compensation from insurers

Unbundling   breaking surgeries into parts to bring more compensation from insurers

Exploding   breaking tests into various parts to bring more compensation from insurers

Code creeps   unbundling, exploding, and upcoding

Miscoding   Routine uncovered tests coded as something else to ensure coverage

Bundling   Insurer's practice of package price for procedures

Case 3.4: MiniScribe and the Auditors

Employee Cooperation in Fraud

1. Shipments to customers are two times the amount that they actually ordered; sales fully booked

2. Manipulation of reserves

3. Pretend inventory (construction bricks wrapped as disk drives)

4. Alteration of auditors' work papers

5. Shipping practices and passage of title and booking of sales

Case 3.7: The Ethics of Derivatives

Entity	Loss
Charles County	$8.3 million (98 percent of its assets in collateralized mortgage
Cuyahoga County	$137 million (leveraged its $1.8 billion fund)
West Virginia	$279 million
Florida	$175 million
Metallgesellschift	$1 billion
Askin Capital Management	$2 billion (firm is liquidated)
Procter & Gamble	$102 million
Gibson Greetings	$23 million
Bankers Trust	$130 million

Lawsuits

Paine Webber	(settled for $33 million)
Piper Jaffray	(settled for $70 million)
Bankers Trust	(pending)
Gibson Greetings	(settled for $23 million)

Case 3.16: Johns-Manville and the Asbestos Exposure

Chronology of Events

1918	U.S. Bureau of Labor statistics monograph
1924-29	Medical studies of asbestos in British journals
1935	Lanza report (Manville changes)
1936	Gardner/Brown silence agreement
1938	U.S. Public Health service study (5 million particles)
1946	Fleisher study of insulation applicators
1947	American Conference of Governmental Industrial Hygienists (follows 1938 study)
1960s	Published reports
1964	Manville warning labels
1965	I.J. Selikoff (first definitive study)
1973	Clarence Borel
1977	Texas suits (445)
1977	Attempted federal legislative protection
1982	Bankruptcy

1991	Trust established for victims
	    $75 million annually; $2.5 billion in stock
	    20% of net income each year

1992	90,000 claims pending
1994	Third party claims increasing

Case 3.17: Electromagnetic Fields (EMF): Exposure for Workers and Customers

Chronology of Events

1950	First studies; U.S. Public Health Service
1968	Navy ELF project in Wisconsin
1972	Becker recommends further study
1973	Power line siting issue erupts in New York
1979	Werthemeier Denver cluster studies on wire configurations and childhood leukemia
1979	PAVE PAWS impact examined
1980-83	Adey studies appear; press coverage of PAVE PAWS on Cape Cod
1985	Houston case on refusal of power lines
1986	Women near PAVE PAWS have higher cancer rate
1988	New studies
1992	EPRI involvement
1994	EPRI study on utility workers

Case 3.18: Video Display Terminals and the Miscarriage and Cataract Cluster Studies

A Look Back at the Findings and Legislation Surrounding VDTs

In the last two years, increasing attention has been paid to the health hazards associated with prolonged VDT use.

March 1979 — An American Journal of Epidemiology study links cancer mortality with children living near high-voltage power lines.

Mid '80s — The Swedish National Board sets a limit on electromagnetic field radiation (EMF) for computer displays at very low frequency (2kHz to 400kHz).

February 1987 — Studies released by Hahon Frolen, a Swedish researcher, link VDT-type fields and abnormal pregnancies in mice.

June 1988 — Kaiser Permanente Medical Care, an HMO in San Francisco, finds women who use VDTs more than 20 hours a week during the first trimester have a heightened risk of miscarriage.

Late 1988 — Suffolk County, NY, passes Resolution 378-1988 requiring businesses to provide adequate eye care, lighting, adjustable furniture and work breaks for employees who spend most of their day working at VDTs.

December 1989 — A Silicon Valley summit brings together II monitor companies, including Apple, SuperMac, DEC, Toshiba and others, to discuss the health hazards of VDTs.

July 1990 — A New York state court overturns the 1988 Suffolk County law that required businesses to provide special conditions for employees using VDTs.

July 1990 — The City of San Francisco approves a VDT workplace bill (405-90) requiring employees to receive 15-minute breaks from terminals every two hours and detachable keyboards, adjustable furniture and anti-glare screens. In addition, a commission is formed to study health hazards associated with VDT emissions.

December 1990 — Apple Computer Inc. testifies in Congress and urges the U.S. government to commit more funds to studying the hazards of extremely low frequency (5Hz to 2kHz) emissions.

1991 and beyond — The Environmental Protection Agency is expected to release a study of health hazards associated with VDTs. The Swedish National Board plans to enforce the extremely low frequency standard (5Hz to 2kHz) for VDT emissions.

Reprinted with permission from *PC Week*, January 28, 1991. © 1991 Ziff-Davis Publishing Company.

Case 3.27: Exxon and Alaska

Damage to Prince William Sound:

Spill covered 1,000 square miles
1,000 dead otters
34,400 dead sea birds
151 Bald Eagles
Fishing industry

Damages Assessed and Costs to Exxon:

$2 billion clean-up
$50,000 fine - Hazelwood
800 civil suits still pending
$180,000 to fishermen (settlement)
$1.15 billion fine (criminal case by U.S. and Alaska)
$900,000,000 (civil case by U.S. and Alaska)
$287 million to fishermen
$9.7 million for damages to Native American land
$1.5 billion for wildlife damage
$20 million to native Alaskans for damages to their
    villages

Case 3.28: The Disposable Diaper Dilemma

PRO

Only 2% of solid waste

Greater environmental
    impact of cloth if
    energy and water
    in laundry included

4 of 5 Americans prefer
    disposable

CON

7,800 diapers/child

2-5 years for plastic to
    break down

20 states regulate
    municipal regulations

Case 4.4: The Obligation to Screen? The Obligation to Reject, *Soldier of Fortune* Classifieds

Ads at Issue

The Hearn Ad

Ex-Marines -- 67-69 'Nam Vets, Ex-Di, weapons specialist -- jungle warfare, pilot, M.E., high risk assignments, U.S. or overseas. (404)991-2684

Note: "Ex-Di" means ex-drill instructor; "M.E." means multi-engine planes; and "high risk assignments" means work as a bodyguard or security specialist.

Previous Ads

Gun For Hire: 37-year-old -- professional mercenary desires jobs. Vietnam Veteran. Discreet and very private. Bodyguard, courier, and other special skills. All jobs considered. [phone number]

Gun For Hire: Nam sniper instructor. SWAT. Pistol, rifle, security specialist, bodyguard, courier plus. All jobs considered. Privacy guaranteed. Mike [phone number].

Case 4.17: Salomon Brothers and Bond Pricing

The Mechanics of the Salomon Squeeze

1. Salomon bids its 35% share in government bond auction (price is high)

2. Salomon bids same high price for customers

3. Government accepts bids

4. Salomon buys bonds back from customers
    Market is cornered

5. Salomon can name its price as other buyers struggle to buy

Case 5.9: Ford and Its Pinto:
Cost Analysis Tables for Pinto Redesign

Table 1

Costs of the 1970 Potential Design Modification
Strategy: Low Estimate[1]

Calendar Year	Sales (1,000)	Estimated Unit Cost ($)	Estimated Total Cost ($ million)	Present Value of Estimated Costs in 1970 ($ million)
1970	76	8.00	.608	.608
1971	328	8.00	2.624	2.385
1972	287	8.00	2.296	1.897
1973	268	8.00	2.144	1.611
1974	192	8.00	1.536	1.049
1975	170	8.00	1.360	.844
1976	106	8.00	.848	.479
		Total		8.873

[1]*Automotive News*, Almanac Issues for 1971-1979, Slocum Publishing Company, Detroit, 1971, and Marketing Services, Inc., Detroit, 1972-1979.

Case 5.9: Ford and Its Pinto

Table 2

Costs of the 1970 Potential Design Modification
Strategy: High Estimate[1]

Calendar Year	Sales (1,000)	Estimated Unit Cost ($)	Estimated Total Cost ($ million)	Present Value of Estimated Costs in 1970 ($ million)
1970	76	18.66	1.418	1.418
1971	328	18.66	6.120	5.564
1972	287	18.66	5.355	4.425
1973	268	18.66	5.001	3.757
1974	192	18.66	3.583	2.447
1975	170	18.66	3.172	1.969
1976	106	18.66	1.978	1.116
		Total		20.696

[1] *Automotive News*, Almanac Issues for 1971-1979, Slocum Publishing Company, Detroit, 1971, and Marketing Services, Inc., Detroit, 1972-1979.

Case 5.9: Ford and Its Pinto:
Internal Memo on Value of Life

The total benefit is shown to be just under $50 million, while the associated cost if $137 million. Thus, the cost is almost three times the benefits, even using a number of highly favorable benefit assumptions.

Benefits:

Savings: 180 burn deaths, 180 serious burn injuries, 2,100 burned vehicles

Unit cost: $200,000 per death, $67,000 per injury, $700 per vehicle

Total Benefits: 180 x ($200,000) plus
180 x ($67,000) plus
2100 x ($700) = $49.15 million

Costs:

Sales: 11 million cars, 1.5 million light trucks

Unit cost: $11 per car, $11 per truck

Total costs: 11,000 x ($11) plus
1,500,000 x ($11) = $137 million

Case 6.5: Levels of Executive Compensation: How Much Should The Boss Make?

Company	CEO	Pay (For 1994)
Wells Fargo & Co.	Carl F. Reichardt	$16,400,000
Colgate-Palmolive Co.	Reuben Mark	$15,800,000
Bear Stearns Cos.	James E. Cayne	$14,600,000
Nations Bank Corp.	Hugh L. McColl, Jr.	$13,700,000
Compaq Computer Corp.	Eckhard Pfeiffer	$13,200,000
Allied Signal, Inc.	Lawrence A. Bossidy	$12,400,000
American International Group, Inc.	Maurice R. Greenberg	$12,100,000
Coca-Cola Co.	Roberto C. Goizueta	$12,100,000
IBM	Louis Gerstner	$12,400,000
AT&T	Robert Allen	$5,490,000
General Electric	Jack Welch	$4,350,000
Eastman Kodak	George Fisher	$5,960,000

Case 7.6: The Degrees-for-Grants Program Comparison of Thesis/Dissertation Language and Contract Reports

1. The most prevailing wind directions at Tower 301 are from the north, northeast, southwest, and northwest especially in the spring and summer. Over 60 percent of the wind is from north. Significant diurnal variation of wind speeds occurs in the summer and fall months.

FWG Associates report to NASA by H.P. Chang and Walter Frost, February 26, 1987.

   In addition to the spatial velocity and reflectivity fields of the JAWS microbursts, which were analyzed and reported by Frost, et al. (1985), JAWS data sets also provided turbulence information in the form of radar-measured pulse, wind, and total standard deviations (defined below).

'Development of a Microburst Turbulence Model' by H.P. Chang and Walter Frost, March 1987

1. The most prevailing wind directions at Tower 301 are from north, northeast, southwest, and northwest especially in the spring and summer over 60 percent of the wind from north. Significant diurnal variation of wind speeds appeared in the summer and fall months.

Peggy S. Potter master's thesis, December 1989.

   In addition to the spatial velocity and reflectivity fields of the JAWS microbursts, which were analyzed and reported by Frost, et al. (1985), JAWS data sets also provided turbulence information in the form of radar-measured pulse, wind, and total standards deviations (defined below).

Dennis A. Faulkner doctoral dissertation, May 1990

Advanced Instructional Module -- Ethics
Teleological Theory

1. Utilitarianism

2. Ethical Egoism

3. Christian Consequentialism

Advanced Instructional Module -- Ethics
Deontology

1.   Rights (Kant)

2.   Justice